SCHUMANN
ON MUSIC
A Selection from the Writings

ROBERT SCHUMANN

Translated, edited and
annotated by
Henry Pleasants

Dover Publications, Inc., New York

Published in Canada by General Publishing Company, Ltd., 30
Lesmill Road, Don Mills, Toronto, Ontario.
Published in the United Kingdom by Constable and Company,
Ltd., 10 Orange Street, London WC2H 7EG.

This Dover edition, first published in 1988, is a slightly corrected
republication of *The Musical World of Robert Schumann: A Selection from
His Own Writings*, originally published by Victor Gollancz Ltd,
London, and St. Martin's Press, New York, in 1965.

Manufactured in the United States of America
Dover Publications, Inc., 31 East 2nd Street, Mineola, N.Y. 11501

Library of Congress Cataloging-in-Publication Data

Schumann, Robert, 1810–1856.
[Literary works. English. Selections]
Schumann on music : a selection from the writings / Robert
Schumann : translated and edited by Henry Pleasants.
      p.   cm.
Translation of selections from Gesammelte Schriften über Musik
und Musiker.
Reprint. Originally published: The musical world of Robert
Schumann. London : Gollancz, 1965.
Includes index.
ISBN 0-486-25748-7 (pbk.)
1. Music—19th century—History and criticism.   2. Musicians.
I. Pleasants, Henry.   II. Title.
ML410.S4A25   1988
780'.903'4—dc19   88-11800
                                                            CIP
                                                            MN

CONTENTS

INTRODUCTION

Robert Schumann founded the *Neue Zeitschrift für Musik* (literally, 'New Periodical for Music') in 1834 when he was not yet twenty-four. He was its owner, editor and principal critic until 1844 when he turned it over to a colleague and moved to Dresden.

Nearly a decade later, after he and Clara had moved from Dresden to Düsseldorf, and when he was once more suffering from symptoms of the mental disease that would soon cost him his life, he began to assemble and edit the hundreds of essays, articles, reviews, feuilletons, aphorisms, etc., that he had written for the *Neue Zeitschrift für Musik*. They were published in 1854 as *Gesammelte Schriften über Musik und Musiker* ('Collected Writings about Music and Musicians') in two volumes.

There have been two previous attempts to translate Schumann into English. The first was by Fanny Raymond Ritter[1] who, in 1876-1880 brought out *Music and Musicians* in two instalments designated, respectively, as First and Second Series. Her arrangement of the material was influenced by the fact that the First Series was published with no certainty that a Second Series would follow. For obvious reasons she selected what appeared to her to be the best of the crop for this First Series, including all the major set pieces such as Florestan's 'Shrovetide Oration', the essays on Berlioz' *Sinfonie Fantastique* and Schubert's Symphony in C major, the 'Letters of a (Music-) Lover', 'A Monument to Beethoven', 'The Editor's Ball', etc.

In so doing she disregarded the chronological order which Schumann had chosen for his book. Lesser items were grouped according to forms, i.e. under 'symphonies', 'overtures', 'studies for the pianoforte', 'concertos', etc. This system was continued more consistently in the Second Series. Schumann had also used it, both in the *Neue Zeitschrift für Musik* and, chronologically, in his *Gesammelte Schriften*, but Mrs. Ritter, in abandoning chronology, also abandoned that continuity of history and style which is essential to an appreciation of Schumann as writer and critic.

Her accomplishment in translating the whole two volumes was formidable, but the English is so dated and the error count so high that her work could not be allowed to stand for ever as the English-speaking music lover's only insight into the literary and critical gifts of

Robert Schumann. The volumes are, moreover, almost totally devoid of annotation.

A second attempt was made under the sponsorship of the New Friends of Music, of New York, in 1946 with the late Paul Rosenfeld as the translator. It was published in the United States by Pantheon Books Inc. and in England by Dennis Dobson. This time no effort at completeness was made, and again the chronological order was disregarded. Instead, the emphasis was on what Schumann had written about the great masters. All that he wrote on Beethoven, for instance, was assembled under the heading, 'Beethoven', and all that he wrote about Chopin under 'Chopin', including fragments culled from articles not solely devoted to the composers concerned. Thus, of 'The Editor's Ball', one of Schumann's most imaginative and literate pieces, we get only an excerpt dealing with Chopin. The English, if hardly exemplary, is an improvement upon Mrs. Ritter's, and the error count is low. The annotation is meagre.

In plotting my own attempt I have been prompted by the conviction that a chronological arrangement of the material selected is essential to an understanding of Schumann's progress as a writer and critic and also of the evolution of music in Germany during a decisive decade; further by the thought that Schumann's position as a critic cannot be gauged simply by the glowing words he had for the masters. If there are comparatively few among us today to whom Spohr, Moscheles, Hummel, Thalberg, Hiller, Herz, Field, Kalkbrenner, Cramer, Henselt, Heller, Loewe, Franz, Bennett and Gade are familiar, it does no great credit to the way musical history is taught nowadays. They were Schumann's contemporaries. Many of them were his friends. They were famous in their time; that they were eventually overshadowed by the larger figures of Liszt, Wagner, Brahms, Chopin, Mendelssohn and Schumann himself is no reason to condemn them to oblivion. In some ways, indeed, a knowledge of their music and the details of their lives are more important to an understanding of the musical life of Europe in the immediate post-Beethoven era than is familiarity with the masterpieces, if only because they were relatively minor figures, lacking that universality which confounds fashion, and therefore most instructively typical. They were all a part of Schumann's life and times, and what he has to say about them tells us much not only about them, but also about himself and the period in which he lived.

I have not, of course, attempted completeness. I have sought rather a cross-section designed to reveal Schumann as fully as feasible, as writer and critic and to place him in perspective among his fellow musicians. He was, with Berlioz, the first of the composer-critics. Unlike Berlioz, he wrote for a periodical that he himself had founded and in accordance with policies of his own which had led to its founding. About the latter there is no need to add to Schumann's own statements included in this selection, notably in the Preface and in the New Year's Editorial for 1835. It should be recorded, however, that Schumann's literary enterprise was successful. The circulation of the periodical was numbered only in the hundreds, and Schumann made no personal fortune out of it. But it was widely and effectively influential, and played a major part in making Europeans, particularly Germans, aware of their musical heritage and the obligations this heritage imposed upon them. It also furthered the early careers of many fine young musicians whose names first came to public notice in its pages, among them Chopin, Henselt, Heller, Hiller, Gade, Bennett and, of course, Brahms.

Translating Schumann is not easy. As a writer he was rather the gifted dilettante than the professional master. In the early years he was decisively and excessively influenced by both the mind and the style of Jean Paul Richter. Among the consequences were numerous passages abounding in metaphors (often mixed), obscure allusions, coy disguises, mysteries, riddles and ambiguous syntax. In other words, he tended to be self-conscious, high-falutin' and pretentious, and succeeded, from time to time, in being only a bit silly. In later years his writing became simpler, more to the point, more professional—and rather less charming. He was composing music at a tremendous pace, and his life was clouded for a time by Friedrich Wieck's desperate efforts to frustrate his courtship of Clara. There also appeared at this time the first manifestations of his mental disorder. Writing was becoming a chore, and he no longer had the time, probably no longer even the desire, to bring to the writing task the enthusiasm, the concentration and the dedication required for those set pieces that so distinguished the first years of the *Neue Zeitschrift für Musik* and which show what a fine writer he might have become had writing been his sole preoccupation.

He should probably be ranked, nevertheless, among the great critics of European music. He lacked Hanslick's easy mastery of the writer's craft, his breadth of experience and the elegance of his prose style. He lacked Berlioz' gift for the imaginative turn of phrase and his infectious pleasure in the ridiculous and outrageous. He lacked Debussy's sense of proportion, and he was rarely as cutting or savage as Hugo Wolf. Many critics, German, French, English and American have surpassed him in learning. He was, indeed, rather provincial. Aside from a youthful vacation trip to Italy and tours with Clara to St. Petersburg and Holland, he knew little of the world outside Germany, and his prejudice against most things Italian and all things French (except Berlioz) was pronounced and benighted. His denunciation of Meyerbeer's *Les Huguenots* merits inclusion among the stuffiest notices ever written. And yet his articles are illuminated by a knowledge and appreciation of the composer's craft unmatched by any other critic, and inspired by the noblest concept of the composer's calling. They are also distinguished by a most uncommon decency. In reading his enthusiastic comments on such men as Hiller, Kessler, Chopin, Mendelssohn, Heller, Bennet, Gade, Henselt, etc., it should be remembered that they were all his competitors. Such generous acknowledgement of their gifts, in most cases inferior to his own, is eloquent testimony of high principle and purpose. And in the case of composers whom he takes to task it is usually for failure to fulfil earlier promise. It is often implied and sometimes stated that Schumann's pen has been sharpened by a sense of having been let down.

He was an idealist, then, who was guided by the most exalted examples, both musical and literary, and who proved himself worthy of his models. If he was, as a critic, not quite a Hanslick—well, Hanslick, in more ways than one, was no Schumann.

H. P.

[1] (1840-1890), a Philadelphian, wife of Frédéric Louis Ritter (1834-1891), an Alsatian musician, active for many years as choral conductor in Cincinnati and New York and, from 1874, Director of the Music Department at Vassar College. Mrs. Ritter also wrote an original work, *Woman as a Musician*, published in 1877.

SCHUMANN
ON MUSIC

PREFACE

(1854)

TOWARDS THE CLOSE of the year 1833 a group of musicians, mostly young, living in Leipzig, established the custom of nightly gatherings. The meetings were informal, as if purely by chance, and primarily social, although they obviously also served the exchange of ideas about the art which was food and drink to them all—music!

The state of music in Germany at that time can hardly be said to have offered any grounds for rejoicing. Rossini still reigned supreme in the theatre; among pianists, Herz and Hünten[1] had the field pretty much to themselves. And yet only a few years had passed since Beethoven, Carl Maria von Weber and Schubert had lived among us! Mendelssohn's star was, to be sure, in the ascendant, and wonderful things were spoken of a Pole named Chopin; but their enduring influence would not be established for some years to come.

One day these young hotheads were seized with an idea: Let us not sit idly by; rather let us do something to improve matters, to restore the poetry of the art to its rightful place of honour! Thus emerged the first pages of a New Periodical for Music (*Neue Zeitschrift für Musik*). The pleasure of a firm and close association of young talents was of short duration. Death claimed one of our dearest associates, Ludwig Schunke. Some of the others left Leipzig for a time. The enterprise was on the point of dissolution when the musical visionary of the group, who heretofore had spent more of his life dreaming at the piano than with books, undertook the direction of the magazine and continued as its editor for ten full years, until 1844. The result was a succession of essays from which this collection is drawn. Most of the views expressed therein are still his own. What he hoped and feared about many an artistic phenomenon has, with the passage of time, come to pass.

It seems appropriate to mention here an association, or league, which was more than secret, since it existed solely in the fantasy of its founder —namely, the League of David (Davidsbund). It had occurred to the founder that in order to express divergent views about art it might be appropriate to invent contrasting characters as their spokesmen. The principal protagonists were Florestan and Eusebius, with Master Raro functioning as an intermediary.[2] The Davidsbündler appear and reappear throughout the pages of the magazine, humorously combining

Dichtung und Wahrheit (poetry and truth).[3] In later years they vanished, not unmissed.

If these collected pages, reflecting a richly active period, should serve to divert the attention of the living to many an artistic apparition since lost in the floods of the present, their purpose will have been realized.

R. S.

[1] Hünten, Franz (1793-1878). He was born in Coblenz, but went as a young man to Paris where he studied at the Conservatoire with Reicha and Cherubini, subsequently settling there as virtuoso, teacher and composer. He returned to Coblenz in 1837, and remained for the rest of his life, composing fashionable pieces for which, according to Hugo Riemann, he was paid 'horrendous sums'. He also wrote a *School of Piano Playing*.

[2] Florestan and Eusebius represent two aspects of Schumann's own nature and temperament. The one fiery, impatient and idealistic, the other moderate, sober, reflective and tolerant. Master Raro usually represents Friedrich Wieck.

[3] The title of Goethe's Autobiography.

AN OPUS 2

(1831)

EUSEBIUS DROPPED BY one evening, not long ago. He entered quietly, his pale features brightened by that enigmatic smile with which he likes to excite curiosity. Florestan and I were seated at the piano. He, as you know, is one of those rare musical persons who seem to anticipate everything that is new, of the future and extraordinary. This time, however, there was a surprise in store even for him. With the words, 'Hats off, gentlemen, a genius!' Eusebius spread out before us a piece of music.

We were not allowed to see the title. I turned the pages idly; there is something magical about this secret enjoyment of music unheard. It seems to me, moreover, that every composer has his own musical handwriting. Beethoven looks different on paper from Mozart, just as Jean Paul's prose differs from Goethe's. Here, however, it was as if I were being stared at oddly by strange eyes—eyes of flowers, basilisks, peacocks, maidens. In certain places it became clearer—I thought I could discern Mozart's 'Là ci darem la mano' being woven through a hundred chords, Leporello winking at me, and Don Giovanni hurrying by in a white cloak.

'Well, let's hear it,' said Florestan. Eusebius obliged, while we listened, pressed against each other in the embrasure of a window. He played as if possessed, conjuring up countless figures of the most vivid actuality. It was as if the enthusiasm of the moment had given to his fingers a dexterity far beyond their normal endowment. Florestan's applause, to be sure, not counting a serene smile, consisted of nothing more than a statement that the variations could have been by Beethoven or Schubert, had either of them been a great piano virtuoso. But then he looked at the title and read: *Là ci darem la mano, varié pour le Pianoforte par Frédéric Chopin, Œuvre 2*, and we both exclaimed incredulously, 'An Opus 2!'

We all started talking at once, our faces flushed with excitement. The general tenor was: 'Something decent, at last—Chopin, never heard of him!—Who can he be?—A genius in any case!—Was that not Zerlina laughing, or Leporello?'

The scene was quite beyond description. Drunk with wine, Chopin and conversation, we dashed off to Master Raro. He laughed sceptically and said: 'Oh, I know you and all your new discoveries. But anyway, bring this Chopin round.' We promised to oblige next day. Eusebius soon took his leave, quietly as always. I stayed behind for a while with Master Raro. Florestan, who has no home for the moment, fled through the moonlit streets to my house. I found him there in my room after midnight, stretched out on the sofa, his eyes closed.

'Chopin's variations,' he began, as if talking in his sleep, 'keep going through my head. Certainly it's all dramatic, and it's all Chopin. The introduction—as complete in itself as it is—(do you remember Leporello's skips in thirds?)—strikes me as the least appropriate to the whole. But the theme (I wonder why he chose B flat), the variations, the concluding episode and the Adagio—genius peeks out at you from every bar. Of course, dear Julius, the characters are Don Giovanni, Zerlina, Leporello and Masetto. Zerlina's answer in the theme is amorously enough defined. The first variation might be described, perhaps, as aristocratic and coquettish—the Spanish grandee flirting amiably with the peasant girl. This becomes self-evident in the second variation, which is more intimate, more comical and more contentious, just as if two lovers were chasing each other and laughing rather more than usual. How it all changes in the third variation! Here is moonlight and fairy-magic, with Masetto standing apart and cursing roundly— and Don Giovanni unperturbed. Now about the fourth, what do you think of it? (Eusebius played it very cleanly, by the way.) Is it not pert and wanton and straight to the point? The Adagio is in B flat minor, to be sure, but I can think of nothing more appropriate. It seems to imply a moral admonition to the Don. It's naughty, of course, but also delightful that Leporello should be eavesdropping—laughing and mocking from behind the bushes; that oboes and clarinets should pour forth their charming seduction, and that B flat major, in full bloom, should signal the first amorous kiss. But all that is nothing compared with the last movement—is there wine left, Julius? That is the whole Mozart finale, complete with popping champagne corks and clinking glasses—with Leporello's voice intruding, and the vengeful, pursuing shades, and Don Giovanni in full flight! And then the ending—reassuring and conclusive.'

Only in Switzerland, he concluded, had he ever experienced such sensations as in hearing this finale (on one of those lovely days when the evening sun reaches higher and higher to the tips of the highest mountains and disappears with one final ray of light, and one senses that the white giants of the alps have closed their eyes, and one feels that he has been vouchsafed a heavenly vision).

'Now, Julius,' he said, 'how about alerting yourself to some new dreams and going to sleep!'

'Dearest Florestan,' I replied, 'these private feelings may well be praiseworthy, if rather subjective; but, obvious as Chopin's genius may be, I, too, bow my head to such inspiration, such high endeavour, such mastery!'

On this we slept.

This article, representing Schumann's debut as a writer, with its subsequently famous 'Hats off, gentlemen, a genius', was published in the Leipzig *Allgemeine Musikalische Zeitung* in the issue of December 7, 1831. It is the only one of the articles presented in this collection not originally written for Schumann's own *Neue Zeitschrift für Musik*, the first issue of which would not appear until April, 1834. It also marked the first appearance of Eusebius, Florestan and Master Raro, the charter members, so to speak, of the Davidsbund.

The variations were composed in 1827 and first played in public by Chopin in Vienna on August 11, 1829. About their reception on that occasion Chopin wrote to his family in Warsaw the next day: 'The applause was so great after each variation that I could not hear the orchestral tuttis.' Haslinger, the leading Viennese publisher, brought them out the following year. Schumann's friend, Julius Knorr (1807-1861), whom Schumann makes the narrator of this article, played them in Leipzig on October 27, 1831—in other words, prior to the appearance of the article but subsequent to its composition, Schumann having submitted it to Gottfried Wilhelm Fink (1783-1846), then editor of the *Allgemeine Musikalische Zeitung*, in September. Schumann himself had become acquainted with the variations in 1830.

From the point of view of style and presentation the article was something utterly new as an approach to music criticism, and Fink appears to have had reservations about both the style and the opinions; so much so, indeed, that he coupled it with another review of the same work by 'a reputable and worthy representative of the older school' who found in it only 'bravura and figuration'. Although Schumann is believed to have submitted other articles to the *Allgemeine Musikalische Zeitung*, none was ever accepted, and the founding of his own magazine was, to some extent, an act of rebellion against the conservatism of Fink and the *Allgemeine Musikalische Zeitung*.

Chopin himself, when the article—or something like it—was brought to his attention, hardly knew what to make of it. In a letter to Titus Woyciechowski from Paris, dated December 12, 1831, he wrote: 'I received a few days ago a ten-page review from a German in Kassel who is full of enthusiasm for them (the variations). After a long-winded preface he proceeds to analyse them bar by bar, explaining that they are not ordinary variations but rather a fantastic tableau. In the second variation he says that Don Giovanni runs around with Leporello; in the third he kisses Zerlina, while Masetto's rage is pictured in the left hand—and in the fifth bar of the Adagio he declared that Don Giovanni kisses Zerlina on the D flat. Plater [Count Ludwik Plater, a leading figure among the Polish *émigrés* in Paris] asked me yesterday where her D flat was, etc.! I could die of laughing at this German's imagination. He insisted that his brother-in-law should offer the article to Fétis for the *Revue Musicale*, and Hiller, a good fellow with enormous talent . . . only just managed to protect me by telling Mr. Brother-in-law that, far from being clever, the idea is very stupid.' (From *Selected Correspondence of Fryderyk Chopin*, translated and edited by Arthur Hedley, Heinemann, London, 1962, and McGraw Hill, New York.)

The German in Kassel was Friedrich Wieck. He and Clara, then twelve, were embarked on Clara's first extended tour with Paris as their ultimate destination. They had stopped in Kassel to pay their respects to Spohr and to receive his accolade. The brother-in-law was the artist brother of Clementine Fechner, Wieck's second wife and Clara's stepmother. If the reader is puzzled as to how Chopin should be writing on December 12 about a copy he had received from Kassel of a notice that had appeared in Leipzig on December 7, the explanation is simple. What Chopin had received was not Schumann's notice but Wieck's. When Schumann's notice appeared it was accompanied not only by the anonymous dissenting voice, but also by a reference to a third notice 'in the same vein as Schumann's' by Wieck, which could not be published because of lack of space. Despite Hiller's remonstrances it was published in the *Revue Musicale* and in the German publications, *Caecilia* and *Komet*.

HENRI VIEUXTEMPS AND LOUIS LACOMBE

(1834)

A PROVIDENTIAL COLLABORATION of two very young French-men, who chanced to meet in the course of their separate tours!

Tout genre est bon, excepté le genre ennuyeux, including theirs. If one should judge their achievements by the applause, then they must have been of the most prodigious sort. There were ovations when they appeared, ovations while they played, and a great tutti of applause at the end. Henri[1] was even recalled. And all that in the auditorium of the Gewandhaus in Leipzig!

A dozen applauding Frenchmen, to be sure, do more than an entire hall full of Germans, lost in blissful communion with Beethoven. With the French every nerve applauds, from head to foot. Enthusiasm crashes them together like cymbals. The Germans do a quick review of musical history, comparing epochs, fleetingly, but well—and then you have that mezzoforte that has ever distinguished our manifestations of approval. This time it was different. And why should one not rejoice in an appreciative audience, particularly since the boys deserved it?

Whoever presents himself before the public should be neither too young nor too old, but rather in full bloom; and not just in one part or another, but all over. With Henri one can comfortably close one's eyes. His playing has the fragrance of a flower. His accomplishment is complete, masterly throughout.

When speaking of Vieuxtemps it is possible to think of Paganini. When I first heard the latter I rather assumed that the sound would be unique right from the start. Nothing of the kind! He began with a tone so thin, so small! Then effortlessly, almost imperceptibly, he cast his magnetic chains. They oscillated from artist to listener, from listener to artist, becoming ever more wondrous, more intricate, while the listeners pressed together in a bond of common fascination. He bound them ever tighter until they had become as one, to face him as a single entity and to receive from him as one from another.[2]

Other artist-magicians have different formulae. With Vieuxtemps it is not the individual beauties that hold us, nor Paganini's gradual concentration, nor yet the gradual expansion worked by other great artists. From the first tone to the last we find ourselves quite unexpectedly in a magic circle drawn around us without our knowing where it began or where it will end.

And now Louis![3] As a small, fiery pianist with courage and talent he appeals to me. An older artist will not, of course, stretch his physical and psychic strings to the snapping point, if only because they will, indeed, snap. What does it matter that under this little fellow's hands Hummel's tender Concerto in A minor became an Orlando Furioso,[4] about whom, so the story goes, men fell dead when his teeth chattered? I have little taste for dainty musical clocks. An over-abundance of energy subsides of itself as one grows older.—In the Herz variations, which would persuade us that they are the most difficult and significant pieces ever conceived, things were more in focus, i.e. brilliant, vivid and incisive, as required by composition and public alike.

While I could not deny that both movements of Hummel's concerto were carefully prepared, and delivered, moreover, with that French spirit and conviction that demand applause, still, I would urge his teacher not to hold him too long with little pieces, and badly composed ones, at that. It kills the young spirit and deters growth. One remarked it plainly in his accompanying of the violin, which contrasted curiously with the rest of his playing. We all know how, from an artist's accompanying, we can gauge to what extent his sensibility has been awakened and developed.

And so continue on your way, you dear young fellows. If today you have not fully understood me—well, wait a while!

FLORESTAN

[1] Vieuxtemps, Henri (1820-1881), who subsequently became one of the greatest violinists of his generation and an outstanding composer for the violin. He had spent the winter studying in Vienna and was returning to Paris via Prague, Dresden and Leipzig.

[2] Schumann, then still a student of law at Heidelberg, had journeyed to Frankfurt-am-Main to hear Paganini at Eastertide, 1830. The experience encouraged him in his resolve to become a piano virtuoso and prompted two sets of Études de Concert on Paganini caprices. They comprise Schumann's Opus 6 and Opus 10.

[3] Lacombe, Louis (1818-1884) had also spent the winter in Vienna, studying with Czerny and Sechter. In his subsequent career he achieved a modest reputation as composer and critic.

[4] A reference to the epic by Ariosto (1516). The Orlando of the poem is identical with Roland of the Chanson de Roland.

THEODOR STEIN

(1834)

WE SHOULD BE less severe in our judgment were the subject of these lines[1] not, in fact, an exceptional talent, if hardly very highly rated. We confess to a predilection for child prodigies. He who accomplishes the extraordinary in his youth will, with continuous learning, rise to extraordinary accomplishments in maturity. Certain skills should be cultivated to the point of virtuosity as early as possible. But that upon which our young artist has concentrated in earning his fame we oppose as utterly false—namely, improvising in public at an early age. In so saying we address ourselves, not to the boy, whose extraordinary talent we acknowledge, but to his guide, or teacher, or however he may call himself.

Who will attempt to reassemble the burst bud? It would be futile. The suppression of an early awakened predilection would seem to be as contrary to nature as it is natural that a certain faculty may appear and develop earlier in some persons than others. But the rare January blossom should be cultivated and cared for in some quiet recess before being exposed to the wide, cold world. We do not wish to anticipate what the future of this young artist may be. It could have been brilliant, and, under certain circumstances, could hardly have been otherwise. But so much appears to have been neglected in his education, and so many blunders committed, that we feel compelled to admonish the teacher not to sacrifice a later and enduring recognition for futile early acclaim.

All his pupil's present virtues are those of talent, his shortcomings those of improper upbringing. Among the former we would reckon the sure grasp of a situation and its translation into the language of music, his usually successful interweaving and disentanglement of his materials, and his often surprising part-writing. Conspicuous among the latter are dull monotony of expression, the passive, melancholy cast of his melodies, and the unceasing recourse to minor tonalities. He shows us countenances, but they are pale and tear-streaked. That should not be.

Granted that all this may not be unassociated with tendencies common to the most recent musical past; still, this should not mean that youth must be deprived of blossoming, robust life. Do not introduce

Beethoven to the young too early on! Drench them and strengthen them with the fresh, zestful Mozart. There are natures who seem to resist the normal course of development, but there are also natural laws, according to which the illuminating torch, once overturned, can disfigure its bearer.

One need not look far to discover the basis of his shortcomings. Our amiable young artist, sensible and musical as he is, must be fully aware that much is still lacking, including even the correct playing of his instrument, the easy security that only good schooling can provide, the sure dexterity that comes only from continuous practice, and, above all, a healthy tone, which no one brings into this world with him. If we are not mistaken, he will one day be thankful to us for having drawn him so sober a picture of the future, and for having pointed out that it is no laughing matter. If, on the other hand, we are mistaken, then we must still add that in him a talent will have been lost which merited a better destiny.

In any case, let him remember an instructive legend. Apollo took up with a handsome ordinary mortal. As the latter then began to display ever more divine attributes, and finally came to resemble the god of youth himself, in body and spirit, he prematurely betrayed his secret to his fellow mortals. The god, displeased, deserted him, and the young man, shattered by the loss, gazed without ceasing into the eye of the sun, the distant beloved, until he died.—So, do not expose your divine gifts to the eyes of mortals until advised to do so by the divinities who so endowed you and to whom you have become an object of value. To the artist, to the lovely mortal, the god appears transfigured as Fantasy.

EUSEBIUS

[1] Stein, Theodor (1819-1893), who went on to enjoy a distinguished career as pianist and teacher, principally in Stockholm, Helsinki and Reval, and finally in St. Petersburg, where he was for many years a highly regarded member of the piano faculty at the conservatory. He was especially noted for his improvising.

J. N. HUMMEL

Études, Opus 125

(1834)

GAIETY, REPOSE AND GRACE, the characteristics of the art of the ancients, are also characteristic of the school of Mozart. As the Greek pictured his thundering Jupiter with a smiling countenance, so Mozart withheld his bolts of lightning.

A real master nurtures no pupils, only other masters. It is ever with a sense of awe that I have approached the works of Mozart, whose influence was so great and so extensive. Should this clear way of thinking and poetizing give way to something more formless and mystical, as suggested by the forces whose shadows now encroach upon all the arts, let us not forget the beautiful epoch which Mozart dominated and which Beethoven then shook until it shuddered in every joint, conceivably not entirely without his Prince Wolfgang's sanction. The throne was subsequently occupied by Carl Maria von Weber and a couple of foreigners. Since their withdrawal from the scene, people everywhere have grown more and more confused, and toss now in an uneasy, classic-romantic semi-sleep.

Time was when artists who seemed to have reached their peak were advised to continue anonymously, since what might be regarded as progress in a younger, unknown artist could be counted against the established and the famous as a sign of failing creative power. If this were also to mean that music long regarded as significant because of its association with a famous name were no longer to be a stimulus to associative error, then the critic would be guilty either of guessing or presumption if he claimed to have identified a culminating peak. How, after Beethoven's Symphony No. 7, for instance, could the critic have anticipated an Eighth or Ninth? The artist, on the other hand, even while continuing to strive onward and upward, would always regard the last, just completed work as this culminating point.

It would be untruthful to rank the work under discussion[1] as equal in beauty to those from Opus 60 to Opus 80, where all the creative forces governed harmoniously. It is still the same stream, to be sure, still majestic and imposing, but already broadening out to be received by the sea, the mountains receding, and the banks no longer restraining the current within a flowering channel. But all honour to it in its course, and let us remember how once it took the world about it to its bosom and faithfully reflected it!

With music developing so rapidly, a phenomenon unexampled in other arts, it must be inevitable that even the best works seldom remain a subject of conversation for longer than a decade. That many of the younger talents forget so quickly and so ungratefully that they are building on foundations laid by others is merely an example of the intolerance of youth, characteristic of the young in every epoch.

As young as I am, I prefer to have nothing on my conscience or in common with a certain Florestan, so-called, if also greatly beloved. Ah, Florestan! If you were a great king and lost a battle, and your subjects ripped the purple from your shoulders, would you not cry out to them in anger: 'Ungrateful wretches!'?

EUSEBIUS

II

O! dear Eusebius, you make me laugh! And if everyone were to set his clock back, the sun will still rise as usual.

As much as I admire your way of allotting everything its proper place, I find you a romanticist at heart—although not without a certain reverence for names, which time will cure.

Really, old man, if some had their way, we would soon be back in the good old days when you had your ears boxed for putting your thumb on a black key.

For the time being, however, I shall not go into the misguidedness of some of your enthusiasms. Let's concentrate on the work itself.

Methods and pedantry may bring rapid progress, but it is one-sided and trivial. O! What sinners you teachers are! With your Logier[2] contrivances you force the buds to premature blossom, or, like falconers, you pluck your pupils' feathers so that they may not fly too high. Guides you should be, showing the way, but not for ever tagging along.

Even with Hummel's School of Piano[3] I began to have my doubts about whether he, fine virtuoso that he was in his time, was also the best pedagogue for those who came after him. Along with much that was useful went much that was aimless and mere padding; along with good advice went much that was simply stultifying. That the musical examples he chose were all by Hummel I readily forgave. One knows one's own things best, and can choose more readily and more appropriately. What I failed to realize was that Hummel had simply not kept up with the times. Maturity—and these études—have taught me better.

Études, Davidsbündler, are studies, i.e. they should help one learn to do what one has not been able to do before.

The estimable Bach, who knew a million times more than we imagine, was the first to write for pupils, but he began so prodigiously that not until many years later was he recognized as the founder of a rigorous but thoroughly sound school, and then only by a few who had, in the meantime, made progress on their own.

His son, Carl Philipp Emanuel, inherited lovely talents. He refined and sharpened, adding melody and song to the predominant harmony and figuration, but never approached his father as a creative musician. As Mendelssohn once said, 'It was as if a dwarf were to appear among giants.'

Clementi[4] and Cramer[5] followed. Because of his contrapuntal, often cold music, the former found little sympathy among the young. Cramer was preferred because of the bright clarity of his études. There were others to whom one granted certain, more specialized virtues, but only Cramer was held to provide an all-round schooling for head and hand.

But then it appeared desirable to provide something for the heart, too. It was recognized that the empty monotony of these études often did damage. It was also recognized, thank God, that one did not have to learn them, goose-like, one after another in order to chalk up progress. The excellent Moscheles composed interesting, illustrative pieces, which also engaged the imagination. And then came Hummel.

Eusebius, I tell you frankly that these études came along a few years too late. When you have plenty of ripe fruit, do you offer the pleading child bitter roots? Guide the child straight to the rich world of Hummel's earlier compositions, and let him partake of the spirit and fantasy that play there in a thousand inviting colours.

Who would deny that most of these études are conceived by a master's hand, that they are perfect in their fashion, that each enjoys a certain distinctive physiognomy, and that, finally, they all derive from that sovereign assurance that only long years of experience can give? Lacking is beauty in the work itself, which we hope might so enchant the young that they would forgive its difficulties—in other words, the stimulus of imagination.

Believe me, Eusebius, if theory—to use your own metaphor—is the accurate but at the same time lifeless mirror which dumbly reflects the truth but which, without the animate object, remains inanimate, then imagination is the blindfolded fortune-teller, from whom nothing is withheld, and who is often most delightful in her errors.—But what do you say to all this, Master?

FLORESTAN

III

My young friends, you are both wrong. A famous name has made the one a captive, the other a rebel. How does it go in Goethe's *Westöstlicher Divan*—

Als wenn das auf Namen ruhte,
Was sich schweigend nur entfaltet—
Lieb' ich doch das schöne Gute
Wie es sich aus Gott gestaltet

(As if 'twere on a name it stood,
All that which silently unfolds—
I'll take the beautiful and good
As God creates and God beholds.)

RARO

[1] Hummel, Johann Nepomuk (1778-1837). A pupil of Mozart, Haydn, Clementi and Salieri, a fellow pupil of Beethoven, the teacher of Czerny, Hiller, Henselt and Thalberg, Haydn's successor as Director of Music for Prince Esterhazy, and one of the foremost piano virtuosos of his time. He was considered to be Beethoven's equal in improvisation and by some to be his superior. Schumann himself thought seriously of becoming his pupil, and would probably have done so had not the injury to his hand put an end to his hopes of becoming a piano virtuoso. There is an instructive letter from Schumann to Hummel, then in Weimar, dated August 31, 1831, in which Schumann says: 'I can play every concerto at sight, but, fundamentally speaking, must begin with the C major scale.' Hummel's curriculum vitae would suggest a key figure in the history of European music, but in fact the transitional figures were Beethoven, Schubert, Liszt, Chopin and Schumann himself, at least in piano playing. The style represented by Hummel pre-dated Beethoven, originating in the 'galanter Stil' and expiring with Thalberg and Moscheles. As Duncan Hume put it in his article in *Grove's Dictionary*, 'his music is almost exactly what one might expect from a brilliant virtuoso in such circumstances. Add to this the fact that he was a public player upon the piano with the old Viennese

action, so eminently suited to a facile execution of light ornamentation, but deficient in expressing depth of emotion, and we have a pretty complete idea of Hummel's method.' Schumann retained the greatest respect for him and had a particular affection for his Concerto in A minor, but, as reflected in the comments attributed to Florestan, was fully aware that Hummel, even in 1834, had become dated.

[2] Logier, John Baptist (or Bernhard) (1777-1846), invented a gadget known as a 'chiroplast' to develop a proper hand position, and made a fortune out of it. Curiously, it was endorsed and even used by such reputable teachers as Clementi, Cramer and Kalkbrenner. For a detailed and amusing account see Arthur Loesser's *Men, Women and Pianos* (Simon and Schuster, New York, 1954, and Victor Gollancz Ltd., London, 1955).

[3] *Ausführliche Anweisung zum Pianofortespiel*, published in 1828.

[4] Clementi, Muzio (1752-1832), a celebrated, many-sided and widely travelled virtuoso who once competed honourably, if not victoriously, with Mozart. Although the latter spoke and wrote disparagingly of Clementi, he adopted a theme from a sonata played by Clementi in this contest for the Overture to *The Magic Flute*. He was variously occupied, mostly in London, as composer, teacher, publisher and piano builder. Among his most distinguished pupils were John Field, Kalkbrenner, Meyerbeer and Moscheles. His most enduring work was the *Gradus ad Parnassum*, which, severely abbreviated, still survives. Like Hummel, he wrote a book on piano playing, *Méthode pour le Pianoforte*. He was also renowned for his stinginess, and died rich.

[5] Cramer, Johann Baptist (1771-1858), a pupil of Clementi. He was born in Mannheim but spent most of his life in London, where he was greatly respected as virtuoso, composer and teacher, and familiarly and affectionately referred to as 'glorious John'. Like Clementi, he was also a publisher. His *Grosse praktische Pianoforte-Schule* was one of the definitive works of piano pedagogy, and the 84 études, later expanded to 100, which form its fifth part, are still widely and profitably used. He was greatly admired as a pianist by Beethoven, and seems to have been one of the true pioneers in the development of a legato keyboard style.

NEW YEAR'S EDITORIAL

(1835)

Our address from the editor's throne shall be brief. It is an old journalistic custom to greet the New Year with fine promises, although not even the journalist can exert any firm control over what the year may bring. Whether we have fulfilled promises already given, or lived up to expectations—which, according to our far-reaching plans, were considerable—is not for us to judge. An acknowledgment of the youth of the venture may also imply such censure as may be warranted. Such body and spirit as heaven may grant shall remain essentially the same. A word of explanation, however, about the continuation of the critical section of these pages is in order.

An age dominated by the custom of exchanging compliments is nearing its end. We confess that there was no desire on our part to contribute to its resuscitation. Whoever will not dare to attack what is bad in a thing can only half defend what is good.—You artists, and particularly you composers, have no idea how happy we have been when we could greet your work with truly unmeasured praise. We know only too well the language appropriate to the discussion of our art; it is the language of benevolence. But with the best will in the world the encouragement or the restraint of the talented as well as the untalented cannot always proceed—benevolently.

In the short period of our activity we have learned a lot. Our basic policy was set forth at the outset. It is simple: to be remindful of older times and their works and to emphasize that only from such a pure source can new artistic beauties be fostered; at the same time to oppose the trends of the more recent past, proceeding from mere virtuosity, and, finally, to prepare the way for, and to hasten, the acceptance of a new poetic era.

Some of our readers understood us immediately and recognized that our judgments were governed by non-partisanship and, above all, by sympathetic enthusiasm. Others gave no thought to the matter, and cheerfully awaited the beginning of the end of the old refrain. It is otherwise sheerly inexplicable that we should have been expected to review things which are beneath criticism. Still others called our procedure 'inconsiderate' and 'inflexible'.

To the latter we prefer to attribute, not base motives, but rather the noblest. Recognizing, for instance, that our artistic contemporaries are not, as a rule, rich in worldly goods, they may, perhaps, feel that one should not spoil the often hard-won fruits of their toil by exposing a glum future. It is painful, they may argue, to be told, after travelling a long distance, that one has chosen the wrong path; for we know perfectly well that the musical artist or, for that matter, any other artist, cannot pursue another, probably more stable, profession or craft without damage to his art.

But we fail to see what it is that we musicians have over other arts and sciences where various parties are openly opposed, and openly carry on their disputes and feuds. Nor do we see how it is compatible with the honour of our art and the truth of criticism to contemplate with equanimity the three arch-enemies of ours and every other art: the untalented, the too versatile and the talented scribblers. This is not to say that we have anything against certain transient celebrities. They have their legitimacy, filling perfectly the role assigned to them by the mighty dictates of fashion. They are, moreover, and we acknowledge it sadly, the sources of the capital with which the publishers—who are also essential—cover the losses incurred in the issuance of the classics. But three-quarters of all the rest is spurious stuff and unworthy of publication. The public is up to its ears in printed music, confused and confounded. Publishers, printers, engravers, players and listeners spend their time vainly. Art must be more than a game or a mere pastime.

Such were our views when this journal was founded. They have doubtless become apparent from time to time. If we have not previously enunciated them so definitively it was because we hoped that the accomplishments of certain noble young spirits whose sponsorship we regarded as a duty, and the intentional disregard of the run-of-the-mill conglomeration, would provide the quickest means of discouraging mediocrity. We confess that we landed on the horns of a dilemma. Many a reader will have noted and complained that the space we allot to criticism bears no proportionate relationship to the number of works being published. He has not been given an opportunity to form an idea of all publications, good and bad. It was the three arch-enemies enumerated above that made it difficult. In order to give the reader a point of view from which he could take in the totality of the scene, we had to devise a procedure which would meet the requirement without impinging upon the consideration due the essential and the important.

Now the productions of the three arch-enemies are, in fact, so similar —the first lifeless, the second trivial and the third routine—that with the characterization of a single composition one has covered the basic features of them all. And so, in consultation with artists who have both the elevation of the art and the well-being of the artist at heart, we shall review those compositions that fall into any one of the three categories with one of three stereotyped reviews, adding nothing but the titles of the compositions—not, mind you, on the basis of a one-sided opinion, but only according to the considered opinion of many. That we hope this feature to be as brief as possible must be as obvious to the reader as our wish to discuss, in shorter or longer essays, every-thing that is distinguished even by just one small felicitous turn.

Thus, let this confession begin the New Year. One often hears, 'the new year, an old year'. Let us hope: 'A better year!'

FLORESTAN'S SHROVETIDE ORATION

(Delivered after a performance of Beethoven's Ninth Symphony)

(1835)

FLORESTAN LEAPED UP on the piano and said:

Assembled Davidsbündler, that is, youths and men dedicated to the destruction of Philistines, musical and otherwise, the bigger the better![1]

You know, men, that I am not one to rave about things. Truly, I know the symphony better than I know myself. Let us waste no words upon it. Least of all having just heard the real thing.

Nor was I the least bit annoyed, as little as I heard. Mostly I was laughing at Eusebius, and the way the rascal went after that fat man who asked him during the Adagio:

"Tell me, sir, didn't Beethoven also write a "Battle" Symphony?'

'I think you mean the "Pastoral", don't you?' suggested Eusebius, indifferently.

'Ah, yes, of course,' said the fat one, and resumed his meditations.

I suppose man deserves his nose; why else would God have given him one? These audiences endure a lot, about which I could tell you the most marvellous stories. For instance, that time, Kniff,[2] when you were turning pages for me in a Field nocturne. Half the audience was already indulging in self-examination, i.e. they slept. I was playing one of the most dilapidated old pianos that ever imposed itself upon an audience. Unfortunately, my foot slipped, and I caught the Janissary[3] stop instead of the sustaining pedal. It was soft enough, fortunately, so that I could turn an accident to profit and, by repeating it from time to time, give the impression of military music heard in the distance. Eusebius, of course, did his best to disseminate the truth, but the audience was ecstatic.

Many similar anecdotes occurred to me during the Adagio when suddenly my musings were interrupted by the crash of the first chord of the Finale. To a trembling neighbour I said:

'What is it but a triad with a suspended fifth, somewhat awkwardly placed, since one doesn't know which is the bass note, the timpani A or the bassoon F? Look at Türk,[4] Section 19, Page 7!'

'Sir, you are speaking very loudly and, most assuredly, joking!'

Speaking softly now, and in awesome tones, I whispered in his ear: 'You must take care in storms, sir. Lightning sends no liveried messengers before it strikes—at best a storm cloud and a peal of thunder. That's its way.'

'Nevertheless, such dissonances should be prepared!'

Then came the next chord.

'Sir, the beautiful seventh in the trumpet forgives you!'

I was exhausted by my own restraint. I had used my fists to administer caresses!

You gave me a beautiful moment there, Mr. Conductor! You caught the tempo of the deep theme in the basses so wonderfully that I forgot much that had angered me in the first movement where, despite the modestly veiled direction, 'un poco maestoso', one hears the deliberately striding majesty of a god.

'What do you suppose Beethoven had in mind there in the basses?'

'Sir,' I replied, 'that's hard to say. Geniuses have their little jokes— maybe a kind of nightwatchman's song.'

Gone was the lovely moment, and the devil loose again! I looked at those Beethoven-lovers, sitting there goggle-eyed and exclaiming:

'That's by our Beethoven. It's a German work. There's a double fugue in the last movement. They said he couldn't do it, but he did it, and how! Yes, that's our Beethoven!'

From another group:

'The work seems to incorporate all the branches of poetry. The first movement is epic, the second comic, the third lyric and the last drama, a composite of all!'

Somebody else observed:

'A gigantic work, colossal, comparable to the Egyptian pyramids!'

Others were graphic. The symphony represented the story of the origins of man—first chaos, then the divine 'Let there be light!' And the sun rose upon the first human, who was delighted with such magnificence—in short the whole first chapter of the Pentateuch!

I grew angrier—and quieter. And how they all eagerly scanned their texts and finally applauded! I seized Eusebius by the arm and dragged him down the steps past the smiling faces.

Down below, in dim lantern light, Eusebius mused:

'Beethoven, what the word alone contains! Just the deep sound of the syllables singing out to eternity. It's as if there could be no other written symbols for this name!'

'Eusebius,' I said quietly, 'do you, too, presume to praise Beethoven? He would rise up like a lion and demand: "How dare you?" '

I don't really mean you, Eusebius. You are a good fellow. But must a great man always have a retinue of a thousand dwarfs? Do they who smile and clap really think that they understand one whose aspirations were so high and who fought those countless battles?

They, who could not explain to me the simplest musical law, presume to pass judgment on a master!

They, who would take to their heels were I to drop the word 'counterpoint' dare to say: 'Ah, that's to our taste!'

They, who talk of exceptions without knowing the rules, who treasure his excesses while ignoring his achievement of proportion in what would otherwise be merely gigantic—shallow creatures, wandering Werthers, depleted braggarts—they presume to love him and to praise him!!

Davidsbündler, I know of nobody at the moment who could do it with the possible exception of a Silesian landowner who recently wrote to a music-dealer as follows:

'Dear sir—My music cabinet will shortly be in order. You should see how magnificent it is. Alabaster columns within, mirror with silk curtains, busts of composers; in a word, splendid! I would ask you to send me the complete works of Beethoven, as I like him very much.'

What more can one say?

---

[1] Davidsbündler. Although Eusebius, Florestan and Master Raro made their debut in Schumann's review of Chopin's 'Là ci darem la mano' variations in Fink's *Allgemeine Musikalische Zeitung* in 1831, their identity as members of a Davidsbund was first disclosed in an article written by Schumann for a periodical called *Komet* and published in the issue of December 7, 1833. Schumann mentions it in his letters of the time as a preparatory work for a periodical of his own that he already had in mind. In this article he has a piece of paper fall into the writer's hand with the following inscription: 'Finder! You have been chosen for deeds both good and great! You must become a Davidsbündler and expound to the world the secrets of the Bund, i.e. the society whose mission it is to destroy the Philistines, musical and otherwise. Now you know all; you have but to act! And now no inhibitions, please! Go about it with a vengeance!'

[2] Kniff. This is the spelling in the *Gesammelte Schriften*. It was the Davidsbündler name of Julius Knorr, and first appeared in the article in *Komet* referred to above as Knif. In this form it was recognized as an anagram for Fink, the editor of the *Allgemeine Musikalische Zeitung*.

[3] Janissary stop. Early continental pianos were often fitted out with pedals for the production of certain sound effects. The word 'janissary', variously

spelled, refers to a kind of Turkish military music, a taste for which among Europeans was a harmless residue of the Turkish invasions of eastern Europe. The stop, or pedal, here mentioned, probably activated a light cymbal, triangle or drum, or some combination of them.

[4] Türk, Daniel Gottlob (1756–1813), highly esteemed composer, teacher and theoretician, a pupil of Johann Adam Hiller and the teacher of Carl Loewe. His most celebrated theoretical work was a Piano School (*Klavierschule, oder Anweisung zum Klavierspielen für Lehrer und Lernenden mit kritischen Anmerkungen*), published in 1789. The work here facetiously referred to is his *Brief Instruction in the Playing of Thorough-bass* (*Kurze Anweisung zum Generalbassspielen*), published in 1791.

FERDINAND HILLER

Études, Opus 15

(1835)

THERE WAS ONE aspect of Beethoven's romanticism that one might term 'Provençal'. Schubert, in his own most inimitable way, cultivated it to a point of virtuosity. Upon it is based, wittingly or unwittingly, a new, not yet fully developed, school that may well prove characteristic of a special epoch in the history of art. Ferdinand Hiller[1] is one of its young disciples and also one of its remarkable manifestations.

In him I discern an entire younger generation, destined, apparently, to liberate an epoch still chained by a thousand links to the past century. With one hand it is still seeking to undo the chain, with the other it points to a future where it will govern a new realm, suspended, like Mahomet's earth, by most marvellously intertwined diamond fillets and harbouring exotic things as yet unseen, although suggested now and then by the prophetic Beethoven and passed on by the splendid Schubert in his childlike, ingenious and elfin manner. In poetry it was Jean Paul who, once his mortal remains had been laid to rest, flowed on invisible in subterranean channels like a healing spring until two young disciples whom I need not name diverted him back to the light of day and proclaimed, all too vehemently, the dawn of a new era. Thus it was with Beethoven. Like a divinity he lived on in a few rare spirits, admonishing them not to miss the propitious moment for tumbling the idols to whom the masses, for so many empty years, had paid homage. He commended to them, if they were to prevail, not the soft, suave diction of poetry, but the free, uninhibited language with which he had often expressed himself. The young disciples employed it in new and profound forms.

The wiseacres sneered and, like the giant in Albano's dream, said: 'Friends, in this realm waterfalls do now flow upwards.'[2] The disciples countered: 'Yes, but we have wings.' Some among the public detected the young voices and said: 'Hear, hear!' The world waits with bated breath.

FLORESTAN

II

In no other field of criticism is it so difficult to offer proof as in music. Science can argue with mathematics and logic. To poetry belongs the golden, decisive word. Other arts have accepted nature herself as arbiter, from whom they have borrowed their forms. Music is the orphan whose father and mother no one can determine. And it may well be that precisely in this mystery lies the source of its beauty. The publishers of these pages have been charged with favouring the poetical aspects of music to the detriment of the scientific. They have been denounced as young dreamers unaware even of how little they know of Greek and other music. This criticism entails just that by which we would like to see our periodical distinguished from others. We have no desire to investigate any further the degree to which this or that approach to criticism more rapidly advances art. We confess, however, that for us the highest form of criticism is that which reflects most closely the impression made by the stimulating original itself. In this sense Jean Paul, for example, could contribute more to an understanding of a Beethoven symphony or fantasy by a poetical counterpart (without even mentioning the symphony or fantasy) than all these art critics who apply ladders to the colossus in order to measure it by ells. All this is, to be sure, more easily said than done, and would be demanded only by a superior poet rival. With études, moreover, from which one should not merely learn but also learn well and, while one is about it, learn something beautiful, there is an additional element. On this occasion, therefore, as little as possible shall be left aside, and Hiller's work examined from many angles—the aesthetic as well as the theoretical and the pedagogical. For as a pedagogue I look for three things in particular: the bloom, the root and the fruit, or the poetical, the harmonic-melodic and the mechanical, or for the profit to the heart, the ear and the hand.

About many things in this world there is simply nothing to be said, as with Mozart's Symphony in C major with the fugue, much of Shakespeare and some of Beethoven. The merely clever, on the other hand, the mannered and the personally idiomatic set one to thinking. Thus I prefer to divide this review, like a proper sermon, into three parts.

Part I (poetical quality of the work, charm and spirit): I doubt that Hiller will ever be imitated. Why? Because, while himself original, he borrows so much from other original composers that the product has the strange taste of hybrid fruit. An imitator, consequently, would have to conform to this inter-relationship of intrinsic and foreign, and to do so would be nonsense. I do not mean to imply that Hiller imitates intentionally. Who does? Nor do I wish to imply that he lacks the strength to secure himself against foreign influences. On the contrary, his strength is such that he fears to leave it unadulterated lest it be misunderstood, particularly in its highest manifestations. He is lured by the finest and best of all the great composers, but would avoid being as complicated as Bach, as ethereal as Mozart (although this is the least of his worries) or as profound as Beethoven (this the greatest). And so he tries to combine the virtues of this composer with those of another. Under the circumstances it is small wonder that things often fail to work out as he had intended them.

Such greedy intent is dogged by discouragement when, as in Schiller's *Berg-Alten*, the giant form bends down to rumble: 'No farther, friend. This is my domain!' Therein lies the basis of an observation that comes to mind in every étude. There is always a sudden stopping, a loss of altitude midway in the ascent. He takes off like a conquering stallion only to stumble before reaching the finishing line; for the latter is stationary and cannot meet us halfway. Indeed, it seems to recede the nearer one approaches. Thus, all the études lack that golden sense of assurance, that anticipation of victory which, with strong natures, one notes at the first word.

While I may be reading too much into all this, or even be in error, still, I feel confident that I can cite with certainty the compensatory virtues. They are imagination and warmth (not effusiveness and enthusiasm as with Chopin, for example), both enveloped in a romantic chiaroscuro that may one day rise to the level of transfiguration. For Hiller should take care with his next step, beyond which kobolds and gnomes reign, and he should reflect upon the overtures to *A Midsummer Night's Dream* and *The Hebrides* (which are to one another as Shakespeare is to Ossian), in which the romantic spirit soars aloft in such a flight that one forgets the material substance and the tools the composer has used. Nevertheless, Hiller is happy in the adventurous and the elfin, although hardly as poetic as Mendelssohn. Add to that a marked inventiveness and a character possibly too wary of the more commonplace and we have the picture of a young artist who deserves the interest already shown in him, but who has not yet learned to exploit the nobility of his musical lineage with the moderation that leads to self-knowledge and with which we have to govern and direct our inherent creative resources.

Part II (theoretical, relationship of melody to harmony, form and structure of periods): Where Hiller's talent is inadequate, so is his knowledge. He has learned a lot, but he also reminds us of certain enterprising spirits rather too eager to make a name for themselves, who will have had a peek at the last page while the teacher was still explaining the first. That one so ambitious would seek ways of disguising his weaknesses was to be expected. Thus he tries to distract us from the flatness of his work by the richness of his harmonies, or goes off into something entirely different, or stops suddenly, etc.

And, indeed, I hardly know what to suggest for one whose poetical talent is so outstanding but whose schooling has been so superficial. It is easier with geniuses. They fall and rise again on their own. But what are we to say to others? Should they go back and start all over again? Should they try to be natural and simple, as is so often suggested? Should they write like Mozart? But who can prescribe that one should go just so far and no further? Should we condemn a lovely idea simply because its intrinsic beauty is not yet fully realized?

I have no idea how far Hiller will go. But for his own good he should be admonished to learn to distinguish between success and failure. He should solicit the counsel of trustworthy friends about what is suitable for publication and what is not, friends who could tell him, 'On ne peut pas être grand du matin jusqu'au soir': One should discipline one's favourite children. Within my own four walls I may do as I please; he who steps out into the sunlight (or the public eye) will be exposed to its glare.

But to return to the études, one thing strikes me again and again. Hiller often seems to be more concerned with words and expressions than with thought and substance. He lays out his jewels, but hasn't the beauty which jewels should enhance. Or, to employ other metaphors, he has finished the crib before thinking of a mother; he is like a jeweller to whom it is a matter of indifference whether his diadem adorn the head of a proud and beautiful Roman virgin or the greying cranium of a faded lady-in-waiting, just as long as somebody buys it.

Thus his melodies are subordinate to his harmonies, the latter rich, even oriental, and often harsh. It is incomprehensible to me how anyone who has lived so much in music and written so much of it, who has heard both the best and the worst and has learned to distinguish between them can allow harmonies in his own things that are not so much false by the old rules as simply offensive. If I did not know him better I would be compelled to say to him: 'You have no ear for music!'

Part III (mechanical): For young composers who are also virtuosos nothing is more tempting than the composition of études, preferably of horrendous difficulty. Novel figurations and complicated rhythms are easy to come by and lend themselves to harmonic extension. At the same time, and almost unwittingly, one learns by composition. One prefers to practise his own pieces. And reviewers dare not complain of the difficulties. What, after all, are études for?

Hiller enjoys a reputation as a virtuoso and has doubtless earned it. A pupil of Hummel, he went to Paris, where there is no want of competition. His acquaintanceship with Chopin, who knows more than anyone about the piano, may have inspired him in one way or another. In short, he sat himself down and composed études. Whether or not he had any particular purpose or objective in mind at the outset is an open question. Who knows? But the piano-playing reader and teacher can ask to be told whether they should buy them and, if so, what to expect from them, how difficult they are, and for what class of player they are best suited.

In response to all these questions this much is certain. Each étude contains an exercise, to be sure, and there is a new difficulty here and there. But on the whole the composer seems to have been more concerned with the composition of characteristic pieces of poetic substance than with the encouragement of mechanical pianism. Thus we find in the entire collection no indications of desired or preferred fingering or pedalling. Aside from the title there is nothing to indicate the mood of a piece, not even a cautionary interpretative hint, such as 'animato , etc. This all seems to assume a degree of perfection beyond that which one brings into the world as a natural endowment. Were I to define the class of player to whom the études could be given with impunity, I would point to those intelligent and imaginative pianists who would hardly need them as an adjunct to achieving mastery of the instrument, being masters already. Or, to put it differently, they are for musical people whose musical cultivation is beyond spoiling.

Let me say in conclusion that I have played and studied these études with attention and interest. If the editors of these pages have granted an unconscionable amount of space to the review, may it be regarded by this young German artist as proof that he has not been forgotten in his native land. Should he find criticism too far outweighing praise, let him be mindful of the standards by which he himself wishes to be judged, i.e. the highest. Should the reader, on the other hand, wish a summary judgment, I can think of no more appropriate valedictory than these words from *Wilhelm Meister* that have been running through my head all the time I have been writing:

'The most insignificant person can be complete as long as he acts within the boundaries of his own abilities and accomplishments; but even the most beautiful attributes can be obscured, invalidated or nullified if that utterly essential factor of proportion is ignored or violated. This iniquity will become increasingly more common in modern times. For who can meet the requirements of the profoundly intensified present—and at a rapid pace at that?'

[1] Hiller, Ferdinand (1811-1885), who went on to become one of the most well-rounded of the great German musicians of the century, distinguished himself as composer (*The Fall of Jerusalem*), conductor (Paris, Frankfurt, Leipzig, Dresden, Düsseldorf and Cologne), piano virtuoso (he introduced Beethoven's Concerto in E flat to Paris), teacher (the Cologne Conservatory became famous under his directorship) and writer (his *Aus dem Leben eines Tonkünstlers* and his correspondence from Paris for the *Kölnische Zeitung* are among the most instructive source materials of the century). He lived in Paris from 1828 to 1835, enjoying the company of Cherubini, Rossini, Chopin, Liszt, Meyerbeer, Berlioz, Heine, etc. He and Schumann became very close friends. Schumann succeeded Hiller as conductor both in Dresden and Düsseldorf, doubtless with Hiller's backing, and Schumann's Piano Concerto is dedicated to him.

[2] From Jean Paul's *Titan*.

JOSEPH CHRISTOPH KESSLER

(1835)

IT IS INADMISSIBLE to appraise an entire life on the basis of a single deed. An instant that threatens the overthrow of a system may often be explained and excused by reference to the totality of which it is but a tiny part. Disassemble a Beethoven symphony with which you are not familiar and see whether even the most beautiful idea is effective as an isolated phenomenon. This is truer of music than of the graphic arts, where a single torso can establish the master. In music everything is dependent upon the relation of the individual part to the whole. This applies to the individual composition, whether large or small, and it applies, also, to the artist's whole life. One often hears, for instance—false and impossible as it may be—that Mozart had only to write *Don Giovanni* to be the great Mozart. He would, to be sure, have gone down in history as the composer of *Don Giovanni*, but he would be far from having been Mozart.

I speak, therefore, with some hesitation about works whose predecessors are unknown to me. I like to know something about the composer's schooling, about the views he had as a youth, even about the circumstances of his daily life—in a word, something about the man and the artist as he has revealed himself thus far. (I am not in this fortunate position in the case of the composer whose works are here under review.)[1] He who sets about the appraisal of an individual without such knowledge may easily write unsympathetically or under constraint. I gladly accept the latter charge. Want of sympathy, however, the composer need not fear, since in the four works of his that I know he can inspire only respect.

I confess, not without regret, that I prefer the two earlier works, not so much because of their content or because of a better rounded form, neither of which was foremost in his mind, but rather because of the spontaneity of their invention and the natural flow of expression. It would be cause for concern were the artist to be tempted by certain models to desert a path which, if not of his own discovery, he had, at least, pursued in his own fashion. I know that one should be careful about reminding young artists to treasure their individuality; they may try in a variety of ways to break away from the model and, in so doing, inhibit even more severely the natural development of their creative resources. But in the case of Kessler we have a poetic spirit so strong that it can, on its own and without outside help, cast off the binding chains of apprenticeship.

Thus, these pieces are the assertive utterances of a spirit still bound, outbursts of pride, even of anger, and enunciated, moreover, by a youth still imbued with respect for his elders: Beethoven and Franz Schubert. When he becomes tender or sentimental one notes how he resists letting his feelings get the better of him; when he attempts to storm the heights we are reminded of young men who think of themselves as steeled when they are, in fact, merely earnest.

I remarked earlier that the two later pieces are inferior to the earlier ones. What I meant was that the earlier ones have more discoveries. On the one hand we have true invention, the unveiling of a creation never previously known; on the other we have the individual finding for himself what is already at hand—the one the work of genius, which, like nature itself, sows a thousand kinds of seed; the other, like the single clod of earth, receiving the seed and processing it in a single image. In calling the expression in the first less contrived, I did not mean to imply that it was thoroughly natural and fully developed. Although the thoughts are, indeed, worthy of being so called, and although he always knows what he is about, he attempts now and then by some singular cadence or rhythm to give them a mystical quality. This may impress the laymen as profundity; the musically educated will recognize the effort to avoid the conventional—sometimes unavoidable, as in certain cadences and conclusions, etc.—or to improve upon it in some way. One must always take care towards the end of a piece, where the thought should flow easily towards its conclusion, not to disturb the listener with anything new to feel or think about. In the form—or non-form—of these pieces the sentiment cannot, to be sure, expand in these gradual vibrations stirred in us in a longer work of art. With such spontaneous productions we must also take care not to choose for our critique a moment out of harmony with the required mood. Nevertheless, we always have on the one hand the master who, even in the smallest forms, can produce that which is fully rounded and fully satisfying; on the other, the mere thought or idea itself, which alone determines whether it catches on at any given moment and imposes itself as dictator of our own thoughts and ideas.

In short, our estimable colleague would appear well advised to examine his resources, to review the path he has travelled thus far and, finally, to desist from seeking refuge in the miniature, however amusing it may be, and in the rhapsodic. One cannot judge the power of

Mount Aetna by the size of the stones it discharges; but people do gaze upwards in astonishment when its pillars of flame leap up towards the clouds. There is an admonishment here for Kessler for having produced (in the metaphor) mere stones; for myself, too, for having picked them up and examined them without awaiting the greater eruption. I know that this is as premature as anticipating the felicitous perfection of an entire picture from a few sketches. But I know, too, that in a time such as ours, crushed beneath the dull, heedless tread of celebrity-ridden war-horses, we must discuss those who, like Kessler, at least betray a sturdy aspiration.

RARO

[1] Kessler, Joseph Christoph (1800–1872), virtuoso and teacher. Certain of his études were incorporated in the pedagogical works of Kalkbrenner and Moscheles, indicating the high regard in which they were held. Chopin dedicated to Kessler the German edition of his Preludes. The works reviewed here were a Fantasy, Opus 23; an Impromptu, Opus 24; Bagatelles, Opus 30, and Twenty-four Preludes, Opus 31.

FROM THE DAVIDSBÜNDLER ARCHIVES

(1835)

PIANO SONATAS

Sonata in C minor by Delphine Hill Handley[1]

COME CLOSER, my dear, and don't be afraid of the big, bad critic! Heaven knows I am no Menzel;[2] rather an Alexander, saying to Quintus Curtius:[3] 'I do not fight with women; only where there are weapons do I reach for my own.'—Like a lily's stem shall my critic's staff be wafted over your head. Or do you suppose that I do not know those occasions when one would speak but cannot from sheer bliss; or when one would press everything to his heart without having found anything to press; or where it is music that shows us what we shall once again lose? If you believe any of these things about me, my dear, you err.

Truly, an entire eighteenth year reposes in the sonata—uninhibited, amiable, thoughtless. Ah, all the things that it is! Even a bit studied! It speaks of the moment, of the present. No fear of what has been, none of what may be. And even if there were nothing to it at all, one would still have to praise Sister Corinna[4] for abandoning miniatures and trying a life-size picture. Could I only have been with her while she was writing it! I would have pardoned everything—false fifths, unharmonic part-writing; in short, everything! For there is music in her nature, and the most feminine imaginable! Indeed, she will develop into a romanticist, and then, with Clara, we would have two amazons in the glittering array.

One thing that still escapes her—the reconciliation of the composer with the virtuoso, whom I remember under her former name. She wanted to show that she, also, had pearls with which to bedeck herself. But there is no need for them in the twilight hour when, to be happy, one needs no more than solitude, and, to make happy, no more than a second soul. And so I lay the sonata down—with many an errant thought!

EUSEBIUS

II

Two Sonatas by Carl Loewe[5]

And now for the lions! Young critics go preferably for the high places, like lightning seeking out church towers and oak trees. Firmly convinced, as I am, that my amiable Eusebius found more in Delphine's sonata than is there, I also know that with these sonatas by Loewe there may be things in them which escaped my notice. . . .

From what I have played of Loewe's thus far, it is fairly clear to me what I shall have to say. Rich in intimate, profound song—which so distinguishes his ballads—he has chosen in the piano an instrument which, if it is to sound and sing, must be handled with other means than are suitable to the human voice. Loewe plays with his fingers what he hears sung in his head. Now it is true that a meagre piano-tune can be made to sound after a fashion when well sung; but a fine vocal melody will be only half as effective on the piano. The older I become, the more I see that the piano speaks essentially and characteristically in three ways: through multiplicity of voices and harmonic variety, as with Beethoven and Franz Schubert; through use of the pedal, as with Field, and through volubility, as with Czerny and Herz. In the first one encounters the large-scale player, in the second the fantasists, and in the third the stringers of pearls. Well-rounded composer-virtuosos, such as Hummel and Moscheles and, more recently, Chopin, employ all three elements and are consequently the most deeply loved. All pianists, however, to whom at least one of these elements does not come naturally, or who have not mastered one of them, are handicapped. Loewe employs them together, but I do not regard him as a fine pianist, and intelligence is not enough.

One can discuss such things with all due seriousness without thinking specifically of the elegiac of the two sonatas, which I love for many reasons, and prefer to the brilliant one, as the composer probably does, too. To gather three parts into a whole is, I believe, the intention of sonata, concerto and symphony composers. With the older composers it was done more formally, or more *pro forma*, the emphasis being on external physiognomy and tonality; the younger composers broadened the individual parts into sub-sections and discovered a new middle movement, the scherzo. One was no longer satisfied to restrict an idea and its development to a single movement. One hid it, in other guises and fragmentations, in the following movements. In short, one wanted to introduce historical interest (don't laugh, Eusebius!) and, as the times grew more poetic, dramatic interest, too. Even more recently the tendency has been to draw the movements themselves more closely together, and to bind them by instantaneous transitions from one to the other.

If in the brilliant sonata the connecting thread is more visible and tangible, in the elegiac its progress is more meaningful. Its F minor character is constant from beginning to end, audible even when the prevailing tonality gives way from time to time to other keys. The transitory quality of Loewe's composing lies in his habit of never lingering with the detail, of inventing it all at once and then finishing it off at one go. That is the only excuse one can find for much inconsequential matter that the listener must accept with the bargain,—as with the herds and clouds that painters put into their landscapes when nature offers better.

One other thing I sense in Loewe's compositions—namely, that when he is finished one would like to know more. Unfortunately, it has often occurred to me that people have asked what I had in mind with some of my own extravagant effusions. I have no answer. But I maintain, nevertheless, that with Loewe something is left behind—or that there is something behind it.

In the introduction certain progressions disturb me, which recur throughout the whole movement. For the rest, however, it is strong-tender, almost too impassioned to be called elegiac. The Andante I call a song, and let it go at that. The Presto I shall pass over, as it displeases me from beginning to end. In the Finale I see a veiled nun peering out at me from behind a barred window; medieval it is for sure!

I have to laugh when Loewe gives fingerings, and often quite singular ones, too. It will be all the same to him with what fingers he is played, or on the G-string? How? Well, I mean . . .

FLORESTAN

III

Grand Sonata by Wilhelm Taubert[6]

'I regard the first movement of this sonata as the first, the second as the second and the third as the last—in descending order of beauty.'

Thus I can imagine you, dear Florestan, beginning your dissertation. But hands off here, young fellows!—Yes, I see you reaching for your asses' jawbones, preparing to slay the Philistine. But if Florestan has a notable faculty of smelling out the flaws of a work in a matter of seconds, Eusebius, with his tender touch, detects their beauties, with which he is often able to cover up the blemishes. But, as youths do nowadays, you both linger longest and most affectionately with poetic compositions in which the element of fantasy is dominant. To this category our sonata does not belong.

We had occasion last spring to discuss a small piano piece by the same composer. We feel under no constraint to take back anything of the opinion we formed at that time. Here, again, we find, if nothing extraordinary, at least universal and excellent truths proposed in a noble form by a cultivated man. He is careful neither to say nor to promise what he cannot support or fulfil, and he will not undertake what might get him in over his depth. So exactly does he know his resources, and so precisely does he understand what to do with them. In this respect many could learn from him.

Now, while the spectacle of an extravagant nature is more exciting, more grandiose, and comparable, perhaps, to the cascading waterfall so favoured by painters, it is pleasant, too, to be carried along by the tractable, unhazardous river, touching gold kernels and pearls as we trace the bottom with our feet. It would be unjust, however, with respect to this sonata, to let the metaphor suffice. The first movement, especially, flows from beginning to end with such lively force that the last, despite its outwardly greater speed, has an almost languid effect; while the current of the one rises up from the depths, in the latter it seems to be confined to the surface. It might be, of course, that one who had never heard the Finale of Beethoven's Sonata in C sharp minor might judge it differently; in which case, I should make the simple statement from which, in the long run, all music criticism stems—namely, that I do not like it.

The first section, on the other hand, I find so beautifully conceived, carried out and finished off that it merits closer examination. And here I shall let Eusebius do the talking, about whose views, in this case, at least, I have no misgivings:

'The sonata sets off at a leisurely pace. It is as if only when all has been prepared do things get under way. The song becomes stronger. As in an orchestra, the tutti enters. A rapid figure emerges. Thus far we have heard nothing extraordinary, but one is carried along without giving too much thought to the matter. Now we note questioning basses in the major tonality. A voice answers, lovely and timid: "Don't look at me so severely,—why wish to hurt anyone?"—and joins company with the first soft song. The earlier rapid figures leap in, tremulous with curiosity. The scene becomes more lively. A tiny, tender, merry strain can hardly make itself felt. Up and down it goes, and forward and backwards; a firm hand takes over and puts an end to it. Two new, rather pale figures appear, male and female, and relate what they have experienced of pleasure and pain. Others join in sympathetically— "Just pull yourselves together, and banish tears and lightning flashes from your eyes"—"But forgive us our laments for the departed."— Now everything evens out. The stranger is assimilated, the familiar goes hand in hand with the unfamiliar; an alto voice asks cheerfully: "Who is so excited, and why?" "Listen to me again," says the first voice. . . .'

So much for Eusebius, who doubtless reads a good deal into it. In the second movement, about which I have said nothing so far, the former principal theme appears in a new guise. As if forgetful of former melancholy, it enters amiably and confidently. Of tears there is hardly a trace, and if you were to ask about them, they would be denied. The whole setting has been changed. Everything seems more practical and down-to-earth. Certain countenances have such tender, original features that I hardly need to point them out to you. The last movement seems to me to have been somewhat clumsily tacked on to the Scherzo. Indeed, I hold the whole movement against the composer, who should have awaited a happier hour.

RARO

IV

Grand Sonata by Ludwig Schunke[7]

Do you remember, Florestan, an August evening in the remarkable year of 1834? We were walking arm in arm, you and Schunke and I. A storm hung over us, with all its beauties and forebodings. I can still see his face illuminated by a flash of lightning, and his upward glance as he said, almost inaudibly: 'A flash for us!'

And now heaven has opened without lightning, and a divine hand has gathered him up, so quietly that he hardly noticed it.—Ah, Mozart, Prince of Spirits in that other world founded by the most beautiful of human faiths, call together one day—and may it be a long time off— all those disciples who, in this world, have borne the German name of Ludwig! See what noble spirits shall ascend to him, and with what joy he shall behold them—Ludwig Beethoven, Cherubini, Spohr, Berger,[8] Schunke!—The first of these was followed by the youngest on Sunday morning, last December 7, before the completion of his twenty-fourth year.

One winter night a year ago a young man joined our group in Krause's cellar. Every eye was focused upon him. Some were reminded of a Johannes figure. Others said that if one were to dig up a statue at Pompei with similar features it would be taken for the head of a Roman emperor. Florestan whispered in my ear: 'There goes the living Schiller as painted by Thorwaldsen,[9] only even more like Schiller.' Everyone was agreed that he must be an artist, so distinctly had nature engraved his calling in his countenance.—You all have known him, the eyes aglow with enthusiasm, the noble, aquiline nose, the mouth with its smile of self-deprecation, the luxuriant head of tumbling curls, and beneath it all a lithe, slim torso that seemed, not so much to bear, as to be borne. Even before he had quietly spoken his name, 'Ludwig Schunke, from Stuttgart', I heard a voice within me saying: 'He it is whom you are seeking'—and in his eye I read something similar. Florestan was in a melancholy frame of mind at the time, and concerned himself less with the stranger. An incident, of which you may not have heard, brought them closer together.

A few weeks after Schunke's arrival, a Berlin composer[10] passed through and was invited to a gathering at which Schunke was also present. Ludwig was proud of the association of his family name with virtuosos, particularly horn players. Somehow, during dinner, the conversation turned upon horns. The Berliner dismissed them rudely, remarking: 'One should give them nothing to blow except C, G and E,' and he asked if the first horn theme in the Symphony in C minor, although very easy, 'did not always sound horrible enough'. Ludwig said not a word. But an hour later he burst in upon us in the cellar and said that this was how things stood, and that he had written the Berliner a letter accusing him of impugning the family name[11] and inviting him to choose between daggers and pistols, and would Florestan be his second? We all broke out laughing, and Florestan was reminded of the famous old lutenist, Rohhaar, who had once said that a musician with courage was a ——. 'Truly, good Louis Schunke,' he said, 'you put the lutenist to shame!'

Schunke was in no mood for jokes. He continued to take it all seriously, and even roamed about the town looking for a gunsmith. Finally, some twenty-four hours later, there came an answer from the Berliner, written on wrapping paper. It said that he (Schunke) must be quite out of his mind; he (the Berliner) would be charmed to shoot it out with him, but at this very moment when he (Schunke) would be reading the letter he (the Berliner) would be well on his way to Naples, etc. I shall never forget the way he stood there, the letter in his hand, a veritable angry Apollo, and so wrought up that one could count the veins in his white hand—and at the same time smiling so roguishly that one wanted to hug him. It all made a great impression on Florestan, and, like a couple of children, they began exchanging views on every-thing from favourite dishes to Beethoven. The following evening drew the bond between them tighter and for ever!

Of his own music we had as yet heard nothing but a brilliant set of variations, composed in Vienna, where, as he himself later expressed it, he had made no progress except as a virtuoso. This progress had, how-ever, been enormous. That he was a master pianist we knew from the first chords. But on that occasion Florestan was unmoved, and on the way home he let loose upon me all his old impatience with virtuosos. A virtuoso, he said, who could not lose eight fingers in order to use the remaining two to write down his compositions was not worth the powder it would take to kill him. And was it not the virtuoso who was to blame if divinely gifted composers starved to death? Etc.

The finely grained Schunke sensed all this. He knew that he had been found wanting, and he knew where. Then came the special evening to which I have referred. A number of Davidsbündler were gathered together, including the Master. No one was thinking of music. It was as if the grand piano had opened itself of its own accord, and as if Ludwig, now sitting there, had been wafted thither on a cloud. All of a sudden we were caught up in a stream of unfamiliar music.—I can see it all now in my mind's eye, the dimmed light, the still walls, as if they, too, were listening, the friends grouped around, breathless, Florestan's pale features, the musing Master and, in the midst of it all, Ludwig, who held us spellbound, as if in a magic circle. When he had finished, Florestan said: 'You are a master of your art, and I pronounce the sonata to be your best work, particularly when it is you who plays it. Truly, the Davidsbündler would be proud to number such an artist among the members of their order.'

Ludwig was ours. Would you want me to tell you more of the happy days that followed? Spare me the reminiscences! They shall be locked away like rosaries in the most secret drawer. Few are the festival days when one shall put them on display!

The Davidsbündler, when they heard the news, gathered together and exchanged anecdotes, gay and sad. Then from Florestan's room issued soft tones, and the friends grew quieter, for they recognized the Sonata. When Florestan had finished the Master said: 'And not another word!—We are closer to him now than ever before. Since he left us there has been a special redness in the heavens. Whence it comes I would not know. In any case, young fellows, it's up to you to light the way!'

About midnight they went their separate ways.

R. S.

[1] Née Schauroth (1814-188?), a pupil of Kalkbrenner, born in Magdeburg, resident of Munich, to whom Mendelssohn dedicated his Concerto in G minor. Mendelssohn's sister Fanny visited her in Munich in 1839 and wrote: 'I have never heard Felix's First Concerto played so well except by himself. In addition to all that, she is a most amiable person.'

[2] Menzel. The reference is presumably to Wolfgang Menzel (1798-1873), who had recently distinguished himself with a violently critical book, *Die deutsche Literatur* (1827).

[3] Curtius, Rufus Quintus, biographer of Alexander the Great (*de rebus gestis Alexandri magni*). The *Encyclopaedia Britannica* describes the work as 'uncritical' and as showing 'ignorance of geography, chronology and military matters'. Since the biography is assumed to have been written during the reign of Claudius (A.D. 41-54) it would seem that Schumann here shows himself to be similarly ignorant, at least in chronology.

[4] Sister Corinna. The reference is to the novels *Corinna* and *Delphine* by Madame de Staël.

[5] Loewe, Johann Carl Gottfried (1796-1869), known primarily as a composer of ballads, of which he was himself an outstanding interpreter. Of the works here reviewed one of them is certainly the Sonata Elegiac in F minor, Opus 32. The other is presumably a sonata entitled *Mazeppa*, Opus 27. Loewe in German means lion, hence the pun in the opening sentence.

[6] Taubert, Gottfried Wilhelm (1811-1891). He spent the greater part of his life in Berlin, achieving early fame as a virtuoso, subsequently devoting himself to teaching, conducting and composition. None of his works, which included a number of operas, has survived, although Schumann was by no means alone as an admirer among his contemporaries.

[7] Schunke, Ludwig (1810-1834), a co-founder with Schumann of *Die Neue Zeitschrift für Musik*. He had been a pupil of Reicha and Kalkbrenner in Paris. Before writing this article Schumann wrote to a friend: 'May heaven give me strength to set him a worthy monument in our periodical.'

[8] Berger, Ludwig (1777-1839), a pupil of Clementi and the teacher, in Berlin, of Mendelssohn, Taubert and Henselt. He was a prolific composer, and his études, particularly, were held in high esteem.

[9] Thorwaldsen, Bertel (1768-1844), famous Danish sculptor.

[10] The reference is to Otto Nicolai (1810-1849), conductor and composer, now remembered as the founder of the Vienna Philharmonic and composer of *The Merry Wives of Windsor*.

[11] Schunke's father and uncle were both celebrated horn virtuosos.

LOUIS SPOHR'S 'WEIHE DER TÖNE'

(1835)

ONE WOULD HAVE TO transcribe a third time in order to give an idea of this symphony[1] to someone who had never heard it. For the poet's words are inspired by music, which Spohr, in turn, has translated back to music again. Could one find a listener, who, unacquainted either with the original poem or the headings for the various movements, could give us an accounting of the pictures they suggest to him, we would have, indeed, a test of the composer's success in achieving his objective. I, unfortunately, was acquainted with the symphony's intentions in advance, and found myself compelled, quite against my will, to submerge the images all too clearly suggested by the music in favour of the still more substantial raiment of Pfeiffer's[2] poem.

Putting all this aside for the moment, I should like today to touch upon something else. And if I attack the subordination of music to this, of all texts, and thus get to the inner core of the matter, it should be understood that I am not impugning what is otherwise a musical masterpiece.

Beethoven sensed the hazards to which he exposed himself in writing the Pastoral Symphony. In those few words, 'more an expression of sensations than a painting', which he placed at the head of the score, lies a whole aesthetic for composers; and it is ludicrous to paint him, as many have done, seated by a brook, his head in his hand, listening to the ripple of the water. With the symphony here under discussion, it seems to me, the danger was greater.

If anyone ever set himself apart from his fellows, or if anyone has ever remained true to himself from his very first note, then it is Spohr, with his lovely, eternal lament. He sees everything, however, through tears, and his ideas seem to dissolve into formless, ethereal images for which it is hard to find a name. It is a kind of perpetual incantation, harmonized and sustained, to be sure, by the spirit and hand of an artist—but we all know that, of course! More recently he has devoted all his resources to opera. And as there is no better advice to offer a primarily lyrical poet who would aspire to greater force of expression than that he should study the dramatic masters and make some attempts on his own; so it is easy to assume that opera, in which he must pursue situations and work out plot and characterizations, might tear him from his melancholy groove. *Jessonda* was straight from his heart. His instrumental music, nevertheless, has remained much the same.

His third[3] symphony differs only externally from its predecessors. He felt that he must try something new. Possibly influenced by Beethoven's Ninth Symphony, whose first movement may rest upon the same poetic basis as the first movement of Spohr's, he sought refuge in poetry. But how strangely he chose—and how true to form! It was not to Shakespeare or Goethe or Schiller that he turned, but to something almost more formless than music itself (if that is not putting it too boldly), to a tribute to music, to a poem that describes the effects of music. In short, he described in tones the very tones described by the poet, and praised music with—music!

When Beethoven conceived and elaborated his thoughts for the Pastoral Symphony, it was not one single, fleeting spring day that inspired him to his joyous outcry, but rather the dark converging mixture of noble songs above us (as Heine, I think, has somewhere put it), creation itself, with its infinite multiplicity of voices. The poet of *Weihe der Töne* caught them in an already rather faded mirror, and Spohr re-reflected the reflection.

---

[1] *The Consecration of Sound*, Spohr's Symphony No. 4 in F major, Opus 86.

[2] Pfeiffer, a poet in Kassel, where Spohr had settled as Hofkapellmeister at the Court of the Elector of Hesse-Kassel. Pfeiffer's sister, Marianne, became Spohr's second wife.

[3] Schumann's error.

CHRISTIAN GOTTLIEB MÜLLER

Symphony No. 3

(1835)

W ERE I A PUBLISHER, I would have the handwritten score[1] in front of me today, and in a few weeks the printed one.

Without those one can, of course, make some observations, but hardly any judgments; for so German a work cannot be readily viewed from all sides. What on the cathedral at Strasbourg, for instance, may appear from the distance to be mere decoration or filling, is revealed upon closer inspection as an integral part of the whole. But there is something to be said for leaving one's first impression of a work to the imagination; large forms have a more magical effect in the moonlight than when sunlight penetrates into every arabesque.

It is a familiar experience that most young composers try right off to do the job too well. They assemble too much material, which, in their less skilled hands, tends to pile up and, when brought together, to merge into featureless globs. One remembers something of this kind as having happened in Müller's two previous symphonies. In this third, however, things are better and less laboriously ordered. We may expect that if this symphony approaches mastery in its outlines, the next may well approach it in coloration, too. Most imposing remains, naturally, the spirit, with its royal retinue; here it often asserts itself proudly (particularly in the last movement). Indeed, the performance is so bold that we rejoice, as for one who has previously been almost too withdrawn and demure and now, sensing himself on firm ground, is doubly assertive. Where we are reminded of Beethoven's manner one is tempted, in a certain sense, to comparisons favouring the younger composer. I mean that what he successfully achieves on his own is happily distinguished from his attempts to emulate foreign models. Among the former I reckon, for example, the utterly tender reminiscense before the conclusion of the whole symphony, which, as if animated by the composer's sense of satisfaction in his own idea, now bursts forth, fully free and uninhibited.

An examination of the score would reveal still other interesting things, along with some pretty details. As it is, I can no longer recall exactly the first theme of the first allegro movement. I remember only that I could not be sure whether it was to be taken seriously or as a joke. Probably a bit of each. But the second theme, with its lovely and insistent rhythm, speaks with greater conviction. In the slow middle movement the stringendo stands out, quickly developing a life full of promise. That at the end one has the feeling of something more to come represents a dramatic advance over the movements of other symphonies, particularly of the old school, where the four parts are rounded off inwardly as well as outwardly. The Leipzigers like to applaud after adagios, and this time the demonstration was fully in order.

The rhythm of the Scherzo is not distinctly grasped at a first hearing, but a glance at the score would easily clarify the matter. The 'alternative' can become a favourite with the symphony public. The heavy emphasis on the weak beats reminds one of a similar procedure in the *Eroica*, but has an entirely different effect. One is only incidentally struck by the superficial resemblance. If I am not mistaken, this movement ends abruptly, as do most of the others. On an earlier occasion I have written: 'One must always take care towards the end of a piece, where the thought should flow easily towards its conclusion, not to disturb the listener with anything new to feel or think about.' These abrupt endings are often called original. In fact, nothing is easier than to write an original ending—or any ending at all. Nor does one have to carry things as far as Chopin, who recently even closed a piece with a six-four chord. I say this as a general observation, and not with particular reference to the symphony under discussion.—The last movement is the most impassioned, interwoven throughout with busy violin figurations, sometimes no longer very pretty, but interestingly conceived and executed.

It is my considered opinion, then, that as a new work and a credit to German talent, this symphony should be rated above most others of its kind. To the composer himself, who has resisted every temptation to court easy popularity, may these observations, volunteered with no claim to infallibility, offer some idea of the high expectation and pleasure with which many music lovers await his future works.

I said at the outset, and advisedly, that were I a publisher, I would have the printed score ready in a few weeks. I would also, however, assuming that I understand something of such things, ask the composer to make a few small changes. To have completed something is, to be sure, a blessed feeling, but much depends upon how something is begun. The hand of genius must be felt there, too. Thus, right in the introduction, which seems to be there only as a bow to tradition, there is much that I would like to change. What is the purpose of this ceremonial, portentous thing? How welcome it is when Mozart (in his Symphony in G minor) and Beethoven (in most of his later symphonies) gives us, right at the outset, and in full flavour, a taste of rich, bubbling life. Yes, I find—even in some of Haydn's symphonies—that sudden plunge from adagio into allegro a greater blemish than a hundred chromatic fifths! I would also shade over certain four-part wind passages; they seem for ever to be saying: 'Look, we are playing in four-part harmony!'—not to mention a certain embarrassment on the part of the audience, which cannot fail to notice the enforced idleness of the violins. Finally, in the last movement, I think I would eliminate some instruments from the crescendo from forte and fortissimo to *fff*, if only to have them in reserve when the *fff* moment is reached. I am reminded of the last movement of Beethoven's Symphony in A major, where, just when the festivities seem to have reached their peak, new voices and new reserves of strength are suddenly released and carry the rioting to what may well be the ultimate of which music is capable.—(I fear that I would be stoned to death by the Beethoven lovers were I to betray the text which I would supply for that last movement of the Symphony in A major.)[2]—And then, were I a publisher, the work should be sent forth into the world.

(Written on the morning after the first performance.)

FLORESTAN

---

[1] Müller, Christian Gottlieb (1800-1863), violinist, composer and conductor of the Euterpe Concerts in Leipzig. He enjoys the possibly unenviable distinction of having been Schumann's instructor in orchestration.

[2] See the third of the 'Letters of a (Music-) Lover (p. 70).

SOME NEW PIANO SONATAS

(1835)

I

Carl Loewe's 'Spring' Sonata

ONE SHOULD BE able to find a bit of spring in any music; this time the imaginative bard lays a special sacrifice at its altar.

From Loewe one would rather have expected a 'winter' sonata, in which I would have anticipated the sound of snow under wagon wheels and of nightbirds around the steeple; but he has caught the sounds of spring, too, if hardly like Beethoven whose Sixth Symphony is to other idyllic compositions as the life of a great man to his biographies, but still as a poet with clear and open eye. And that alone is welcome in a time and in an art ever more given to Faustian introspection and preferring dark mysticism to life's fresh pleasures. Whoever, therefore, expects night scenes and northern lights will find himself mistaken. In their stead he sees meadows in the incipient green of springtime, and here and there a bud with a butterfly. So much for the music as poetry.

As a composition it can hardly be described as either profound or new. Melody and harmony come together naturally, often even simply. The whole is, perhaps, too fleetingly felt and conceived. We hope that the composer will understand us correctly. Beethoven, in his Pastoral Symphony, sings in melodies so simple that one can imagine some childlike spirit's having invented them. Certainly, however, he did not write down everything that occurred to him in the first rush of inspiration, but rather chose from among many. And it is that to which we take exception in this and many of Loewe's other works. They put forth big claims with the softest of voices, and we are asked to accept the commonplace and the hackneyed just because it is an eminent composer who is repeating them, and for the sake of the central idea. We doubt that any other living composer in Loewe's class would have permitted some of the details of this sonata to be published. Such passages as the first theme of the first movement, the beginning of the second section of the same movement, etc., may be excused as appropriate to the setting and the terrain in which it is all played and painted; but, as we have often said, there must be music enough in the painting to be effective on its own merits, and to leave the ear independent of the eye. Thus we find the second movement the most self-sufficient, musically, and the Introduction the least successful episode of all.

Be that as it may, we recommend this sonata to teachers, particularly. They should let their younger pupils play it. Its thoroughly clear and natural sentiment should be both pleasing and improving.

II

'Spring' Sonata by Count von Pocci[1]

Had I not seen the title page, I should have guessed the sonata to be by a woman, and would have reviewed it as follows:

'Whatever your name—Adèle or Zuleika—I love you sight unseen, as I love all who write sonatas. If only you could end the way you begin, as, for example, on the very first page, where one is met by the fragrance of March violets. . . . But while your eye is dreamily exploring the moonlit sky, or your heart is lost in Jean Paul, you are also distracted by your girl-friend's becoming pink ribbon. In a word, you are a good little seventeen-year-old girl, full of affection and vanity, or ardour and caprice. Nor can I scare you with such words as "tonic" and "dominant", not to speak of "counterpoint". You would only laugh and say that's the way you made it and there's nothing to be done about it, and, anyway, one should be nice to you.

'But if I were your teacher, and a clever one, I would give you Bach and Beethoven to play (but not Weber, whom you so adore) in order that your ear and features be sharpened, your tender sensibilities be firmly channelled, and your thoughts be given shape and security. And then I hardly know what even a *Neue Zeitschrift für Musik* could find to say about you that did not rhyme with "lovely" and "pretty".'

EUSEBIUS

How slyly my friend Eusebius evades the issue. Why not come right out and say: 'Count von Pocci has much talent and little schooling?'

FLORESTAN

III

Sonata by Franz Lachner[2]

If the sonata had been composed by a Frenchman, or even an Italian, one would have been astonished by its earnestness and profundity.

There is, as yet, no world art, and, therefore, no criticism whose criteria are not governed by the degree of cultivation attributed to the respective nation and associated with its national characteristics. Lachner is a German, and should be content to be addressed in straight-to-the-point, unambiguous German.

We hardly know whether to be sorry or glad that, aside from this sonata, many songs and a symphony, which we have heard only once, we know nothing more of Lachner's compositions. He poses a most difficult problem for criticism, not because he is so darkly profound that he is difficult to get at, but rather because of the snake-like slipperiness with which he glides away whenever and wherever one tries to take hold of him. If he says something dull, there is something fine to make up for it; if one is annoyed by some reminiscence of Spohr or Franz Schubert, it is soon followed by something fully his own; if it all seems, for a time, to be deception and vain show, he suddenly becomes candid and straightforward.

You can find in this sonata whatever you want: melody, form, rhythm (in which, however, his invention is weakest), fluency, clarity, facility, correctness—everything is there. But nothing touches you, hardly anything penetrates beyond the ear. We thought the fault might lie in our own mood of the moment, and conscientiously put the sonata aside for some time, in order to compare a later impression with the first one. We consulted the opinion of others. The result was always the same.

It is not a trifling matter. High hopes were entertained for Lachner. Because of his talent, criticism has been indulgent. It is time now that he learned vigilance, lest he become even more deeply enmeshed in his slipshod ways. There are certain semi-geniuses, who, uncommonly aware and receptive, absorb everything extraordinary and proceed to handle it as if it were their own. They have one wing of genius and the other of wax. When circumstances are favourable—under the stress of excitement, for instance—the good wing may assist the other aloft; but under normal conditions of repose the wax wing drags the other down.

One often repents such severe criticism of people of this kind—for some of their flights are crowned with success. One is often tempted to suggest that they desist from creative endeavours altogether, because they do not know how badly they deceive themselves and others. They live in a state of perpetual tension, in a continual crisis. One is constrained to leave them there to work out their own salvation; for criticism just gets their backs up, and praise may easily go to their heads.

Most of them are greedy for fame, and have not sufficient self-control to withhold their works from the world. It follows that the world, in turn, can hardly fail to note the crudity and ambiguity of the works thus exposed. For the very same reason, i.e. because in such persons and compositions there is no definitive system or style, one is often misled about them and their future, and may, indeed, predict worse than eventually occurs. This may be the case with Lachner, and we devoutly hope so, renouncing all divinatory criticism. Let him accept these observations—which apply more to a whole class of composers, and only partly to him—as the utterance of many who are fully aware of his artistic predilections, but who cannot suppress the feeling that more might be expected of him were he to forgo the applause of the multitude in favour of the more rewarding praise of his artist contemporaries.

[1] Pocci, Count Franz (1807-1876), better known for his small choruses for children, to which he contributed his own texts and his own illustrations. He lived all his life in Munich.

[2] Lachner, Franz (1803-1890), a pupil of Stadler and Sechter in Vienna and an intimate friend of Schubert, he was principal conductor of opera successively at the court theatres of Vienna, Mannheim and Munich, and a prolific and successful composer.

'FURY OVER THE LOST PENNY'

(1835)

It WOULD BE HARD to conceive of anything more amusing than this little escapade. How I laughed when I played it for the first time! And how astonished I was when, a second time through, I read a footnote telling me that this capriccio, discovered among Beethoven's manuscripts after his death, bore the title: 'Fury over the Lost Penny, Vented in a Caprice.' . . . O! It's the most adorable, futile fury, like that which seizes you when you can't get a boot off, and you sweat and swear and the boot looks up at you, phlegmatically—and unmoved!

I've got you at last, you Beethoven fanatics! I'd like to vent my feelings about you in quite another fashion, and pummel you with the softest of fists when I see you beside yourselves, your eyes bulging, lost in rapture, and gasping: 'Beethoven strives ever for the rapturous, from star to star he flew, free from this earth!'

'I'm really unbuttoned today', was his favourite expression when his spirits were high. And then he would laugh like a lion and let loose about him—for he was unruly in all circumstances.

Well, with this capriccio I shall be unruly with you, my friends. You'll call it common, unworthy of a Beethoven, just like the tune to 'Freude, schöner Götterfunken' in the D minor Symphony, you'll bury it deep under the *Eroica*.

Should there one day be a resurrection of the arts, and Genius hold the scales with the capriccio about the penny balanced against ten of the newest dramatic overtures, well, I tell you, the overtures would flip skyward!

And you composers, young and old, there is one essential thing that you could all learn from it, something you need to be reminded of from time to time: nature, nature, nature!

CHARACTERISTICS OF THE KEYS

(1835)

THERE HAVE BEEN arguments for and against; the truth, as always lies in the middle.

One can as little say that this or that sentiment can be expressed only in this or that key (rage in C sharp minor, etc.) as that every key is capable of expressing anything, as Zelter[1] maintained.

Analysis of key characteristics began in the last century. It was the poet, Christian Schubart,[2] in particular, who professed to find certain expressive properties in certain keys. Poetically attractive as this idea may be, Schubart overlooked entirely the basic distinctions inherent in the major and minor modes; he also assembled too many ultimately particularized designations. He called E minor, for instance, a maiden dressed in white with a pink bow on her bosom; in G minor he found dissatisfaction, uneasiness, wrestling with an unworkable plan, gritting of the teeth in anger, etc. Now just listen to Mozart's Symphony in G minor, with its buoyant Hellenic charm, or to Moscheles' Concerto in G minor!

Granted that through transposition from the original key into another a composition will achieve a different effect, and that this would seem to indicate a fundamental difference between one key and another! Transpose Schubert's *Sehnsucht* Waltz[3] from A flat into A, or the Bridal Chorus from *Der Freischütz* from C into B—the new tonality will seem to be incompatible with the mood, if only because the mood which produced those pieces is asked to sustain itself in a strange environment. The procedure by which the composer is prompted to choose this or that basic tonality for the expression of his feelings is as inexplicable as the creation of the genius himself, whose very idea embodies the form, the vessel, so to speak, within which it will be securely contained. The composer hits upon the correct key immediately, much as the painter chooses his colour, and without giving much thought to it.

If it is, indeed, true that in various epochs certain stereotypes have come to be associated with certain keys, then we should assemble all the masterpieces set in any given key and compare their prevailing moods. The difference between major and minor may be assumed at the outset. The one is masculine and active, the other feminine and passive. Simpler emotions have simpler tonalities. Compound emotions move better in strange keys, less familiar to the ear. The emotional rise and fall can best be discerned by tracing one's course through the circle of fifths, moving upward from C, the high point will be reached with F sharp, midway in our journey from octave to octave, from which it descends through the flat keys back to C.

[1] Zelter, Karl Friedrich (1758-1832), violinist, composer, conductor and teacher, founder (in Berlin) of the first Liedertafel (men's chorus). He was an intimate friend of Goethe, who is said to have preferred Zelter's settings of his poems to Beethoven's and Schubert's.

[2] Schubart, Christian Friedrich Daniel (1739-1791), organist, composer, theorist and poet, now best remembered as author of the words to Schubert's 'Die Forelle'. Schumann here refers to his theoretical work, *Ideen zu einer Aesthetik der Tonkunst*, published posthumously in 1806.

[3] Better known outside Germany as 'Mon Désir'.

LETTERS FROM A (MUSIC-) LOVER[1]

(1835)

To Chiara

'MIDST ALL OUR musical soul-feasts, there appears the head of an angel, bearing rather more than a mere likeness to a certain so-called Chiara, right down to the roguish cut of the chin. Why are you not with us? And how you must have thought of your friends in Firlenz last evening, from *Meeresstille* to the blazing Finale of Beethoven's Symphony in B flat!

I know nothing lovelier than a concert, unless it be the hour before one, when you go about on tiptoe, humming ethereal melodies and performing whole overtures on windowpanes.

The clock strikes a quarter-to. . . .

And I climb the steps with Florestan.

'Sebb,' he says, 'there is much to look forward to this evening. First, the mere fact that we shall be hearing music. The summer drought leaves one thirsty. And then we have F. Meritis, leading his orchestra into battle for the first time. I look forward, also, to our soloist, Maria,[2] with her vestal voice, and, finally, to the whole expectant audience—and you know what I normally think of audiences. . . .'

As he spoke the word 'audience', we found ourselves confronted by that ancient attendant with a face like Mozart's Commendatore. He had his hands full, and was rather peevish about letting us pass, Florestan, as usual, having forgotten his ticket. I stepped into the glittering auditorium, and if anyone could have read my face he would have interpreted it as follows:

'I step softly, for about me I sense the presence of those rare men to whom it is given to move and enchant hundreds at a time. I see Mozart during a symphony, beating time with his foot so hard that his shoe-buckles break. There is Hummel, that fine old master, improvising at the piano. And there is Catalani,[3] tearing off her shawl because someone has forgotten to spread her a carpet. And there are Weber and Spohr and many others! Then I thought of you, Chiara, peering down from your box, as you are wont to do, with that becoming lorgnette!'

While such thoughts were coursing through my head, I suddenly became aware of Florestan, stationed, as always, near the doorway, his eyes flashing fire, and seeming to say:

'I've got you all together again, dear public, and can set you at each other's throats. For years I have dreamed of organizing concerts for the deaf and dumb, that you might learn from them how to behave yourselves at concerts, especially when they are very beautiful. You should be turned to stone pagodas, like Tsing-Sing,[4] if you were so much as to think of discussing what you have seen in the magic wonderland of music.' And so on. . . .

My reflections were interrupted by a sudden deathly silence as F. Meritis entered. Instantly, hundreds of hearts went out to him.

Do you remember that evening when we drove along the Brenta from Padua?[5] The oppressive Italian night air sent us off to sleep. And then in the morning there was a sudden cry: '*Ecco, Ecco, signori, Venezia!*'—And the sea lay stretched out before us, motionless and monstrous; far out on the horizon a distant tinkle, as if the little waves were conversing in a dream. Thus it coils and shimmers in *Meeresstille*. One dozes, more lost in thought than thinking. Beethoven's chorus, also based on Goethe, with its accentuation of every word, sounds almost rough compared with this sounding spiderweb of the violins. A harmony is unleashed towards the end that seems to suggest a daughter of Nereus casting a seductive eye at the poet, as if to lure him down. But then, for the first time, there comes a higher wave, and little by little the sea grows everywhere more sportive, and sails flutter in the breeze, and gay pennants, and now away, away, away!

'Which of F. Meritis' overtures,' some simpleton asks me, 'do you like the most?'

The tonalities of E minor, B minor and D major[6] blend suddenly into a triad of graces, and I can think of no better answer than:

'Each of them!'

F. Meritis conducted as if he had composed the overture himself, and the orchestra played accordingly. And yet I was struck by Florestan's comment that the orchestra played rather as he himself had played when, fresh from the provinces, he had begun his studies with Master Raro.

'My worst crisis,' he said, 'was the middle stage between native gift and art. Accustomed to grasp things impulsively, but handicapped by inadequate technique, I now had to play slowly and distinctly. There followed such a period of hesitancy and stiffness that I began to despair of my own talent. Fortunately, it didn't last long.'[7]

For my part, I was disturbed, both in the overture and in the symphony, by the conductor's baton,[8] and I agreed with Florestan that in a symphony the orchestra must be like a republic, subordinate to no higher authority. Still, it was a joy to watch F. Meritis, and note how with his eye he anticipated and communicated every meaningful turn and nuance, from the most delicate to the most robust, an inspired leader plunging ahead—in contrast to those conductors who threaten with their sceptres to thrash the score, the orchestra and even the audience!

You know my impatience with disputes about tempi, and my conviction that the inner substance of the movement is alone decisive. Thus, the faster adagio of a cold player sounds more sluggish than the slower tempo of a player with warm blood in his veins. With orchestras, however, one is dealing with large bodies. Rougher, thicker ones are able to give more emphasis and more meaning, both to detail and to the whole. With small, more delicate orchestras, as with our Firlenz Orchestra, one must compensate the lack of resonance by driving tempi. In a word, the Scherzo of the symphony seemed to me too slow. One noticed it quite plainly, too, in the orchestra's restlessness in seeking repose.

But what is all this to you in your Milan? And what is it, indeed, to me, who can always imagine the Scherzo just as I would have it?

You were curious as to whether Maria would be as well received in Firlenz as formerly. How could you doubt it?—Except that she had chosen an aria that earned her more honour as an artist than applause as a canary. And there was a Westfalian music director[9] who played a violin concerto of Spohr, quite well, if a bit pale and lean.

Everyone felt that the composition of the programme reflected a change of policy. Where, from the very beginning, Firlenz concerts had found Italian butterflies fluttering around German oaks, the latter now stood alone, so sturdy and dark. Some chose to see a reaction in this. I rather attributed it to chance. We all know how imperative it is to defend Germany against the intrusions of your beloved Italians. But let it be done with discretion, and more through the encouragement of the German young than through futile resistance to a power that comes and goes like a fashion.

Florestan came by at midnight with Jonathan,[10] a new Davidsbündler, the two of them deep in a dispute about the aristocracy of the spirit as against the republic of opinion. Florestan has finally found an opponent who gives him diamonds to crack!

Enough for today. Don't forget to keep track of your calendar, and to look out for August 13, when Aurora will unite your name with mine![11]

EUSEBIUS

II

To Eusebius

. . . My pulse is pounding in feverish excitement, and Felicita's[12] melancholy cadences are still echoing inside me.

That was not the applause of a delighted public, but rather the exultant delirium of an unchained mob! The noise of one of your northern music festivals is like the pious murmur of a *Dona nobis Pacem* compared with this full chorus of the enchanted Milanese. The men deported themselves like supple-jointed puppets, and let you know with their hands and feet that they were sheerly beside themselves. The ladies took their fragrant bouquets and threw them by the hundred at Desdemona's feet. The double-bass player laid aside his bow, and beat out an approving after-tutti on his instrument, while the timpanist, where he had nothing to play, improvised a furious storm. Nor were we idle ourselves. Even Livia seemed to forget herself for a few minutes.—The Marquis offered his sweet sufferer his arm, and I had to follow.

I have just read—and heard—your letter through. Your thoughts about the orchestra as a republic I understand perfectly. I cannot think of that masterly adagio in the *Meeresstille* otherwise than with every instrument, and particularly the basses, seeming to drift in by chance, just as from the ocean one broad eternity seems to emerge after another. I passed your idea on to Fritz Friedrich.[13] It was all very well, he observed, but to play the overture with proper spiritual truth you would have first to send the whole Firlenz Orchestra out to sea.

Ali Baba[14] I do not understand. I told you once before how bored I was when I heard it in Paris. That reminds me of one of Florestan's aphorisms: When a great poet tells long nursery tales in his old age, it is but natural; but to see blue sky when it is raining, that is unnatural.

But now to Felicita. The woman is truly incomprehensible, as amiable as she is extraordinary. She invited us to a rehearsal, and we stole away from the Marquis. You should see how this creature is not only a distinguished member of the company but even the animating soul of the whole stage. In this she may be compared with Schröder-Devrient.[15] She supervises the costumes, the placement of the chorus, the stage business of the principals and gives the orchestra the tempi;

and in the same instant she is embellishing her aria with the loveliest of ornaments. Without song she would be the greatest actress of the century, and without speech the greatest mime.

This example of genius unchained confirms again what Master Raro has said about genius: 'It often has to be awakened rudely, and—up to a certain point—pedantically developed.' For Felicitas had a severe teacher in her father, who almost always greeted her youthful accomplishments, already quite admirable, with dissatisfaction, criticism and still higher demands. In New York,[16] where she sang a Desdemona to his Otello, he threatened to stab her in earnest if she did not develop more expression in her singing and acting. This threat from so severe a teacher had such an effect upon the sixteen-year-old girl that her father, after the performance, rapturously predicted her future greatness. She told me the story herself, expressing her gratitude for her father's superior insight. If you show all this to Master Raro I can see him already, an exultant smile on his lips, passing the letter on to a certain——

CHIARA

III

To Chiara

The postman suddenly became a flower in my eyes as I detected 'Milano' in shimmering red letters on the envelope.

I, too, recall with pleasure, my first visit to La Scala, where I heard Rubini and Meric-Lalande.[17] Italian music should be heard in the company of Italians. German music, of course, can be enjoyed under any sky.

I was right in assuming that the programme of the opening concert did not reflect a change of policy, for since then we have been offered Hesperian[18] fare. I have had to laugh at Florestan. He is bored to distraction. But if only to spite those Handelians and other -ians[19] who talk as if they themselves had composed *Samson* in their nightgowns, and without absolutely damning everything Hesperian, he compares it with 'fruit salad' and 'Titian flesh without souls', etc.—and all in such a comical way that one would burst out laughing were it not for the sobering glare of his imperious eagle eye.

'Truly,' he is wont to observe, 'the time is long past when it was considered good form to work oneself into a rage about Italian music. And, indeed, why go after errant pollen with a club? I hardly know which epoch to prefer, one full of obstreperous Beethovens, or one full of dancing Pesaro swans.[20] But I am curious about two things: first, why female singers, who never know what to sing (excepting all or nothing), don't cut their capers on small things, say a song by Weber, or Schubert, or Wiedebein;[21] secondly, why German song composers, instead of complaining about how little they are sung in concerts, don't compose pieces suitable to the concert hall—arias, scenas, etc.?'

Our singer (not Maria),[22] who did something from Rossini's *Torvaldo e Dorliska*, so trembled as she began her 'Dove son? Chi m'aiuta?' that I said to myself: 'In Firlenz, dear, the good Lord helps those who help themselves!' But she got into stride, and the audience applauded her cordially.

'If our German female singers,' Florestan interjected, 'would only stop behaving like children who think that by closing their eyes they become invisible! Most of them hide themselves behind the music so stealthily that one is really curious to know what they look like. Now compare them with the Italians, whom I have seen singing at each other in a Milan concert with eyes rolling so eloquently that I was worried lest artistic passion give way to something else. That is an exaggeration, of course, but I would still like to see something of the dramatic situation reflected in German eyes, some expression of pleasure and pain in the music; beautiful song from a marble countenance leaves one in doubt as to what is inside. I mean that merely as a general observation. . . .'

Then you should have seen Meritis playing Mendelssohn's Concerto in G minor! He sat down at the piano like an innocent child, and then took one heart captive after another, drawing them after him in droves. When he finally released them they knew only that they had been flown past a Greek isle of the gods and were now safely set down again in the concert hall in Firlenz. 'You are a master blessed in his art,' said Florestan to Meritis afterwards. And they were both right.

Florestan has said not a word to me about the concert, but I caught a characteristic glimpse of him yesterday. I found him leafing through a book and making notes. When he left, I read in his diary: 'There are some things in this world that just cannot be talked about: Mozart's Symphony in C with the fugue, for example, most of Shakespeare and some of Beethoven!' On the margin he had added: 'And Meritis when he plays Mendelssohn's concerto!'

I shall spare you my comments on that which reappears year in, year out—excepting symphonies. I remember how you once said of Onslow's[23] Symphony in A that, having heard it only twice, you know it from memory, measure for measure. I have had the same experience, although without knowing what it is about it that lends itself to such ready assimilation. I see, on the one hand, that the instruments stick too close together, and are too indiscriminately piled on top of one another; and, on the other, that both principal and secondary subjects, the melodic strands, emerge so strongly that I am at a loss to reconcile their clarity with the thick instrumentation. There is some governing element here, but to me it remains an undisclosed secret. What I have said may set your mind to work upon it. . . .

I feel most at ease in the courtly ballet festivity of the Minuet, where everything glistens with diamonds and pearls. In the Trio I find myself in a small ante-room. The door to the main ballroom keeps opening and closing, and through it one hears the violins and floating fragments of amorous exchanges. . . . All of which reminds me of Beethoven's Symphony in A, which we heard a little while ago. . . .

Only moderately enchanted, we went, late in the evening, to Master Raro. You know Florestan, how he sits at the piano and, while improvising, talks as if in his sleep, and laughs and cries and gets up and begins again, and so on? Zilia[24] was sitting in the bay window. Other Davidsbündler were grouped around here and there. Much talk, and then——

'I had to laugh,' said Florestan, at the same time beginning the A major Symphony, 'at a certain dry notary who professed to find in the first movement a battle of giants and in the last their destruction. He slid over the Allegretto, as it did not fit in with his conception.[25] And I laugh at those who are forever talking about the innocence and absolute beauty of music. I concede that music should not repeat the hapless consecutive octaves and fifths of life, but rather cover them over. And I concede that I often find—in the arias from Marschner's *Hans Heiling*,[26] for example—beauty without truth and in Beethoven —rarely—truth without beauty. But usually I find my fingers itching for the throats of those who assert that Beethoven in his symphonies always devoted himself to the noblest sentiments, the loftiest reflections about God, immortality and the courses of the stars. The blossoms in his floral crown may, indeed, have pointed to heaven, but the roots of that great genius were firmly planted in his beloved earth.

'To return to the symphony, the following scenario is not mine at all. It was originated by somebody in an old issue of *Caecilia*, with the setting transferred to the reception hall in the country estate of a count, or something of the kind—possibly out of too great a reverence for Beethoven; in any case, a superfluous nicety. . . . It is the gayest of weddings. The bride is a heavenly child with a rose in her hair, but only one. Unless I am very much mistaken, the Introduction pictures the guests gathering, exchanging greetings profusely and with inverted commas; the merry flutes remind us that the whole village, full of may-poles with varicoloured ribbons, rejoices with the bride. Again, unless I am very much mistaken, the pale mother's trembling gaze seems to be asking the bride: 'You realize, don't you, that this also means our parting?'—at which Rosa, suddenly quite overcome, throws herself into her mother's arms, but with one hand in that of the bridegroom, drawing him behind her. . . .

'Now it suddenly becomes very still in the village outside.'—Here Florestan took up the Allegretto, picking out bits of it here and there.—'Nothing stirs except a transient butterfly or a falling cherry blossom. . . . The organ sounds. The sun is high, and its rays create long diagonal columns of dust particles within the church. The bells ring wildly. Churchgoers arrive. Pews are opened and shut. Some of the peasants gaze intently into their hymnbooks, others upward to the choirloft. The procession draws nearer—first choirboys with lighted tapers and censers; then friends of the groom, looking back from time to time at the bridal pair, the latter accompanied by the priest; then the parents, friends of the bride and finally all the youth of the village.

'I need hardly picture for you the rest, how they all assemble in their appointed places, how the priest walks up to the altar and speaks, first to the bride and then to the happiest of bridegrooms, admonishing them about the responsibilities of their union and its purposes, urging them to find happiness in harmony and love, and finally soliciting the bride's fateful "I do", which she enunciates deliberately and resolutely. . . . Don't let me carry it any farther,' concluded Florestan, 'Picture it for yourselves in the Finale as you will!'—and he broke off, ending the Allegretto abruptly. It seemed as though the sexton had slammed the door so hard that the whole church resounded.

Enough. Florestan's description rather moved me, too, and now the words are blurred as I write. There is much more that I could tell you, but the outdoors summons me. May the interval until my next letter faithfully await a more beautiful beginning.

EUSEBIUS

IV

To Chiara

'What we first heard took flight before our eyes, like a young phoenix soaring up from its own ashes.

SCHUMANN ON MUSIC

'Here white yearning roses and pearling lily calyxes inclined their heads; there orange blossoms and myrtle nodded, while alders and weeping willows spread out their shadows. In the midst of it all gently moved a maiden's radiant countenance, seeking flowers for a garland. I often spied little boats, hovering daringly over the water. There lacked only a master's hand at the helm, a smartly spread sail, to send them cutting swiftly, triumphantly and surely through the waves.

'Thoughts I heard here, that wanted only the right interpreter to reveal them in all their true radiance; but the ardent spirit that animated and guided them finally bore them safely to their goal. And now appeared a young Saracen hero, like an oriflamme, complete with lance and sword, who jousted in such a manner that it was a joy to see; and finally a French knight pranced by, and every heart beat faster. . . .'

This is as far as Eusebius got. I found him last evening with his head on this sheet of paper, fast asleep. He was something to paint—or to kiss. He looked as if in his dream he were hearing all over again that concert of Zilia's which he was attempting to describe to you. We enclose the programme. Just don't laugh at old Sebastian's Concerto for Three Keyboard Instruments, which Zilia played with Meritis and Walt, the gentle Davidsbündler. Be rather like Florestan, who observed that now it must be clear to everyone what clods we all are.[27]

I must tell you, however, how our weekly Firlenzer concert, which occurs every week with such satisfactory regularity, was recently most dangerously disturbed. Right after the symphony there was a fire alarm. Fire engines clanked away, bells were rung, and panic swept the hall. A lot of people had their heads tucked under their arms. A little singer with only one tail to his frock coat (the other had been ripped off in the crush) was trying to make his way over the seats to the great out-doors. He cut a miserable figure, as did a female colleague down on her knees to the fat timpanist, begging to be rescued in tones that had little to do with *bel canto*. You should have seen your Davidsbündler. They stood like granite, pointing to their tickets and calmly demanding music. Meritis, too, his eyes flashing lightning, swung his baton high above every head; one courageous trumpeter even blew his part solo. But it was all to no avail. There was no getting the audience back together again. But there was a good deal of riotous laughter next day when we heard that somebody had ignited the sentry-box over the head of a sleeping municipal sentinel.

Before the next concert Florestan made sure that there was no danger, for the programme contained a world of music, and he didn't want to miss a note of it. But eyes are more incendiary than flame. In the hall he found himself between two brunettes, and his heart, squarely hit, beat more feverishly than F. Meritis' baton—which may be why he found almost all the tempi of the *Eroica* too slow and stiff. Florestan, by the way, calls the *Eroica* the 'Roman' and the Fourth, in B flat, the 'Grecian'.

A bravura aria with violin obbligato had more crinoline and long train than youthful cheeks.

'How do you like our new soprano?' asked my neighbour.

'An elegant method, pure intonation and a tractable *mezza voce* are not to be despised in such lean times as these, and I think . . .'

'Apropos, have you heard,' interjected my neighbour to the left, 'that a convention of German female singers has met to offer a prize for an explanation of how it is that one can still sing absolutely perfectly with the mouth closed and without articulating any words?'

A flute concerto was just ending.

'I wish,' said my neighbour to the right, 'that the flautist had played the fiddle.'

'Right you are,' added the neighbour to my left. 'I like the flute, but particularly the piccolo. It cuts so pleasureably right into your . . .'

At this moment the Chorus from *Clemenza di Tito* cut into my ear— we were sitting right up against the young Romans—and I missed the words of my sensitive companion. I was again aware of how difficult it is to set up an operatic ensemble in a concert hall, happy as I was with today's choice, for *Tito* has practically vanished from the repertoire. The absence of scenery and the movement of the characters on the stage have an irremediable effect on the spiritual warmth and harmony of the presentation, so that technical shortcomings, too, easily become weakening and unsettling.

Finally, Francilla[28] has been here, whose art so binds her to you and Livia. Your words from Munich echoed in our memory. You are right. This is a diamond of the purest fire, which ignites, as it illuminates, hazardously; a heaven-stormer, who, with bold strides, goes straight for the heights. During her concert the whole audience was a single countenance, radiant with genuine delight. And how they all listened in breathless silence, as if they wanted to sip the siren sounds from her lips. It seemed to me as if I heard the tic-toc of their hearts, and saw secret sighs and blissful smiles hovering over them. An old accountant let go with salvos of applause, like a young buck. And why not? For the first time in twenty years he was reminded of warm youth and the happy pangs of love. It was, perhaps, the last poetic strophe in his restricted life.

On our way home Raro said he would not wish, at any price, to be a singer who had heard such a performance. She reminded Jonathan of Malibran. Florestan complained about decorum and 'Why should we not fall straight away about each other's necks?' Eusebius said very simply that it was a debt of honour instantly to bestow upon her the diploma of the Davidsbund. As for myself, I can only report that next morning when I went to see her I knew not what I should say, nor know now what I said, unless it was plainly enough written in my eyes that silence can also be a language. In short, at the moment, I hardly envy you your Venice, with its lustrous waters, its women and its marble palaces—although I do envy Venice you.

SERPENTIN[29]

PS. A word more before Florestan comes in. After Francilla's concert I heard Jonathan say to Florestan: 'If I am not mistaken, Florestan, I saw something moist on your cheek after the Donizetti aria.'

'Possibly,' Florestan replied, 'but it was only perspiration.'

Back home I heard Florestan pacing furiously up and down in his room, exclaiming in disjointed phrases:

'O! eternal shame! O! Florestan, have you lost your senses? Have you studied Marpurg,[30] dissected the 'Well-tempered Clavier', and learned Bach and Beethoven from memory only to weep at a miserable aria by Donizetti, heard for the first time after many years? And this Jonathan has to see it! If those tears were still there I would crush them with my fist!'

At this he rushed to the piano, and with horrible moans and groans proceeded to play the aria as though it were a beer cellar ditty, ludicrously and grotesquely, so that he was finally able to calm himself and say:

'Truly, it was only the tone of her voice that so went to my heart....'

S.

[1] The German title is 'Schwärmbriefe', which has previously been translated, more literally, as 'Letters of an Enthusiast'. Schumann included only the first and third in his *Gesammelte Schriften*. They are fancifully disguised reviews of Mendelssohn's first concerts as conductor of the Gewandhaus Concerts in Leipzig in October, 1835. The other two have been included as appendices by the editors of subsequent editions. Chiara is, of course, Clara Wieck, who was not in Italy at the time. Meritis is Mendelssohn, and Firlenz is Leipzig.

[2] Maria, i.e. Henriette Grabau (1805-1852), a very popular soprano who spent

the greater part of her career in and around Leipzig, where she had a fixed engagement.

[3] Catalani, Angelica (1780-1849), one of the great sopranos of history and, by all accounts, also one of the most difficult. A British critic who heard her towards the end of her long career remarked: 'Her powers were undiminished, her taste unimproved.' Another described her taste as 'vicious'. It is doubtful that Schumann ever heard her.

[4] Tsing-Sing, a comical figure in Auber's opera, *Le Cheval de Bronze*.

[5] Schumann draws here upon his experiences during a trip he took to Milan and Venice as a student in 1829.

[6] The key signatures of Mendelssohn's overtures, *A Midsummer Night's Dream*, *The Hebrides* and *Meeresstille*.

[7] Obviously a reference to Schumann's own experiences when he gave up his law studies at the University of Heidelberg to devote himself to the piano as a pupil of Friedrich Wieck.

[8] Although Mendelssohn was not the first conductor to use a baton, he appears to have been the first to do so in Leipzig. Spohr had used one when he conducted the London Philharmonic fifteen years earlier.

[9] Gerke, Otto (1807-   ?), a pupil of Spohr.

[10] The identity of this Davidsbündler is uncertain. It may have been Chopin, who visited Leipzig in early October, 1835, and who was undoubtedly qualified for honorary, associate, corresponding or even full membership in the Davidsbund.

[11] August 12, 13 and 14 were the name days of Clara, Aurora and Eusebius in the Saxon calendar.

[12] Felicita, i.e. Malibran, Maria Felicita (1808-1836), a daughter of Manuel Garcia and the most celebrated contralto of her time, which was short. She was the sister of the equally celebrated and longer-lived Pauline Viardot. She did, in fact, appear as Desdemona in Rossini's *Otello* in Milan on October 12, 1835, but neither Schumann nor Clara was there, and there is no evidence or any reason to believe that Schumann ever heard her.

[13] Fritz Friedrich, i.e. J. P. Lyser, a deaf painter and writer, an intimate friend of Schumann and an occasional contributor to *Die Neue Zeitschrift für Musik*.

[14] An opera by Cherubini.

[15] Schröder-Devrient, Wilhelmine (1804-1860), a very celebrated German singing actress, particularly renowned for her Leonore in *Fidelio*.

[16] The Garcias went to New York at the close of the London season of 1825, and Maria did, indeed, sing Desdemona to her father's Otello. The rest of the story, however, suggests that press agentry did not come in with the twentieth century.

[17] Rubini, Giovanni Battista (1795-1854), the most celebrated Italian tenor of his time, and Meric-Lalande, Henriette-Clementine (1798-1867), a French-born, Italian-trained soprano of less memorable attainments, both of whom Schumann had heard in Milan in 1829.

[18] Hesperian, referring to the Greek designation of Italy.

[19] I.e. Italians.

[20] Pesaro swans, i.e. Rossini's. Pesaro was Rossini's birthplace.

[21] Wiedebein (Gottlieb (1779-1854), a prolific and, in his time, popular composer, whom Schumann frequently mentions with respect.

[22] A Mlle. Weinhold from Amsterdam.

[23] Onslow, George (1784-1853), a French composer of mixed French and English descent, who divided his life, appropriately, between France and England and who succeeded to Cherubini's membership in the Institut.

[24] Zilia, one of several Davidsbund names for Clara Wieck.

[25] The reference is to an article by Carl Friedrich Ebers (1770-1836) in a periodical called *Caecilia*, published in 1825. The concept of the A major Symphony as representing a village wedding, subsequently expounded here by Florestan, was supported by Gustav Nicolai (1770-1836), a composer and critic who, in his book, *Arabesken für Musikfreunde*, attributed the idea to Beethoven himself. The attribution is not commonly accepted.

[26] Marschner, Heinrich (1795-1861), a very successful opera composer who, with Spohr, Flotow and Lortzing, dominated the musical theatre in Germany between the generations of Weber and Wagner. *Hans Heiling* was the finest and most successful of his operas, and is still revived from time to time in Germany.

[27] The reference is to the concert given by Clara Wieck on November 9, 1835, in which she played her own Concerto in A minor and Bach's Concerto in D minor for Three Keyboard Instruments with Mendelssohn and Rakemann (Walt).

[28] Francilla, i.e. Pixis, Franzilla (1816- ?), née Göhringer, an adopted daughter of the famous pianist, Johann Peter Pixis (1788-1874). She had a distinguished career, appearing in both concert and opera in Germany, Italy, France and England. Chopin had an amusing encounter with her which he describes in a letter to Titus Woyciechowski from Paris, dated December 12, 1831: 'I simply must write to you about my little adventure with Pixis. Just imagine, he keeps in his house a very pretty fifteen-year-old little person whom (he says) he intends to marry and whom I met at his place in Stuttgart. On his arrival here Pixis invites me to come and see him, without saying a word about the young lady (whom I had already forgotten) having come with him. If he had, I might have visited him sooner! He asks me to visit him, so I go during the week. Well, on the stairs his young ward, with great satisfaction, asks me in, says, "It's all right, Mr. Pixis is out—come in and sit down—he won't be long, etc." (A nervous trembling came over both of us.) I make some excuse, knowing the old man is jealous: I say I'll call again later, etc. Meanwhile, as we were chatting so cosily and delightfully on the stairs in the innocence of our hearts, up comes little Pixis, glares (just like Soliva in Warsaw) through his huge spectacles to see who is up there talking to his belle. He rushes wildly up and stops in front of me with an abrupt *"Bonjour!"* for me and "What do you think you're doing here?" for her, followed by a tremendous outburst of curses in German for daring to receive young men in his absence. I too, feeling blameless, smilingly back up Pixis and reproach her with coming outside so lightly clad in

nothing but a silk dress. At length the old fellow calmed down, recovered himself, took me by the hand and showed me into the drawing-room, not knowing how to make enough fuss of me—he was terrified that if I lost my temper I might play a dirty trick on him when he was out, or rather on his ward. Later on he came downstairs with me to the door, and noticing that I was still endeavouring to suppress a smile—I couldn't conceal my joy in feeling for the first time that someone could think me capable of such a thing—he went, as I observed, to the housekeeper's lodge and asked whether I had been upstairs a long time, etc. From that moment Pixis cannot praise my talent enough to all the publishers, particularly Schlesinger who has commissioned me to write something on themes from *Robert le Diable* which he paid Meyerbeer 24,000 francs for. How do you like that? Me, a seducer!' (From *Selected Correspondence of Fryderyk Chopin*, translated and edited by Arthur Hedley, Heinemann, London, 1962, and McGraw Hill, New York.)

[29] Serpentin was the Davidbund name of Karl Banck (1809-1889), Schumann's associate and his successor as editor of the *Neue Zeitschrift für Musik*. Schumann frequently used the names of other Davidsbündler for his own pieces, and it is assumed, although not with certainty, that this letter is by him.

[30] Marpurg, Friedrich Wilhelm (1718-1795), after Rameau, with whom he was associated for a time in Paris, the outstanding theoretical writer of the eighteenth century. His *Handbuch beim Generalbasse und der Composition* was standard for several generations, as was his *Abhandlung von der Fuge*.

BERLIOZ' 'SINFONIE FANTASTIQUE'

(1835)

Let us enter the fray, not with wild cries as our old German fore-fathers did, but rather like the Spartans, with merry flutes. He to whom these lines are dedicated needs no shield-bearer, to be sure, and it is to be hoped that his destiny will be the reverse of Homer's Hector. But be his art the flaming sword, then let these words be its protective scabbard.[1]

A first glance at the symphony inspired me with the most extraordinary sensations. As a child I used to place the music upside down on the music stand and revel in the strangely intertwined notational structures —as I subsequently revelled in the upside-down palaces reflected in the canals of Venice. The writer was reminded of other scenes from his earliest childhood. There was, for example, that occasion when, late at night, and with everyone in the house asleep, he crept as in a dream, and with eyes shut, to his old piano, now ruined, and played chords and wept. When told about it next day he could recall only a strangely sounding dream and many odd things that he had heard and seen, and he could distinguish clearly three mighty names, one in the south, one in the east and one in the west—Paganini, Chopin and Berlioz.[2]

The first two have soared to the peaks with eagle's wings; they had the easier task, combining in their persons both poet and showman. The orchestral virtuoso, Berlioz, will have a more difficult time of it, and many a hard battle, but perhaps the more sumptuous laurel wreaths in the end. Let us hasten the moment of decision. Time presses on, always eternally. Whether forward or backward, for better or for worse we leave to the future to decide. No one has yet persuaded me, however, that our own time is headed for the worse.

Now that I have gone through Berlioz' symphony countless times,[3] astonished at first, then horrified and, finally with wonder and admiration, I shall try to sketch it for you. I will show the composer as I have come to know him, with his virtues and his shortcomings, in his vulgarity and his intellectual sovereignty, as a spiteful instrument of destruction and as a lover. For I know that what he has given us here can no more be called a work of art than can nature without the ennobling hand of man, or passion without the discipline of a higher moral force.

With old Haydn character and talent, religion and art experienced a uniform ennoblement. With Mozart the ideal artistic nature developed independently, but side by side with the sensual man. In other poetic spirits the outward course of life has sometimes been in a direction diametrically opposite to that of the artistic production. Berlioz belongs rather to the type exemplified by Beethoven, whose artistic development is inseparable from his life story, a change in the one being reflected immediately in the other. Music is to Berlioz like the snake to Laocoön. He can take no step without it. He rolls with it in the dust. It is with him as he drinks in the sun. If he were to cast it from him, he would have to do it musically. Were he to die, his spirit would expire in those strains that we hear echoing on the horizon at noon.

We have here a young man of French blood, so musical, bursting with strength, already struggling with the future and, perhaps, with other formidable passions, suddenly pinioned for the first time in his life by the god of love—not, mind you, by that modest sensation which tends to confide in the moon, but rather by the dark flame that one sees pouring at night from Mount Aetna. . . . There he sees her! I picture this feminine creature as I picture the main theme of the whole symphony,—pale, slender as a lily, veiled, still, almost cold;—but the word grows sleepy and its tones burn into the vitals.—Read in the symphony itself how he plunges towards her, seeking to entwine her in all the tentacles of his soul, and how he recoils breathlessly before the chill of this Briton,[4] and again how he would humbly bear her train and kiss its hem, only to stand proudly upright and demand her love because he—loves her so extravagantly. Read it through. It is all written in drops of blood in the first movement.

A first love may well make a warrior out of a coward, but 'a heroine does a hero much damage', as Jean Paul has said. Fiery young men whose love remains unrequited tend, sooner or later, to throw out the inner Plato and render countless sacrifices on epicurean altars. But Berlioz is, by nature, no Don Juan. He sits among the profligate companions glassy-eyed. With every popping champagne cork a string within him snaps. As to one running a high fever, the familiar, beloved countenance appears to him from every wall and fastens itself oppressively to his heart. He repels her, and a whore, laughing loudly, throws herself into his lap and asks what ails him.

Genius of art, here you rescue your darling, and he understands full well the smile quivering on your lips. What music there is in the third movement! This intimacy, this remorse, this passion! The metaphor of the deep refreshing breath after a storm is overworked, but I know none other more beautiful or more appropriate. Creation still trembles from the embrace of heaven, and melts from a thousand eyes, and the fearful flowers tell of the strange guest who still looks back from time to time, thundering.

And here is the place where one who wished to earn the name of 'artist' would have wound it up and celebrated a victory of art over life. Tasso continued on into an insane asylum. But in Berlioz the old lust for destruction is doubly awakened, and he lays about him with a titan's fists. As he pictures the taking possession of the beloved and as he passionately embraces the automaton figure, so does the music, ugly and vulgar, cling to his dreams and the attempted suicide. The bells toll to it, and skeletons play the organ to a wedding dance. . . . Here genius turns away, weeping.

FLORESTAN

II

I have read Florestan's words and the symphony with the utmost attention, the latter down to the last grace note. And yet it strikes me —inclined as I am to agree with this initial judgment—that this psychological approach to the critical appraisal of the work of a composer known to us only by name, and about whom, moreover, there are so many conflicting opinions, is inadequate. This review, favourable as it is to Berlioz, could arouse suspicion simply by its utter neglect of the actual musical composition.

It is plain to me now that a more than merely poetical head is required to place this remarkable work in its proper historical perspective, i.e. a man who is not only a philosophically cultivated musician, but also at home with the history of the other arts, one who has himself given thought to the significance and inter-relationship of their various manifestations and the meaning of their order of appearance.—So let the words of a musician be heard who, as an individual, has adopted the direction of the new generation and defended with body and soul the best that is in it, but who will nevertheless not be deterred, before the court, from breaking his staff over the head of his beloved, even when, privately, he would gladly pardon him. This time there are, to be sure, more laurels to break than staffs.

Form is the spatial envelope of the imagination.[5] The larger the form the grander the imagination required to fill it. In instrumental music the term 'symphony' has heretofore signified the largest of forms.

In appraising something we are accustomed to take its designation into account. We apply certain criteria to a 'fantasy', others to a 'sonata'. With second-rate talents it suffices that they abide by the traditional forms. With first-rate talents we acknowledge their right to extend them. Only the genius may fly free.

With Beethoven's Ninth Symphony, the greatest of all purely instrumental works in respect of sheer size, it seemed that the ultimate had been reached in terms of both proportions and objectives.

None has dared any essential departures from the inherited form, excepting an occasional experiment here or there, as in the newest symphony of Spohr.[6] Mendelssohn, an important artist in terms both of output and content, seems to have concluded that there was nothing to be gained in this field, and has struck out upon a new path—reconnoitred before him, to be sure, by Beethoven in his great *Leonora* Overture. With his concert overtures, compressing the symphonic concept in a smaller area, Mendelssohn has achieved pre-eminence over all other instrumental composers of the day. One almost feared that the term 'symphony' might soon become a thing of the past. From abroad nothing but silence! Cherubini tried his hand at a symphony many years ago, but is said to have concluded, possibly prematurely and too modestly, that it was too much for him. Everyone else in France and Italy has been composing operas.

Now, in an obscure corner of the northern coast of France, a young medical student has thought up something new.[7] Four movements are not enough for him. He prefers the five-act form of the theatre. My first assumption was that this symphony of Berlioz' was a sequel to Beethoven's Ninth. But not at all! It was first performed at the Conservatoire in Paris in 1820, before Beethoven's was published.[8]

I should make it clear at the outset that I can judge only by the piano score, assisted, to be sure, by the fact that the instrumentation for the most decisive passages is indicated. Even were this not the case, however, it is all so orchestrally conceived and thought out, with every instrument used exactly as and where its use would seem to be inevitable, that any good musician could make a tolerable score of it excepting, of course, those new combinations and orchestral effects in which Berlioz is said to be so productive.

If any judgment ever struck me as unjust, then Fétis'[9] on Berlioz: '*Je vis, qu'il manquait d'idées mélodiques et harmoniques.*' He may deny Berlioz everything—fantasy, invention, originality—as, indeed, he has. But harmonic and melodic richness? If I express myself polemically about Fétis' notice, brilliantly and imaginatively written, by the way, it is not because I find it hostile or unjust but rather because it betrays a blindness, an absolute lack of comprehension for this kind of music.

As for the harmonic quality of this symphony, one notes the eighteen-year-old,[10] rather clumsy composer who glances neither to right nor to left but heads straight for his objective. If Berlioz, for example, wishes to go from G to D flat, he does so, without any modulatory formalities. One may shake one's head as one will at such stunts; musically sophisticated persons who heard the symphony in Paris have insisted that at this particular juncture nothing else would do, that it could not be otherwise. Indeed, somebody has said about Berlioz' music—rather curiously: '*Que cela est fort beau, quoique ce ne soit pas de la musique.*' A bit far-fetched, perhaps, but there is something to it. I would add that such oddly contrived passages are the exception rather than the rule. I would even go so far as to say that his harmonies, despite a diversity of combinations conjured from this material, are characterized by a certain simplicity, certainly by a pithiness and terseness encountered—in a more highly developed form, to be sure—in Beethoven. On the other hand, one encounters vulgar and commonplace harmonies—even faulty ones, at least by the old rules, although it must be conceded that some of them have a splendid sound—and some that sound badly, tortured, disfigured. May the day never dawn when such passages will be sanctioned as beautiful!

And yet there is a curious thing about Berlioz. Try to change something, or to correct it, as any practised harmonist can easily do, and see how dull it seems by comparison. The first utterance of a strong, youthful spirit, has a certain individual, indestructible vitality; it may be rough, but is the more effective the less one tries, through criticism, to bring it into conformity with what are accepted as the canons of art. It is simply not susceptible of artistic confinement, short of learning from its own resources to accept discipline and to establish objectives and procedures. What he hates he seizes rudely by the scalp; what he loves he smothers with affection—more or less. Well, indulgence is called for with a tempestuous young fellow whose dimensions are not measurable with a shopkeeper's yardstick. Let's not overlook much that is tender and of original beauty, balancing the rough and the eccentric.

Although he tends to favour the whole over any of its parts, he is by no means unacquainted with artistically conceived and finely executed detail. He does not squeeze his themes of the last drop, nor spoil one's pleasure in a felicitous idea, as many others do, by working it to death. There are many indications that he could work things out more rigorously if he wished to, and where it might happen to suit him—sketches of the imaginative, terse kind that Beethoven used to make. His best thoughts are usually expressed only once, almost in passing.

If Fétis asserts that even Berlioz' best friends have little to say for his melodies, then possibly I should count myself among his enemies, although I am not thinking of those Italian melodies that one knows before they have begun. True, the principal melody of the whole symphony is a bit common, and Berlioz goes too far in attributing to it 'un certain caractère passionné, mais noble et timide'. But then one should remember that it was not his intention to represent a great thought, but rather a persistent, torturing idea, the kind of thing one carries around for days without being able to get it out of one's head; and this suggestion of something monotonous, maddening, could hardly have been more successfully accomplished. Fétis finds the principal motive of the second section trite and trivial. But again, Berlioz (like Beethoven in the final movement of the Seventh Symphony) is showing us a dance hall—nothing more, nothing less. It's the same with the opening melody of the third section, which Fétis dismisses as gloomy and tasteless. Wander through the Alps or any other herding country, and listen to the pipes and horns. That's the way they sound. Thus it is with all the melodies of the symphony. They are characteristic and natural. In certain episodes they drop their descriptive roles—step out of character, so to speak—and soar on to a universal, sublimer beauty.

If there is something for which Berlioz might be taken to task, it would be his neglect of middle voices. But here again one is confronted with a singular circumstance, one which I have encountered in few other composers. His melodies are distinguished by such an intensity of each individual note that, like many old folk tunes, they simply cannot accommodate any harmonic accompaniment, and would often be the poorer, tonally, for being assigned one. Berlioz harmonizes them accordingly, with a ground bass, or with chords derived from the surrounding lower and upper fifths. One should not, to be sure, listen to these melodies with the ear alone. They will pass unheeded by those who cannot sing them inwardly—not mezza voce, but with full voice. For those who can, they will have a meaning whose significance will seem more profound the more often they are repeated.

Lest we be accused of overlooking anything, a few words about the symphony as an orchestral composition. A born virtuoso of the orchestra, Berlioz makes appalling demands upon both the individual player and the ensemble—more than Beethoven, more than anyone. Nor is it mere mechanical perfection that he is after; he requires sympathetic interest, study and love. The individual must give way to the orchestra as a whole, and the latter, in turn, to the will of the supreme authority. Nothing can be accomplished with a mere three or four rehearsals; as music for the orchestra this symphony may be said to occupy a position similar to that of the Chopin concerto in music for the piano, although this is not to compare the two pieces.

Even Fétis acknowledges his instinct for instrumentation. As I have noted above, one can pretty well divine the instruments just by reading the piano score. But even the most imaginative reader can hardly have an idea of all the various combinations, contrasts and effects. Admittedly, Berlioz blanches at nothing that makes a tone, a sound, a noise or a clang. He uses muted trombones and horns, for example, and harps and English horns and even bells. Florestan says he hopes that Berlioz will one day have an entire orchestra whistle in tutti—although in that case he might just as well write rests, since they would all be laughing too hard to purse their lips. He (Florestan) says that from now on he will read scores with an eye for singing nightingales and storms. Enough! Reading the score is not sufficient. It must be heard. Experience will show whether the composer is justified in posing such demands, and whether the net profit in pleasure increases in proportion to the outlay. Whether Berlioz could also accomplish anything with more modest means need not concern us here. Let us be satisfied with what he has given us.

Berlioz himself has told us in an accompanying programme note what it is all about. As a German, I can only say that he might have spared himself—and us. There is something unseemly and charlatan-like about such guideposts. He might at least have confined himself to the headings for each of the five sections. The more detailed circumstances, interesting in so far as they reflect the composer living the symphony, so to speak, could have been handed down by word of mouth. In a word, the German, with his sense of tact and his distaste for intimate detail, does not like such explicit instruction. Even with the Pastoral Symphony there was some resentment against Beethoven for not having trusted us to figure it out for ourselves. One prefers to be spared the intimacies of the genius' workshop—the origin of creation, the tools and the secrets. After all, even nature betrays a certain delicacy by covering roots with earth. So, let the artist keep his labour pains to himself. God knows what monstrous things might be disclosed to us could we but witness the moment of conception of every work of art!

Berlioz was writing for his own French compatriots, of course, who are little impressed by ethereal modesty. I can picture them sitting there, reading the programme note and applauding their countryman for having got it all down so trenchantly; the music itself concerns them not at all. Whether it would suggest similar pictures to a listener unacquainted with the composer's intention I cannot say, having myself read the outline before hearing the symphony. Once the eye has been directed to a certain object, the ear is no longer an independent judge. If, however, one were to ask if this music really accomplishes what Berlioz asks of it, then try associating it with other, or even contrary images. I confess that at the outset my familiarity with the programme spoiled my pleasure and inhibited my imagination. But as the written outline receded more and more into the background and my own imagination took over, I found it all there, and much more besides, almost always alive and warm.

As to the difficult question of how far instrumental music should go in the representation of thoughts and occurrences, I think many listeners are too apprehensive. Certainly it is erroneous to suppose that composers avail themselves of pen and paper with none other than the ignoble intention of describing or painting this or that. But fortuitous influences and impressions should not be underestimated. Alongside the purely musical fantasy there is often, all unwitting, an idea at work; side by side with the ear the eye, and this ever-active organ retains, amidst the sound, certain contours and outlines which, as the music itself takes shape, crystallize and develop into distinctive images. When music-related elements contain within themselves thoughts and images tonally produced, the expressive character of the composition will be the more poetic or the more plastic as the case may be—the more keen and imaginative the composer's perception, the more gripping and elevating the work.

Why might not Beethoven, preoccupied by his fantasy, suddenly be seized by the thought of immortality? Why might not the recollection of a fallen hero inspire him to a composition? Why not share with another the remembrance of a blessed experience? Or should we be ungrateful to Shakespeare for having inspired in the breast of a young composer a work fully worthy of its source?[11] Or withhold from nature our gratitude, and deny that we draw upon her beauty and nobility? Italy, the Alps, the sea, a sunset in spring—has music told us nothing of all this? Yes, even smaller, more specific subjects can give to music a character so charmingly substantive that one is surprised to find music demonstrating such expressive capacities.

A composer once told me how he had been obsessed, while writing down a composition, with the image of a butterfly adrift on a leaf in a brook; this, he said, had given to the little piece a tenderness and *naïveté* which the actual sight may or may not have had. Franz Schubert was a master of this sort of tone-painting, and I cannot refrain here from passing on an illustrative little anecdote. A friend and I were playing one of Schubert's four-hand marches, and I asked what it suggested to him. 'To tell the truth,' he replied, 'I was in Seville, but more than a hundred years ago, amongst strolling Dons and Donas with trains and pointed shoes and daggers, and so on.' Believe it or not, our visions were identical down to the very city. Let no reader wish to rob me of my little example!

If one wishes to oppose a modern mentality that tolerates a parody of the Dies Irae, then it would be only to repeat what has been written for years against Byron, Heine, Victor Hugo, Grabbe[12] and others. There have been times in history when poetry has donned the mask of irony to hide her tears; perhaps the friendly hand of a genius will one day remove it.

One might continue at length about the good and the bad in this symphony, but for the time being—enough! What has thus far been said will have served its purpose if it may encourage Berlioz to moderate his eccentricities; if it will have introduced his symphony, not as the masterpiece of a great artist but as a work whose originality distinguishes it from all others of its kind, and, finally, if it may serve as a spur to German artists to whom Berlioz extends the firm hand of an ally in the struggle against talentless mediocrity.

[1] This was the longest and most detailed review that Schumann ever wrote. It appeared originally, as here, in two parts, the first signed by Florestan. In editing it for the *Gesammelte Schriften* Schumann eliminated Part I and made considerable cuts in Part II. Although throughout this selection of essays I have generally accepted Schumann's maturer editing and abided by the text of the *Gesammelte Schriften*, I have, in this case, restored most of Part I and made further cuts in Part II—H.P.

[2] A highly fanciful reminiscence. Schumann, as a child, had certainly never heard of Chopin and Berlioz, and can hardly have known much more of Paganini than the mere name.

[3] It should be kept in mind that Schumann had never actually heard the

symphony, and that he was working exclusively from Liszt's piano arrangement, published in 1834.

⁴ Harriet Smithson, an Irish actress whom, unhappily, he subsequently married.

⁵ German original: 'Die Form ist das Gefäss des Geistes.'

⁶ *Weihe der Töne.*

⁷ Schumann's ignorance or his imagination got the better of him. Berlioz had, indeed, studied medicine, but he was born and grew up in La Côte-Saint André in the Department of Isère, near Grenoble.

⁸ An astonishing error. The *Sinfonie Fantastique* was first played at the Conservatoire in 1830—in other words, six years after the first performance of Beethoven's Ninth. It is unlikely, however, that Berlioz was familiar with it. He knew little of Beethoven at that time, and his models were Gluck and Spontini.

⁹ Fétis, François Joseph (1784-1871), the foremost French critic and historian of his generation and author of two definitive works, *Biographie Universelle des Musiciens*, and, *Histoire de la Musique*, of which it has been said: 'Easy as it may be to find fault with these two standard works, it is impossible to do without them.' He was also founder of the *Revue Musicale*. Schumann here refers to Fétis' review of the *Sinfonie Fantastique* in the *Revue Musicale*, which he caused to be reproduced in translation in the *Neue Zeitschrift für Musik*. Fétis' opinion was shared by Mendelssohn.

¹⁰ Again Schumann was off, this time by eight years.

¹¹ The reference is to Mendelssohn's overture to *A Midsummer Night's Dream*.

¹² Grabbe, Christian Dietrich (1801-1836), poet and playwright, one of the most important figures in the history of the German theatre in the nineteenth century.

PIANO SONATAS BY MENDELSSOHN AND SCHUBERT

(1835)

THE DAVIDSBÜNDLER have recently given considerable coverage to newly published sonatas. They can imagine no nobler diamond clasps with which to close the chain than these sonatas by Mendelssohn and Schubert.

Of the former we have his Opus 6; of Schubert the Sonatas in A minor, Opus 42, in D major, Opus 53, in G major (Fantasie), Opus 78, and the Sonata for Four Hands in B flat, Opus 30. They are the loveliest examples of the sonata form—which the Davidsbündler cherish above all other forms—since Beethoven, Weber, Hummel and Moscheles. When one has finally worked his way through the accumulated rubbish that comes one's way, such things loom up behind the music stand like palm-shaded oases in the wilderness.

We could review them from memory—because of the solemn tone with which we plan to close this notice, we are adopting, today, the editorial 'we'—having known them by heart for years. We hardly need to point out that these compositions have been in print for, perhaps, eight years, and were composed even longer ago. But it occurs to us, by the by, that it might not be a bad idea if everything were to be released later rather than sooner. It would be astonishing how little there would be to review, how thin the musical journals would be, and how much wiser we had all become.

Only that which has intelligence and poetry vibrates on into the future, and the slower and longer the vibration, the deeper and stronger the strings that were struck. And even if the greater part of Mendelssohn's youthful works strike the Davidsbündler as preliminary studies for his masterpieces, the overtures, still, there are individual pieces that contain so much that is poetical, and in such an original way, that the composer's great future was foreshadowed with certainty. It is only a mirage, of course, if they seem to be clinging with the one hand to Beethoven, looking up to him as to a saint, and with the other to Carl Maria von Weber—doubtless the more companionable of the two— imagining themselves being led. And it is only a mirage, again, if they seem to behold him awakening from the loveliest of his dreams, the 'Midsummer Night's Dream', and seem to say to him, as Beethoven or Weber might have done, 'You have no further need of us; go your own way'—and suddenly he is off on his own. . . .

If there are reminiscences in this sonata—the first movement, particularly, suggests the gloomy reflections of the last movement of Beethoven's last A major sonata, while its own last movement has a generally Weberian cast—it is not a reflection of weak dependence but rather of spiritual kinship. For the rest, how it all surges forward and drives and gushes forth! Everything is as green and auroral as in a spring landscape. What touches and attracts us is not the exotic or the novel but precisely the lovely and the familiar. It puts on no airs, nor seeks to astonish. It merely finds the right words with which to express our feelings, and in such a way that we think that we have found them ourselves.

We come now to our favourites, the sonatas of Franz Schubert, familiar to many only as a composer of songs, to the majority hardly even as a name. We can only scratch the surface. Were it our purpose to demonstrate in detail why we regard his works so highly it would require whole volumes—for which there may, one day, be time. Although we would describe all these sonatas as 'absolutely wonderful', and without taking a thousand words to it, the 'Fantasie' sonata strikes us as the most perfect in form and substance. Everything here is of a piece, breathes the same air. Let him avoid the last movement who lacks the imagination to solve its riddles. Most closely akin to it is the Sonata in A minor, its first part so quiet and so dreamy; it could move to tears, but at the same time is so easily and simply put together from two pieces that one can only salute the magician who could combine them and contrast them so wondrously.

Life of another sort bubbles forth from the Sonata in D—one thing after another, exciting and irresistible. And then an Adagio, very Schubertian, so bursting with rapture that it seems unable to sing itself out. The last movement is farcical, and difficult to reconcile with the rest. Anyone who tried to take it seriously would only make himself ridiculous. Florestan calls it a satire on the 'nightcap style of Vanhall' and 'Pleyel'.[2] Eusebius finds in the contrasted strong passages those grotesque faces that grown-ups make to frighten small children. The humorous motive is common to both.

We regard the four-hand sonata as one of Schubert's least original compositions, although there are lightning flashes where he stands fully revealed. But for how many composers would one fashion a laurel wreath from this one work alone! In Schubert's wreath it is no more

than a modest twig. Thus severely do we judge the man and the artist
by his best accomplishments!

If Schubert reveals himself, perhaps, with even greater originality in
his songs than in his instrumental compositions, we treasure the latter
equally as purely musical and self-sufficient. As a composer for the
piano, particularly, he excels others—sometimes even Beethoven, as
acute as was the latter's mental hearing in deafness—in that he writes
more pianistically, i.e. everything seems to well up from the depths of
the instrument, while with Beethoven, for example, we must first
borrow colours from the horn, the oboe, etc. If there were something
that we still wished to say in general about the inner substance of these,
his creations, that would be it.

He has sounds for the finest sensations, thoughts, even events and
situations. As manifold as are man's poetic dreams and aspirations, so
variously expressive is Schubert's music. What his eye sees, his hand
touches, turns to music. From the stones that he tosses behind him
spring living human figures, as with Deucalion and Pyrrha.[3] Arch-
enemy of all Philistines, he was, after Beethoven, the most distinguished, and one who practised music in the finest sense of the word.

And so let it be he, as the bells ring out the year, whose hand we
press in spirit once again. Should you bemoan the fact that his hand
has long been cold and cannot return the pressure, just remember that
if there be any such as he still living among us, life is still worth living!
But then see to it that, like him—you remain true to yourselves and
to the best that lies within you. . . .

[1] Vanhall, or Wanhal (1739-1813). Bohemian violinist and composer, a
pupil of Dittersdorf and contemporary of Haydn in Vienna, also the latter's
equal, if not in the quality at least in the amount of his production.

[2] Pleyel, Ignaz Joseph (1757-1831), pianist, composer and conductor, a pupil
of both Vanhall and Haydn, later (1807) founder of the piano factory in Paris
which still bears the family name. Like Vanhall, he was prodigiously productive and, also like him, as the reference suggests, rather old-fashioned.

[3] Deucalion and Pyrrha, King and Queen of Thessaly, the only human
survivors of a flood sent by Zeus. An oracle told them to restore the race by
throwing the bones of their mother behind them. They cast behind them
stones, earth being their mother, from which sprang men and women.

A MONUMENT TO BEETHOVEN

FOUR VIEWS

(1836)

I CAN SEE the mausoleum already, this object of our future veneration —a tolerably high stone slab, surmounted by a lyre with the dates of birth and death. Above it the sky, nearby a few trees.

A Greek sculptor, approached about a monument for Alexander the Great, suggested that Mount Athos be carved out to form his statue, a city held aloft in one of its hands. The idea was denounced as mad; I find it less so than these German penny subscriptions.[1] O happy Napoleon, at rest far out in the ocean, how fortunate you are that we Germans cannot persecute you with a monument commemorating the battles you won from us and with us! You, too, would rise from the grave with the proud register, 'Marengo, Crossing of the Alps, Simplon, Paris', and the mausoleum would ignominiously collapse. Poor Beethoven! Your Symphony in D minor, and all your fine songs of pain (and joy)—we do not consider them great enough to justify letting you off without a monument. Our homage is inescapable!

Eusebius, I see that you are annoyed, that from the goodness of your noble heart you would gladly let yourself be turned to stone as a statue for a Karlsbad fountain if it would only serve the committee. But do I not also bear the misfortune of never having seen Beethoven, of never having pressed my fevered brow into his hand—and would I not have given years of my life if only? . . .

I slowly climb the steps of No. 200 Schwarzspanierstrasse.[2] Not a breath is stirring. I step into his room. He raises himself up, a lion, a crown upon his head, a splinter in his paw. He speaks of his sufferings. At that same moment thousands of delighted people are passing beneath the columns of the temple of his Symphony in C minor.

But the walls are about to collapse; he must leave. He complains that he is left so much alone, that one bothers about him so little.

At this moment the basses come to rest upon the lowest note in the Scherzo; not a breath; from a thread above a fathomless chasm are suspended a thousand hearts. The thread snaps, and the grandeur of the noblest things builds rainbow upon rainbow.

But we just dash through the streets. Nobody knows him, nobody greets him. . . .

The last chords of the symphony resound. The public claps its hands, and the Philistine cries out: 'That is true music!'

Thus you celebrate him in life! No one offers himself—or herself—as his companion. It was his tragedy to die like Napoleon, without a child at his heart, in the wilderness of a big city. Build him a monument, then, if you must; perhaps he earned it. But when one day this slab is overturned, let Goethe's words be inscribed upon the ruin:

> Solange der Tüchtige lebt und tut,
> Möchten sie ihn gern steinigen;
> Ist er hinterher aber tot,
> Gleich sammeln sie grosse Spenden,
> Zu Ehren seiner Lebensnot,
> Ein Denkmal zu vollenden.
> Doch ihren Vorteil sollte dann
> Die Menge wohl ermessen,
> Gescheiter wär's, den guten Man
> Auf immerdar vergessen.

(As long as one still lives and does,/a hail of stones is one's reward;/at last when one is dead and gone,/a call goes out for sums of gold,/to build a splendid monument/in honour of his earthly woes./The world may judge your own return/from this acknowledgement of debt./ 'Twere shrewder far, I do believe,/the once forgotten to forget.)

FLORESTAN

II

If we must recall someone from limbo, then I would propose the critic of the *Allgemeine Musikalische Zeitung* who wrote of Beethoven in 1800 (page 151): 'If Herr Van Beethoven would only cease to deny his own true self, and would follow the path of nature, he could, with his talent and industry, give us many good things for an instrument which', etc.

Thirty-seven years have gone by, and Beethoven's name has spread like a divine sunflower, while the critic in his attic has shrunk like a lifeless nettle. I would like to meet the fellow, however, and raise a subscription for him—maybe to save him from starvation.

Börne[3] says: 'We shall end up by raising a statue to God.' I say that a monument is a ruin facing forward (the ruin a monument facing backward), and questionable at that, not to speak of two monuments or three. For let's assume that the Viennese are jealous of the Bonners, and insist on raising a monument of their own, what fun we would have deciding which was the right one! Both cities have a claim to him. He is entered in the church registers of each. The Rhine calls itself his cradle, the Danube (sadly) his coffin. The poetically disposed prefer the latter; if only because it flows to the east and empties into the great Black Sea. Others point to the lovely banks of the Rhine and to the majesty of the North Sea. And then there is Leipzig, a sort of midway harbour of German civilization, with the distinction of being the first city to have interested itself in Beethoven's compositions—a distinction which has also afforded Leipzig a wealth of heavenly pleasure. And so, I hope for three . . .

I went one evening to the Leipzig cemetery to look for the grave of a great man; for hours I searched up and down—and found no 'J. S. Bach'. When I asked the gravedigger about it, he shook his head, the name meaning nothing, and said, 'There are many Bachs.'

On the way home I said to myself: 'How poetically chance ordains! The ashes are scattered to the four winds, that we should not concern ourselves with perishable dust or the image of common death.' And, indeed, I prefer to picture him seated upright at his organ in the prime of life, the music swelling out from under his feet and fingers, the congregation looking up at him raptly, and possibly a few angels among them.

You, Felix Meritis, a man of equally superior intellect and character, played one of his chorale preludes on that organ; the text was 'Schmücke dich, o liebe Seele'. The *cantus firmus* was hung with wreaths of gilded leaves, and flooded with a spirituality that prompted you to confess: 'If life had deprived you of hope and faith, then this single chorale would replenish you with both.' I had nothing to add, and returned almost mechanically to the graveyard. I felt a twinge that I could lay no flower upon his urn, and I lost some of my respect for the Leipzigers of 1750. So, don't urge me now to express my feelings about a monument to Beethoven.

JONATHAN

III

One should move on tiptoe in church—but you, Florestan, offended me with your heavy tread. At this moment many hundreds are listening to me. The question is a German one. Germany's noblest artist, the supreme spokesman of German thought and spirit—not even Jean Paul excepted—is to be commemorated. He belongs to our German art. A monument to Schiller has been under way for years. A statue of Gutenberg has just been begun. You all deserve the jibes of a French Janin,[4] the abuse of a Börne, the kicks of a haughty Lord Byron if you let the project lapse or push it half-heartedly.

I hold a mirror up to your eyes. Look at yourselves! Four poor sisters came to Leipzig a long time ago from Bohemia. They played the harp and sang. They had talent, but of schooling not a trace. An accomplished musician took them in hand, instructed them, and made distinguished and happy women of them. The man had long since passed away, and only his nearest relatives remembered him. Some twenty years later there came a letter from the four sisters, now living in a distant land, providing enough money for the erection of a memorial to their teacher. It stands today under Bach's windows. Those who come looking for the latter are immediately struck by the simple little statue, a touching remembrance both of the author of the good deed and of the gratitude with which it was rewarded.[5]

Should not an entire nation, which teaches great aims and patriotism on every page, raise to a Beethoven something a thousand times grander? Were I a prince, I would dedicate to him a temple in the style of Palladio. Within would be ten statues. Thorwaldsen and Dannecker[6] could not do them all, but they could supervise the work done by others. Nine of the statues would represent the nine muses and the nine symphonies. Clio would be the *Eroica*, Thalia the Fourth, Euterpe the *Pastoral*, and so on, with Beethoven himself as the divine Apollo. Here would be gathered from time to time the singing people of Germany. There should be contests and festivals, and his compositions played with the ultimate perfection. Or another idea! Take a hundred century-old oaks and replant them in a flat space in such a way as to spell his name in those colossal letters. Or one could picture him in a gigantic frame, like St. Borromeo on his island in the Lago di Maggiore, so that he might look to the mountains as he did in his lifetime.—And when the ships passed by on the Rhine, and strangers asked what the giant meant, any child could answer: 'It's Beethoven!' —And the strangers would assume that it was a German Emperor. Or, if one were to prefer something useful to the living, found an academy in his honour, an 'Academy of German Music', in which his concept would be taught—that concept according to which music is not a thing to be practised by all and sundry like any common craft, but

rather a hallowed realm to be administered by priests and reserved for
the elect, a school for poets, or better, a school of music in the Greek
sense. In a word: Get on with it, and remember that the memorial will
be your own!

EUSEBIUS

IV

Your ideas have no handle. Florestan destroys, and Eusebius lets
things drop. Surely, all this attests to our veneration and gratitude to
departed and beloved heroes. Even you, Florestan, concede that we
must somehow make an outward show of our homage, that if no
beginning is made, another generation will condemn our indolence.
And under the bold cloak that you throw over the whole thing, there
may linger some base caution and greed, perhaps a nagging fear of
being taken at one's word if one goes about praising monuments too
recklessly. So join forces!

Let there be collections in every German land, from hand to hand,
recitals, concerts, opera performances, church musicals, and so on. It
would not be unseemly even to solicit donations at all major musical
events. Ries in Frankfurt, Chelard in Augsburg,[7] L. Schuberth[8] in
Königsberg, have made a most commendable beginning. And so let a
high obelisk or some pyramidal edifice proclaim to future generations
that the contemporaries of a great man, contemporaries who treasured
his works above all else, were mindful enough of their debt to acknowledge it by an extraordinary symbol.

RARO

[1] The *Bonner Verein zu Errichtung eines Monuments für Beethoven* issued an
appeal for contributions on December 17, 1835. Schumann's *Fantasie für
Pianoforte*, Opus 17, was originally conceived as a 'Grosse Sonata von Florestan
und Eusebius', the proceeds to go to the building of the monument. The
campaign was not a success, and the project was subsequently taken over by
Liszt. The monument was unveiled on September 12, 1845, and still stands.

[2] The house in Vienna where Beethoven died. It was also known as the
Schwarzspanierhaus.

[3] Börne, Ludwig (1786-1837), a brilliant polemicist, famous for his attacks on
Goethe. A German Jew who, early in life, was dismissed from a job in Frankfurt-
am-Main because of his faith. His writings, including some famous correspondence from Paris (1832-1834), to which Schumann here refers, were generally
anti-German.

[4] Janin, Jules (1804-1874), famous French dramatic critic, author of *Histoire de la littérature dramatique en France*.

[5] The musician was Johann Adam Hiller (1728-1804), Cantor of the Thomaskirche from 1789 to 1801 and founder of the German Spieloper. The story is essentially true. One of the sisters, Thekla Podlesky, became a successful opera singer. From her savings she built the monument to her benefactor. It was unveiled June 26, 1832.

[6] Dannecker, Johann Heinrich (1758-1841), the most famous sculptor of his generation. Neither he nor Thorwaldsen had anything to do with the monument, which was executed by Lorenzo Bartolini, a pupil of Canova.

[7] Chelard, Hippolyte (1789-1861), French violinist and composer, who settled in Munich, and conducted German opera there, in Augsburg and Weimar. He took a German opera company to London in 1836, and even wrote a German opera, *Hermanns-schlacht*.

[8] Schuberth, Ludwig, a pupil of Weber, and at one time conductor of German opera at St. Petersburg.

THE PRIZE SYMPHONY

(1836)

I

CONSIDERING THE richness of my inventory of day-dreams, why should I hesitate to add to it and here record a truly nocturnal one that occurred to me last night and in which I won the prize for a symphony recently offered by the Vienna *Concerts Spirituels*?[1]

I felt certain that the Viennese judges would tend this time to favour the new artistic fashion recently come to flower in France and already beginning to haunt Germany, and I had decided, therefore, to adopt it myself. This is accomplished more easily in a dream than when wide awake, and so, having recast myself faster than another would have changed his shirt, I declaimed:

—Gluck, the Ritter, when he composed his *Iphigenie*, sat himself down in a green meadow, beneath whose flowering umbels he had cached his champagne bottles. Sarti[2] worked in the late hours of the night, shutting himself up in empty rooms, while Cimarosa developed the ideas for his *Secret Marriage* amidst the noise and tumult of a merry social gathering. Sacchini[3] was inspired in his creative endeavours by the company of a young wife. Traetta[4] used to vanish into the pillared forest of the cathedral to abandon himself to his thoughts. The source of Paer's[5] inexhaustible strains flowed freely only when he was in the company of his friend, and Papa Haydn had to fix his wig and seat himself at the piano, properly groomed, in order to enter into his own musical realm. Zingarelli[6] read the scriptures for inspiration for his *Romeo and Juliet*, while Marcantonio Anfossi[7] loaded his table with delicacies and turned roast capons and suckling pigs into music according to the pulse of his enthusiasm. Mozart, an elfin spirit, on bright moonlit nights gathered the dew-soaked buds of his art in magic groves. Rossini wrote when, where, how and for whatever purpose was required. Paisiello,[8] finally, in the pursuit of his ideas, took his stand preferably where I have just taken mine—in bed!

None of these artists, however, nor many others unnamed, if no less celebrated, was properly situated to write the kind of symphony now running through my head and required by the latest dictates of progress. For such a symphony one must repair to the scaffold or climb

the gallows. All the normal experiences of life have long since become
so hackneyed that no one wants to write them down any more, not to
speak of reading about them. To catch the public's attention today one
must tell of the extraordinary; and Paris serves us cleanly written gun-
powder plots, infernal machines and pillories, which can hardly fail to
have the desired effect on the ordinary mortal. All this applies to music,
too, and it is old-fashioned of us Germans to suppose that with such
bards as Haydn, Mozart and Beethoven an epoch has been cleanly
rounded off, or that there is any longer any spice in such things, or
that cultivated people would waste their time listening to it. Let us
concede that the Frenchman, Berlioz, has broken a new path and has
brought to fulfilment what good Papa Haydn groped for in his *Toy
Symphony* and what Beethoven hit upon in his *Battle of Vittoria*.

The important thing to remember is that a well-chosen sign or
coat-of-arms fills the inn and the store, that man cannot be nourished
by bread alone but needs words, too. Our works must have titles, and
good ones. But rather than dope my bardic hero in opium, or deliver
him to the galley or the scaffold—indeed, rather than search for a bard
altogether—I shall simply choose a clever name appropriate to the
whole affair.

My introductory movement, long drawn out and often interrupted,
I shall call 'Lamennais',[9] and in it all hell shall break loose, lest my
eccentric patron priest be offended. Balzac shall be the main stream
into which this first apparition blends. Life is merrier there, and mixed
with a bit of the devil and a bit of madness. It cannot fail to be effective,
particularly since in the following slow movement I shall present
Victor Hugo. Under his banner begins a dance of death beyond anything ever conceived by the living, including even a Holbein. Nor shall
I forget my minuet. In order to make it properly repulsive I shall
dedicate it to Mme. Dudevant, that clever dodecadulteress[10] and lewd
entertainer who, with her symbolic leg-lifting, delights high society.
Then, in my final movement, I shall conjure up Eugene Sue,[11] stirring
the flood of my melodies into a veritable pirates' orgy, spiced with the
extravagances of their bestial fury and atrocities, the scene brightened
by the fires of Lima and Bengal! Hell and damnation! It will be a
masterpiece. Mozart and Beethoven already lie far below me like
heaven-reflecting alpine lakes, and Haydn like a herdman's hut at the
foot of my avalanche-thundering glacier!

Get on with it! . . . Just not to get sick of it! . . . Indeed, I understand
now how easily they work, those who like to think of themselves as
strong creative spirits soaring above those laws and precepts on which

normal men lean lifelessly and wear themselves down. Just throw
everything overboard with one sweep of the broom, that what comes
afterwards may sound new and imposing! Errors of syntax, consecutive fifths and octaves—let them stand like fresh weeds among the
fruitful seed! For no one knows what a good ear can accommodate.
The old Florentine masters of the allegedly corrupt school did their
painting in cellars in order to make every effect of light the more
powerful and dominant. Composers of our ilk should work in crush-
ing-mills and forges, so that after all the din they could learn and teach
the sweetness of a simple tune!

There have always been, heretofore, poor weak souls who regarded
the flow, the surge of a movement as something wonderful in itself,
obviously overlooking the fact that imagination does not flow but
rather sprays itself to heaven in a thousand directions at once, simple
fellows who hide the paucity of their invention under a certain simplicity. I regard such simplicity as positively deformed! Like everybody
else today I want to amuse myself. Novelty is the thing! And when
one new tune turns up in my music, like those frozen airs in Baron
Münchhausen's post horn,[12] the world of fashion will thank me for it.
What is duller for most people than to have to swirl around within the
circle of a mere couple of ideas, even if these often be well worked out
and developed? My music is like a banquet, offering new delights with
every course from soup to dessert. Cleverness is the main thing, but
one cannot be both clever and lazy. Once at work you must remember
what you have to work with. Do not fail to use that variety of tone-
tools. Hit the orchestra like a storm, blanketing everything from kettledrums to fiddles. Inventing instruments for the tonal stage may appear
to be difficult; but it is essential for the likes of us if we are to unleash
our whirlwind of ideas. And there is comfort in the thought that many
an instrument may sound fresh and new, and even pass for an invention, if only it is forced to play beyond its natural strength and outside
its natural range. This is something that many a soft-headed composer,
shaking his head in amazement while reading one of my scores, may
find it hard to swallow. I mean, I make clarinets out of trumpets,
flutes out of clarinets, oboes out of horns, fiddles out of basses and vice
versa. Through such a confusion of voices I transform the public into a
thousand-voiced choir—and so the prize must be mine, even ahead of
those who, from the banks of the Seine, have been throwing sand in
your eyes. . . .

God knows what I would have written down had I not awakened!
As I peered from my bed my eye fell upon the newspaper, which told

me that my exertion was too late, that the prize had, in fact, been won
by a countryman, by Lachner, of Munich. Congratulations to my
German brother—although the symphony is certainly set in a manner
far different from what I have just imagined. And now that I am awake,
my competitive urge has subsided, and I shall gladly join Lachner in
turning away from all temporal idols and towards the cloud-dispelling
illumination of the old masters!

GOTTSCHALK WEDEL

II

Our gentle Wedel has worked himself into quite a rage over that
Frenchman Berlioz! We artists cannot all be such pious parish priests
as you! Various peoples pray to their various divinities in a variety of
ways; indeed, each individual to his own in his own way. Berlioz may
indulge in human sacrifice, or conduct himself like an Indian fakir, but
he is just as sincere as Haydn humbly offering up a cherry blossom. We
should not presume to impose our faith upon others.

As to the Messiah which you hoped to herald in Lachner's symphony,—alas, you erred. I grant that you will encounter there none
of the spirit of Lamennais or Victor Hugo, which so fills you with
horror, although there are parts of it which remind me of those half-
baked creatures of Meyerbeer, mermaids and flying fish, for example,
which astonish the multitude for a while, if only because of their
singular physiognomy, but which are, in fact, nothing more than
unlovely freaks of nature.

In a word, the symphony is without style, like the Romantsch
language of the Engadin,[13] a mixture of German, Italian and French.
Lachner uses German for his beginnings and his canonic imitations,
Italian for his *cantilene* and French for the joints and endings. Where
this is accomplished with much skill, often one on top of the other, as
in Meyerbeer, one can listen to it if tolerantly disposed. But when it is
all transparent to the point of boredom, as evident in the faces of the
Leipzig audience, only the most indulgent criticism can do other than
repudiate it. And it is the sprawling breadth that would have made it
impossible for the work to insinuate itself into the good graces of the
public, even had the artists and connoisseurs chosen to overlook it.
Someone once said of the great Adagio of Beethoven's E flat Quartet
that he had feasted on it for a whole year. Well, one could say of this
symphony that he had spent an eternity there—but in quite a different
sense!

In the needless extension (Beethoven's Ninth Symphony runs to 226 pages, this prize symphony to 304), one is appalled by an unexampled rhythmic monotony. Thus the first and second movements proceed throughout in a familiar rhythm set off by three quavers, to which many other composers have already fallen victim. When Beethoven manages this in the Symphony in C minor there is no reason why we should not fall at the composer's feet. But here we cannot, in all honesty, overlook the fact that the substance of the idea is so trivial that it vanishes in vacuum and sand. It is too thin to support developmental treatment. This is particularly true of the Adagio, whose point is made in the first part of Schubert's *Sehnsucht* waltz far more tellingly that in this whole movement, which is a hundred times longer, ends on every page and never stops! If there were bad mistakes, structural weaknesses or extravagances they could be discussed, improved or enlivened. But here one can say no more than, 'It's dull', or 'Quite good', or sigh—or think about something else.

The best and freshest in the symphony is in the first movement. There is a kind of passion here, if perhaps not of the most poetical origin. Someone observed: 'The beginning expresses the struggle for the prize, the Adagio the first doubts of a successful outcome, the Scherzo a glimmer of hope and the last movement a surge of cheerful confidence.' Be that as it may, it would seem to be inevitable that works written under such circumstances should have some element of inhibition and anxiety, and that many of the competitors would have written symphonies of a different complexion had their muses not been diverted by the tempting fragrance of laurel wreaths. More would be accomplished if, in the future, prizes were awarded for works already completed. Still, it should be disturbing if we were to assume—it is difficult to do more—that there was really nothing more original or more distinguished among the greater number of works submitted. Nor should one imagine that we have judged the Lachner symphony the more severely because it was chosen above so many others, or that we have heard it and read it with greater expectations than we would apply to any other composition. Every announcement of a new symphony is an occasion for rejoicing, and we approach any new work of such dimensions already prejudiced in its favour.

The first movement, containing many lovely details as well as many weak and boring stretches, left us in a sceptical frame of mind, particularly since it was clear that certain big climaxes had left little in reserve for the subsequent movements. And in the Adagio any last glimmer of hope was extinguished. The Scherzo was without a trace of humour, the Trio even without a trace of wit. In the last movement, finally, there were a couple of attractive motives, nicely interwoven and subjected to traditional fugato-like treatment. But the audience's receptivity was already so diminished that even the most massive effects fell upon deaf ears. A few applauded perfunctorily, probably as much for the impeccable performance as for the symphony itself. The majority heaved a sigh of relief to have it all—at long last—behind them!

[1] A competition for a symphony with a prize of 50 ducats was announced by the Vienna *Concerts Spirituels* in January 1835. The first of the two articles here concerned with the subject was written, not by Schumann, but by Anton Wilhelm Florentin von Zuccamaglio (1805-1860) over his Davidsbündler name, Gottschalk Wedel. It is, of course, a satire on Berlioz' *Sinfonie Fantastique*, prompted by Zuccamaglio's assumption that the prize would go to some young composer of Berlioz' aesthetic persuasion. It didn't. The prize went to Lachner, whose symphony is reviewed by Schumann in the second essay.

[2] Sarti, Giuseppe (1729-1802), a very celebrated opera composer and the teacher of Cherubini. He was also a mathematician and physicist, and fixed a 436 A as the normal pitch for an orchestra.

[3] Sacchini, Antonio (1734-1786), one of the foremost opera composers of his generation, described by Burney as 'the graceful, elegant and judicious composer'.

[4] Traetta, Tommasso (1727-1779), like Sacchini a pupil of Durante at Naples. He was, about 1775, also Sacchini's unsuccessful rival in London.

[5] Paer, Fernando (1771-1839), a favourite of Napoleon. Although born in Parma, he spent the better part of his career in Paris. He composed the bridal march for the wedding of Napoleon and Josephine.

[6] Zingarelli, Niccolo (1752-1837), a prolific composer of operas and masses and, like Paer, a favourite of Napoleon.

[7] Anfossi, Pasquale (not Marcantonio) (1729-1797), a pupil of Piccini and a successful opera composer.

[8] Paisiello, Giovanni (1741-1816), the most famous of the many fine pupils of Durante and also a favourite of Napoleon, who seems to have had a weakness for Italian opera composers. Paisiello wrote the lovely and justly famous 'Nel cor piu non mi sento'.

[9] Lamennais, Hugues Felicité Robert de (1782-1854), a French priest and philosophical and political writer, a liberal who broke with the Church and was buried without funeral rites. The reference is presumably to his *Paroles d'un croyant* (1834), written after he had been denounced in an Encyclical.

[10] I.e. George Sand. Dudevant was the name of her husband.

[11] Sue, Eugène (1804-1857), French novelist. At the time of this essay he had

not yet written his *Les sept péchés capitaux*, which contained stories to illustrate each sin.

[12] Baron Münchhausen was the notional author of a collection of tall tales by Rudolph Eric Raspe (1785).

[13] A district in south-central Switzerland. Romantsch is still spoken there and is, indeed, one of the four official languages of Switzerland.

THEODOR DÖHLER

(1836)

FOUR-FIFTHS OF THE newest piano concertos are in minor keys; one begins to fear that the major third may be doomed to vanish from our tonal system.

Thus, as I opened up Döhler's[1] Concerto in A major, the key which, more than any other, overflows with youth and vigour, and saw laurel branches on the title page, I had hopes of meeting, at long last, a friendly person who might have much to tell me of the beautiful Italy where he has been travelling about for so long. I even hoped that I might, in gratitude, be able to plait the laurel branches into a crown for the composer.

It began tolerably well, but by the time I reached the middle I found myself, while playing one page, glancing hopefully at the next, for the fellow displeased me more and more. I had, finally, no choice but to conclude that he has not the faintest conception of the dignity of the art for which nature has provided him, indeed, with certain talents. The latter are hardly prodigious, to be sure, which makes it even more incumbent upon him to use them judiciously.

If someone wants to write a merry little rondo, he has every right to do so. But if someone is courting a princess, it must be assumed that he is of noble birth and disposition; or, without wishing to be superfluously metaphorical, if one wishes to work in so grand a form, one which the best of our composers approach with humility and trepidation, he should know the requirements. And that is what makes this concerto so infuriating. Even the most talented of hacks, Herz and Czerny, for instance, have tried to achieve something worth while in their larger works. Such presumption on the part of a younger and far less talented composer calls for special distinction—which shall herewith be accorded him.

For the composer's own sake may his guardian angel will it that these lines find their way into his hands before he packs his bags for a second trip to Italy, and that he give due consideration to our plea to remain outside a radius of twenty miles of that land which almost invariably returns our strongest talents to us softened and incapable of decent work.

Italy has its siren songs. It also has its own composers to write them.

Thus, there is no need for us to enrol ourselves among them as mercenaries, least of all to do so for the purpose of participating in an invasion of our own country—and not to speak of the contempt in which such deserters are held by their new friends. If one wishes to make the most of Italy, then he should at least have insight enough not to spoil the gain by a tenfold loss, not to sacrifice strength for weakness, beauty for mere attire, the nut for the shell.

And you, too, gay Vienna, who have counted many a fine artist as your own! You should rather remind your young artists, and often, that one of the greatest artists of the time lived within your walls, than encourage them, as in your amiable, easy-going fashion you are wont to do, to pursue a path leading to quicksand, into which they sink with heavenly ease, deeper and deeper, their ears ringing to the last with your thousandfold 'bravo!'.

---

[1] Döhler, Theodor (1814-1856). Schumann seems to have been unaware that Döhler had been born in Italy and, with the exception of a period as pupil of Czerny and Sechter in Vienna, had spent most of his life there. Disregarding Schumann's advice, he spent most of the rest of it there, too, and died in Florence.

JOHN FIELD

Piano Concerto No. 7

(1836)

THE BEST WAY to review this concerto would be to add a thousand copies of it to this issue of the *Neue Zeitschrift* as a special supplement— and an expensive one, of course. . . .

For I am full of it, and can think of hardly anything sensible to say about it except unending praise. When Goethe says that to praise is presumptuous he is right, as always. I shall simply let Field bind my hands and eyes, if only to express my total surrender, and my willingness to follow him blindly.

Only were I a painter would I presume to attempt a critique— possibly in a picture showing one of the graces defending herself against a satyr. Were I a poet I would attempt it only in Byronian stanzas, so angelic [*eng(e)lis(c)h*] do I find the concerto.

The original score lies opened before me. One should see it!—browned, as though it had crossed the equator—notes like stakes—clarinets peering through in between—thick cross-beams covering whole pages—in the middle a moonlight nocturne 'woven of rosedust and lily-snow', which reminded me of old Zelter and how, in a certain passage in *The Creation* he found the moonrise and, ironically rubbing his hands in the time-honoured gesture, exclaimed blissfully: 'This fellow will make a name for himself!'—and then again a *nota bene* with crossed-out measures and above them in capital letters: '*Cette page est bonne.*'

Yes, everything is good; indeed, good enough to be kissed, and particularly you, you whole last movement, with your divine tedium, your charm, your clumsiness and your beautiful spirit, good enough to kiss from head to toe. Away with your forms and your thorough-bass conventions! Your schoolroom desks were carved from the cedar of genius, and not just once! Do your duty, i.e. have talent, be Fields,[1] write as you wish, be poets and persons, I beg you!   .

FLORESTAN

[1] Field, John (1782-1837), Irish pianist and composer. A pupil of Clementi, he accompanied the latter to Russia and remained there for most of the rest of his life. Chopin's nocturnes were modelled on Field's.

IGNAZ MOSCHELES

Piano Concertos Nos. 5 and 6

(1836)

THE VOCABULARY OF disparagement has a million more words than that of praise; consequently, this notice shall be meagre in proportion to the virtues of the two concertos (Concerto No. 5, in C, Opus 87 and Concerto No. 6 (*Fantastique*), Opus 90).

We have often heard them played by Moscheles[1] himself, and have thereby been reminded that no one, not even the most practised and cultivated musician, can presume to arrive at a proper judgment from mere hearing alone. Certainly these two concertos sparkle just as his earlier ones do, if less brightly. That they were less exciting than they would probably have been at the hands of a more inspirational pianist may, perhaps, be charged to the familiar composure and precision of Moscheles' playing. It occurs to us that many compositions of a fanciful sort gain more immediate effectiveness from a certain bluntness of performance than from the fashionable neatness and smoothness of contemporary virtuosity.

Moscheles' later compositions have, however, discarded much of his former superficial glitter, much to their artistic advantage, and require, in order to grasp and be grasped, a musician capable of projecting an image in which detail is subordinated to the whole. That the virtuoso can still feel at home in them, can display his wares and make his points, is simply an additional advantage shared by few other compositions in such judicious moderation.

We profess to discern three periods in Moscheles' artistic development. To the first period, say, from 1814-1820, fall the *Alexander Variations*, the Concerto in F and parts of the Concerto in E flat. It was the time when the word 'brilliant' gained currency, and when legions of young girls became infatuated with Czerny. Moscheles at that time was no more stingy with his brilliants than others, but, as was to be expected of a young man of such exceptional cultivation, his brilliants were more finely cut. His dazzling virtuosity did, however, tend to obscure the better musician in him.

With his four-hand Sonata in E flat he entered upon a second period where composer and virtuoso were allied as equal partners, as in the

Concerto in G minor and the Études, two works which, alone, would suffice to place him among the first rank of contemporary composers for the piano. The bridge to the third period, where the composer's poetical tendencies appear to gain the upper hand, begins with the Concerto No. 5, in C; its first important work is the Concerto No. 6 (*Fantastique*).

If we term these two works 'romantic', we refer to the magical, sombre illumination that hovers over them. It is intangible and difficult to identify in terms of any particular passage, but one senses it throughout, and especially in the unique E minor Adagio of the Concerto No. 5, which interposes an almost churchly character between the other two movements. The latter are more fiery, more practicable and, when one looks into them, more interesting.

A genuinely musical art form always has a focal point towards which all else gravitates, on which all imaginative impulses concentrate. Many composers place it in the middle (like Mozart), others reserve it for nearer the close (like Beethoven). Wherever it lies, the effect of any composition is dependent upon its dynamic influence. If one has been listening, tense and absorbed, there should come a point where, for the first time, one breathes freely; the summit has been reached, and the view is bright and peaceful—ahead and behind. In the middle of the first movement this point is reached at the place where the orchestra enters with the principal motive; one senses that the thought has finally achieved expression, and that the composer has exclaimed exultantly: 'That's what I wanted!' In the last movement it is to be found, rather less elaborately prepared, in the passage where the violins begin fugally, the orchestra briefly identifying the theme, and the piano repeating it. Everything is very much *à la Moscheles*. He has certain stylistic traits which makes his authorship unmistakable, even in passages played out of context.

The *Concerto Fantastique* consists of four movements played without interruption, each in a different tempo. Our objections to this form have been recorded on previous occasions. While it may not appear impossible to make of it a satisfactory whole, the aesthetic hazards, measured against the possible gains, are simply too great. And in any case, there is a lack of smaller concert pieces in which the virtuoso can exploit the Allegro-Adagio-Rondo sequence in a single movement. One imagines a type of one-movement composition in moderate tempo in which an introductory or preparatory part would take the place of a first allegro, the cantabile section that of the adagio and a brilliant conclusion that of the rondo. It may prove an attractive idea.

It is also one which we would prefer to realize in a special composition of our own. The one movement could also be for piano alone.[2]

Aside from the question of form, then, this *Fantastique* is well made, original, self-sufficient and, despite the rather ill-defined form, fully effective. With the orchestra it makes for an imaginative exchange, each instrument having its own role, its own say and its own significance. We look forward with real pleasure to this composer's new *Concerto Pathétique* and to a new cycle of études, for which we asked some time ago.

[1] Moscheles, Ignaz (1794-1870), one of the most famous and beloved pianists and composers for the piano of the first half of the century, until overshadowed by Chopin and Liszt. He was a friend of Beethoven, who entrusted him with the piano score of *Fidelio*. He lived for many years in London, and translated Schindler's biography of Beethoven into English. In 1843, at Mendelssohn's request, he returned to Germany to head the piano faculty of the newly formed Leipzig Conservatory.

[2] Schumann undoubtedly had in mind his own *Concerto without Orchestra*, Opus 14, which was composed at about this time and which was dedicated to Moscheles. Curiously, this work was originally conceived as a sonata. The idea of calling it a *Concerto without Orchestra* originated with its first publisher, Haslinger, in Vienna. In order to make the piece suit the title Schumann omitted a Scherzo. The composition was subsequently re-titled 'Sonata in F minor' and the Scherzo restored. The last movement has the famous tempo direction, 'as fast as possible'.

HENRI HERZ

Piano Concerto No. 2

(1836)

About Herz[1] one can write (1) sadly, (2) gaily, (3) sarcastically or, as now, all three at once. One can hardly believe how cautiously and shyly I avoid any discussion of him, and how I try to stay at least ten paces away from him, lest I praise him too loudly to his face. For if anyone has ever been honest with his fellow-man and himself, then it is Henri Herz, our countryman!

What more does he wish than to amuse—and grow rich? Has he ever implied that those who like him should therefore like Beethoven's last quartets less? Does he ever ask that his own compositions be compared with them? Is he not rather the gay blade who never so much as crooked a finger for any other purpose than to play the piano—or to hold fast to his fame? How ludicrous the wrath of those classical Philistines who for full ten years have been standing with glaring eyes and lances at the ready, defending their children and their children's children from his unclassical music—which the latter secretly adore!

Had the critics, at the first appearance of this startling comet, correctly estimated its distance from the sun, and had their indignation not been so vehement as to attach to Herz a significance of which he himself would never have dreamed, then this artistic malaise would have been of brief and harmless duration. That he now approaches his end with seven-league strides is in the nature of things. The public has had enough of its toy and tosses it, rather the worse for wear, into a corner.

Moreover, a new generation has emerged, with strength in its arms and the courage to use it. It is like a social circle long dominated by charming worldly Frenchmen. Suddenly a real personality enters, and the charmers crawl off into a corner while the group gives its attention to the newcomer. Herz can no longer talk and compose with his former freshness. He is no longer fêted, and so feels uncomfortable and ill at ease. His tricks fail to come off. He belabours the piano, to borrow from Jean Paul, with brass gloves, aware that better players are peering over his shoulder and marking down every wrong note—and much else!

Yet we should not forget that he has kept millions of fingers busy, and that the public, by playing his variations, has achieved a dexterity which can be employed to advantage in the performance of better and even diametrically opposed things. We are convinced that he who has mastered Herz's bravura pieces can play a Beethoven sonata more easily and freely; and we would, with good conscience, give our pupils —at the right time and not often—real Herz things to study. When an entire audience greets these splendid leaps and trills with shouts of 'Bravo!' we can join in, adding: 'There's good in it even for us Beethoven-lovers!'

Herz's Second Concerto is in C minor, and is recommended to those who liked the first. Should it by chance be placed in a programme also containing a certain Symphony in C minor, one prays that the symphony will follow the concerto.

[1] Herz, Henri (1803-1888), actually born Heinrich in Vienna. He was educated in Paris and from 1825-1835, according to Riemann, was 'the most celebrated pianist and composer of piano pieces in the world'. His star was not sinking quite as fast as Schumann wishfully thought. To recoup losses sustained in a piano factory in Paris, Herz set off in 1846 to tour North and South America (his adventures are recounted in *Mes voyages en Amérique*), and with such success that when he returned in 1851 he could re-establish the factory and compete successfully with Erard and Pleyel at the World's Fair in 1855. He was Professor of Piano at the Conservatoire from 1842 to 1874. While his fame was at its height his compositions sold more than those of any other composer, and he was paid at a rate four times higher than his competitors.

CHOPIN'S PIANO CONCERTOS

(1836)

REJOICE, YOUNG ARTISTS, at the sound of the first voice lifted against you! Welcome it as proof of your talent, and assess the significance of the latter in proportion to the vehemence of the opposition.

Still, it is odd that in the drought years before 1830, when one should have thanked heaven for the meagrest kernel, even the critics, instead of recognizing Chopin, were inclined to shrug him off. Criticism, to be sure, usually brings up the rear, unless it issues from creative heads; one critic, indeed, went so far as to state that Chopin's compositions were barely worth tearing up! Enough of all that! Or should we mention a certain petticoat journal which flirts with us from behind the mask with eyes like daggers, and only because we once observed, laughingly, to one of its correspondents, who had written something about Chopin's *Don Giovanne* variations, that like a bad verse, he had a couple of feet too many, and that it would seem a kindness to him to cut them off? At least, so we are told. We don't read it, and flatter ourselves that we bear some slight resemblance to Beethoven in that respect![1]

But should we be thinking of such things today, fresh from Chopin's F minor Concerto? God forbid! What are an entire year's issues of a musical journal against a concerto by Chopin? What are the ravings of a pedant against those of a poet? What are ten editors' crowns against the Adagio of the Second Concerto? And truly, Davidsbündler, we should count you unworthy of any respectful salutation could you not yourselves dare the kind of work about which you write—with certain exceptions, of course, including this Second Concerto, which none of us can presume to approach, unless it be with the lips to kiss the hem!

Away with musical journals! The triumph and ultimate objective of a good one would be to achieve that high estate where people would read it for some higher reason than for want of anything better to do, or to have encouraged such musical productivity that the world would have neither the time nor the desire to read what is written about it! The music critic's noblest destiny is to make himself superfluous! The best way to talk about music is to be quiet about it!

Odd thoughts to be coming from a journalist! But critics should not suppose themselves to be supreme among artists. They live from artists, after all, and the latter could let them starve to death if they chose to. If criticism is good for anything, then only as a tolerable fertilizer for future works; and God's own sun provides enough of that. Again, why write about Chopin? Why not create at first hand, do one's own playing, one's own writing, one's own composing? For the last time, away with the musical journals, this one and all the rest!

FLORESTAN

II

If things were ordered according to that lunatic Florestan, one could call the above a review—and let it stand as an obituary for this periodical. Florestan should remember that we also have an obligation to Chopin, about whom we have heretofore said nothing.[2] We, ourselves, may regard our silence as the ultimate homage, but the rest of the world may interpret it quite differently. If the homage of words is still outstanding (and a thousand hearts have offered him the most beautiful homage of all!), it is due partly to the hesitancy one feels when confronted with a phenomenon one would prefer to approach through the senses; partly to an awareness of one's own inadequacy vis-à-vis the majesty of the subject and the impossibility of encompassing it from every side at once and in all its height and depth; partly to the inner artistic affinity we feel with this composer, and partly, at last, to the fact that Chopin, in his most recent compositions, appears to be striking out upon a higher path, if not a new one, about whose direction and presumable destination we hoped to get some clearer idea before rendering an accounting to our absent allies.

Genius creates empires, whose smaller states are distributed by higher authority among Talents. To the latter falls the task of organizing and perfecting details, while Genius remains preoccupied with grander productions. Just as Hummel, for example, followed the voice of Mozart, and clothed the master's thoughts in a more brilliant, more buoyant covering, so Chopin follows the voice of Beethoven. Or, to dispense with the metaphor: just as Hummel adapted Mozart's style to the purposes and pleasures of the piano virtuoso, so Chopin introduces the spirit of Beethoven into the concert hall.

He made his entrance, not with an orchestral army, as great geniuses do; he entered with a small following, but his own right down to the last hero. His teachers had been the best—Beethoven, Schubert and Field. The first, we may assume, developed his spirit in daring, the second his heart in tenderness, and the third his hand in dexterity. Thus he stood, equipped with profound knowledge of his art, confident of his own strength and armed with courage when, in the year 1830, the mighty voice of the people arose in the west. Hundreds of young men were awaiting this moment. But Chopin was one of the first to scale the wall, behind which lay a cowardly restoration, a dwarfish Philistinism fast asleep. Blows fell to right and left; the Philistines awoke, angrily, and cried: 'What impudence!' In the rear of the attackers others shouted: 'What splendid courage!'

This was not all that fate ordained to distinguish Chopin from all others. There was also a strong and original nationality—namely, Polish! This was an important element in a favourable coincidence of time and circumstance. Now that the Poles are deep in mourning, their appeal to us artists is even stronger. It is probably just as well that neutral Germany did not immediately appeal to him, and that his genius diverted him straight to one of the world's great capitals, where he could freely compose—and freely rage. For if the mighty autocratic monarch in the north[3] could know that in Chopin's works, in the simple strains of his mazurkas, there lurks a dangerous enemy, he would place a ban on music. Chopin's works are cannon buried under flowers!

In his origin, in the fate of his country, one may find the explanation of his virtues and also of his failings. Who does not think of him when the talk is of passion, charm and spontaneity, of fire and nobility? But who, also, does not think of him when the talk is of eccentricity, of sickly idiosyncrasy—yes, even of savagery and hate?

These evidences of extreme nationalism mark all of Chopin's earlier works. But art demands more. The parochial concerns of the homeland had to give way to the interests of the outside world. The physiognomy is no longer too specifically Slavic in his later works, and tends little by little towards that universal ideal pictured for us most congenially by the heavenly Greeks. Thus, following a new path, we may in the end celebrate a reunion with Mozart. We said 'little by little', for he should never entirely deny his origin. But the more he distances himself from it, the more significant will he be for the art as a whole.

If we must explain in words the significance which in part he has already achieved, then we should say that he contributes to an insight whose confirmation seems ever more urgent: that progress in our art is possible only with the artist's own progress towards a spiritual aristocracy according to whose statutes a command of the mere craft is not only demanded but is taken for granted as a prerequisite, with admittance denied to all insufficiently talented themselves to do what they require of others; in other words they must have imagination, temperament and intelligence. All this is required in order to bring about a higher epoch of general musical cultivation, an epoch in which there can be as little doubt about the truly genuine as about the various figures in whom the truly genuine might appear. The term 'musical' would be understood to mean that inner, living will and capacity to participate, that active sympathy, that ability quickly to give and to receive! All this in order that the moulding of creation and re-creation into a society of artists may lead us closer to the higher goals of art!

EUSEBIUS

[1] Schumann is having his little joke at the expense of the *Allgemeine Musikalische Zeitung* and its editor, Fink.

[2] What he had previously written had been, not for the *Neue Zeitschrift für Musik*, but for the *Allgemeine Musikalische Zeitung*.

[3] I.e. Russia.

WILLIAM STERNDALE BENNETT

(1837)

HAVING GIVEN MUCH thought to the question of what I might offer the reader at the beginning of the year 1837—something that might also stimulate the reader's benevolence towards us—it occurred to me to offer him, along with many wishes for his happiness, a happy personality.

He[1] is no Beethoven, with years of struggle behind him; no Berlioz, preaching revolution in heroic accents and leaving horror and destruction in his wake. He is rather a quiet, lovely spirit, who, whatever may be raging inside him, works alone and above, like a stargazer, tracing the course of the planets and absorbing the secrets of nature.

His name is the one which appears above, his fatherland the home of Shakespeare, whose Christian name he also shares. Indeed, it would be strange if the arts of poetry and music were such strangers to one another that the celebrated country that gave us Shakespeare and Byron could not also produce a musician! Old prejudices have been weakened by the names of Field, Onslow, Potter,[2] Bishop,[3] etc.; they should be further shaken by this individual, at whose cradle a kindly providence stood watch.

It may well be true that great fathers seldom beget children who grow great in the same art or science; but still those are fortunate who are chained to their talent through birth and whose calling is never in doubt—Mozart, Haydn, Beethoven, etc., whose fathers were simple musicians. They drank in music with their mother's milk, learned it in their childhood dreams; with the first emerging awareness they felt themselves members of the great family of artists, into which others often have to purchase admittance with sacrifices. Fortunate, therefore, the young artist of whom we now speak, who must have listened, in astonishment and delight, while his father played the great organ in Sheffield, in Yorkshire.[4]

Probably no other nation is as familiar with Handel as the English, who love everything about him except his German name. He is heard with reverence in the churches. His music is sung at banquets. Lipinski[5] told me he had once heard a postilion blowing Handel arias on his horn. In this favourable environment, even a less fortunate personality must have developed naturally and purely. How much was further contributed by a thorough education at the Royal Academy in London under such teachers as Cyprian Potter and Dr. Crotch,[6] and by unrelenting self-education I do not know. I can say with certainty only that from the cocoon of the school has flown so splendid a Psyche that one can only wish to fly after it, arms outstretched in supplication, as it bathes in ether and flies from flower to flower, giving and receiving. As the native soil cannot for ever satisfy so winged a spirit, he has yearned for the land where the first in music, Mozart and Beethoven, first saw the light of day. Thus, recently, he has lived among us, this darling of the London public, this musical pride of all England.

If I were to say anything about the character of his compositions, it would be that anyone hearing them must be struck by their eloquent fraternal resemblance to Mendelssohn's. The same structural beauties, the same poetic depth and clarity, the same ideal purity, the same benevolence towards the outside world—and yet they are different. The distinctive element is more readily apparent, however, in their playing than in their compositions. The Englishman's playing is, perhaps, more tender (greater attention to detail), Mendelssohn's more energetic (greater concern for the composition as a whole). The one shades even in the quietest passages, the other gathers new strength from the grandest strong passages. If, with the one, we are subdued by the transfigured expression of a single countenance, with the other we are overwhelmed by hundreds of angels' heads flooding forth from a Raphaelesque heaven.

Something of the same is true of their compositions. Where Mendelssohn gives us the whole mad witchery of *A Midsummer Night's Dream* in the most fanciful outlines, Bennett is inspired rather by the individual characters of *The Merry Wives of Windsor*; where Mendelssohn, in one of his overtures, spreads before us an immense, deep-dozing sea, Bennett gives us a softly breathing lake in the trembling moonlight. This last brings me straight to three of Bennett's loveliest pictures, recently published in Germany, along with two other works. They are called *The Lake, The Millstream* and *The Fountain*. In coloration, fidelity to nature, poetical conception, they are Claude Lorrains in music—living, sounding landscapes. The last of them, particularly, under the hands of the poet, has a truly magical effect.

Much else I would like to tell you—how these small pieces compare with Bennett's larger works, his six symphonies, for instance, and his three piano concertos, his overtures to *Parisina* and *The Naiads*, etc., and how he knows Handel from memory and plays all the Mozart operas on the piano in such a way that you seem to be seeing a live performance. . . .

But I cannot hold him off any longer. For some time now he has been peering over my shoulder, and for the second time he has asked:

'But what are you writing?'

Dear friend, I shall write no more than:

'If only you knew!'

[1] Bennett, Sir William Sterndale (1816-1875), who achieved early fame as a child prodigy and went on to become one of England's most distinguished musicians. Mendelssohn heard him play his own Piano Concerto in D minor in London in 1832 and insisted on his coming to Germany, which he finally did in 1836, remaining for a year and a half. If Schumann's prophecy seems extravagant in retrospect, it is not because Bennett did not have a great talent, but rather because the life of a fashionable musical leader in London was too much for it. He taught at the Royal Academy, becoming its Principal in 1866. He also conducted at the Philharmonic, founded the Bach Society, was elected Professor of Music at Cambridge and, in 1871, was knighted.

[2] Potter, Philip Cipriani (1792-1871), composer and pianist, of whom Beethoven wrote to Ries in 1818: 'Potter has visited me several times; he seems to be a good man and has talent for composition.' He succeeded Dr. Crotch as Principal of the Royal Academy of Music in 1832.

[3] Bishop, Sir Henry (1786-1855), prolific composer of music for the theatre, one of the founders of the London Philharmonic Society, and successor to Dr. Crotch as Professor of Music at Oxford.

[4] Certainly with astonishment, his father having died on November 3, 1819, when Bennett was three.

[5] Lipinski, Karl Joseph (1790-1861), eminent Polish violinist, to whom Schumann dedicated his Carnaval.

[6] Crotch, Dr. William (1775-1847), organist, composer and teacher. He was Principal of the Royal Academy of Music from its founding until 1832.

THE MUSEUM

(1837)

UNDER THE ABOVE HEADING we recently received a communica-
tion from the Davidsbündlerschaft asking if its members might not
contribute a collection of interesting heads to this periodical. They
feared that in the type of collective review now becoming fashionable
some important figures might be overlooked. They did not, they
insisted, have anything in mind that smacked of aristocracy. We told
them to go ahead!

THE EDITOR

I

Adolf Henselt: [1]

Variations for Piano, Opus 1

I admire you the more, my good Florestan, for the skilful way in
which you choose the best from the crowd of younger composers and
introduce them into the world (that is, into this periodical) as future
bearers of orders, if not of laurel wreaths. They have been an exotic
lot, lately—Chopin, a Pole, Berlioz, a Frenchman, Bennett, an Englishman, not to mention others of less significance. When, Oh when, I
have often thought, sadly, will a German come along?

Well, one has arrived, a splendid fellow with head and heart in the
right place. I agree fully with our female associate, Sara.[2] Despite the
fact that he has been little heard and has, indeed, hardly an Opus 1
behind him, she places him among the best of the younger artists. You
know, Florestan, we have studied piano together, have revelled in
finger exercises, and sought to secure a beautiful tone. But what I call
euphony, or enchantment in sound, I have never encountered in
higher degree than in Henselt's compositions. This euphony, however,
is only the echo of an inner amiability expressing itself with forthright-
ness and candour rare in these secretive and hypocritical times. Some
other young artists share this virtue with him, but they do not know
their instruments as he does, nor how to present their thoughts so
delightfully.

I am not speaking here of the variations. One can, at most, become infatuated with them, without really being more deeply moved, and, indeed, they have no more serious intention. But there are some people in whom one senses a good heart and a harmoniously cultivated spirit even when they have said but little, nor shown their best. I recently heard a number of his smaller pieces, played by Clara Wieck and by a friend of the composer, and my eyes filled with tears of joy, so directly did they penetrate to the heart.

While such virtues cannot make me forget the more profound characteristics of others, such as the highly passionate Chopin, any more than Walter Scott can make me forget Lord Byron, still, they merit imitation and the most affectionate recognition at a time when a distorted and distorting Meyerbeer celebrates his public debauches and a blinded multitude acclaims the performance. So rejoice in this artist's prospects; beautiful nature will prevail. He, too, should rejoice in his stature and continue, in his music, to spread pleasure and happiness.

EUSEBIUS

II

Stephen Heller: [3]

Three Impromptus, Opus 7

Lest my friend Eusebius bubble over like an over-full glass of champagne, I hasten to present another, equally young German talent, Stephen Heller. He may not share Henselt's virtues in such high degree, but he has versatility of invention, imagination and wit in abundance.

Six years ago a stranger wrote to us, asking if the Davidsbündler would also take up the cudgels for 'miserable manuscripts'.

'This thought', the letter went on, 'cannot be gratefully enough acknowledged. Through fair reviews of such manuscripts the attention of some hard-hearted publisher could be drawn to young talents, and the heart softened or further hardened accordingly. In me you behold one of the many who would like to see their works published, and, at the same time, one of the few who do so, not just to be printed or engraved, but rather to be judged, to profit by instructive criticism, to receive encouragement, etc.'

The whole letter bespoke a clear, fine head, simplicity and modesty. Finally, the manuscript came, again with a letter, from which I recall the following:

'I shall enjoy great respect in your eyes if I introduce myself as an excellent seer and—hearer! I have seen Beethoven, I have seen Schubert, often, in Vienna. I have been to the best Italian opera there and—what a juxtaposition!—heard the quartets of Mozart and Beethoven played by Schuppanzigh. I have heard the Beethoven symphonies played by the Vienna orchestra. Seriously, Davidsbündler, am I not a rare, blessed seer, a hearer favoured by fortune?'[4]

Good friends, I said to mine, after reading such things there's nothing for it but to have a go at the compositions, get to the roots of this fellow whose name is such a fatal reflection of its owner.[5]

I am sick to death of the word 'romanticist', although I have not spoken it ten times in my life.—And yet, if I were to give our young seer a title, that is what I would call him. I hasten to add that there is about him none of that vague, nihilistic disorder behind which some seek the romantic, nor of the crude, spluttering materialism which so delights the French neo-romanticists. On the contrary, he senses things naturally, and expresses himself cleverly and distinctly. Moreover, one feels something more in the background, a characteristic, inviting twilight, rather dawn-red, that lets one see the otherwise solid figures in a bizarre light. One cannot define such things precisely in words. Pictures are better. Thus, I shall compare that mystical light with the rings that one sees during a morning shower on certain days around the silhouettes of certain heads. For the rest, there is nothing inhuman about him except a sensitive soul in a living body. He carries out his ideas carefully and well. His forms are original, imaginative and free. He has no fear of finishing something, itself a sign that there is something there. That harmonic euphony so pleasing in Henselt, he does not possess in the same degree. He is more imaginative, however, and he knows how to blend contrasts into a whole. Some details disturb me, but then he chokes off criticism by some felicitous turn at the right moment. These and other things, Eusebius, distinguish my candidate. Nor do I overlook the dedication! The coincidence is remarkable. You remember that we once dedicated something to Wina in Jean Paul's *Flegeljahre*; the dedication of the Impromptus is also to a character out of Jean Paul—Liane von Froulay! And we have many other things in common. The confession should not be misinterpreted. It is all too plain. And so I recommend to you the Impromptus. Truly, this talent has a future!

FLORESTAN

III

Clara Wieck:

Soirées for Piano, Opus 6

There should also be a female head to adorn our museum. And how better could I celebrate this day, the eve of a beloved's birthday, than by devoting myself to one of her creations. It may well be that her works derive from so exotic an imagination that mere practice alone will not suffice to pursue these rarely interlaced arabesques—or from so profoundly tempered a spirit that, once the graphic, the representational in her compositions recedes into the background, one does not immediately grasp the dreamlike and the introspective. Thus, the majority will lay them aside after a quick glance; indeed, it is easy to believe that contest juries will award these Soirées, among a hundred entries, the last prize rather than the first, so far below the surface lie the pearls and laurel wreaths. Nevertheless, I should be more than usually curious about the verdict of the academicians. For the Soirées betray, on the one hand, and plain for anyone to see, a life effulgent and tender, apparently responsive to the slightest stirring; on the other hand, a wealth of unconventional resources, an ability to entangle the secret, more deeply twisting threads and then to unravel them, something one is accustomed to expect only from experienced artists—and males!

About her youth we would agree. To evaluate the rest one must appreciate her position as one of the supreme virtuosos of the time, with insight into everything. Let Bach penetrate to a depth where even the miner's lamp is threatened with extinction; let Beethoven lash out at the clouds with his titan's fists; whatever our own time has produced in terms of heights and depths—she grasps it all, and recounts it with a charming, maidenly wisdom. At the same time, she has raised her own standards to a degree that leaves one wondering anxiously where it all may lead. I venture no predictions. With such talents one is confronted with curtain after curtain; time lifts them one by one, and what is revealed always differs from what was expected. That one cannot contemplate such a wondrous phenomenon with indifference, that one must follow her spiritual development step by step, may be expected of all those who, in this singular time, acknowledge the natural intimate relationship of kindred spirits, past and present, rather than mere accident or chance.

What do we have, then, in these Soirées? What do they tell us? Whom do they concern? Are they comparable with the work of a master? For one thing, they tell us much about music, and how it surpasses the effusions of poetry, how one can be happy in pain and sad when happy. They belong to those who can delight in music without the piano, whose hearts swell to the bursting point at the sound of intimate yearning and inner song. And they belong to those already versed in the fraternal language of a rare species of art.

Are they, finally, a result? Yes, the way a bud is a result before it breaks out in the splendid colours of the blossoms, fascinating and important as is everything that harbours a future.

And then, of course, to hear them as she plays them! One hardly knows what has struck him, or imagines how such a thing can be recorded in symbols and written out. This, again, is an astonishing art, and it is all hers. Whole books could be heard on the subject. I say 'heard' advisedly. Suspicious of our Davidsbündler resources, we recently asked a good connoisseur to write something about the character of her playing. He promised to do so, and after some two pages concluded: 'It would be desirable, some day, to learn something tangible about this artist's virtuosity', etc. We know where he came to grief, and why we, too, shall stop right here. Not everything can be told in the letters of the alphabet.

FLORESTAN AND EUSEBIUS

September 12, 1837

IV

Felix Mendelssohn:

Preludes and Fugues, Opus 35

A certain hot-head (now in Paris) liked to define the term 'fugue' as denoting a 'composition where one voice races away from the other—and the listener from them all.' He, himself, he would add, made it a point to talk loudly when such things were played in public, and to mutter insults.

In fact, he understood very little about it, rather resembling the fox in the fable; that is, he could not write one himself, no matter how much he secretly wished to. Those who can, of course, define the fugue differently—choir directors, graduate music students, etc. According to them, 'Beethoven never wrote nor could have written a fugue; even

Bach allowed himself liberties at which one can only shake one's head. The best instruction is to be found in Marpurg', etc. How different again, is the view of still others, myself included, who can revel for hours in the fugues of Beethoven, Bach and Handel and who have reached the conclusion that—with the exception of diluted, tepid, miserable, patchwork stuff—fugues can no longer be written.

That was my view, at least, until it was moderated by these fugues of Mendelssohn. Purists deceive themselves when they profess to find in them some of the fine old tricks, such as *imitationes per augmentationem duplicem, triplicem,* etc., and *cancrizantes motu contrario,* etc., just as do those far-flying romanticists who perceive phoenixes rising from the ashes of an old form. But if any of them have a taste for sound, natural music, they will find it here in abundance.

I do not wish to indulge in blind praise, and I know perfectly well that Bach made fugues of quite a different sort. But if he were to rise from the grave today, he would, I am sure—having delivered himself of some opinions about the state of music in general—rejoice to find at least flowers where he had planted giant-limbed oak forests. In a word, the fugues have a lot of Sebastian in them, and might even lead the most sharp-eyed editor astray were it not for the song, the more refined sweetness characteristic of modern music, and here and there certain unmistakably Mendelssohn-esque touches.

Whether other critics agree with this or not, it is still plain that these fugues were not written merely to while away the hours, but rather to remind pianists of that fine old form and to accustom them to it. It is equally plain that this purpose has been well served by the avoidance of all those unfortunate, useless structural contortions and imitations in favour of a melodic line, at the same time retaining the Bachian form. Whether the form itself might not also be reshaped to advantage without depriving it of the character of a fugue is a question that many will attempt to answer. Beethoven gave it a jolt, but he was otherwise engaged, and already too high up in the construction of the domes of new forms to give time to laying the cornerstone of a new fugal edifice. Reicha[6] had a go at it, but his creative gifts obviously did not match his intentions; still his often curious ideas should not be overlooked entirely. In any case, the best fugue is the one that the public takes for a Strauss waltz; in other words, a fugue where the structural underpinnings are no more visible than the roots that nourish the flower. Thus a reasonably knowledgeable music-lover once took a Bach fugue for a Chopin étude—to the credit of both! Thus, too, one could play for many a maiden the last part of one of the Mendelssohn fugues and call it one of the *Lieder ohne Worte*. The charm and tenderness of the figures are such that she would never be reminded of churches and fugues.

In short, they are not just fugues, cerebrated according to formula. They are musical compositions, born of the fancy and poetically executed. And just as the fugue is equally suited to the dignified and the gay and merry, so this collection also contains some of that short, fast variety of which Bach, with his master's hand, dashed off so many. Everyone will find them. They betray the finished, inventive artist, who can play with chains as with floral wreaths.

As for the preludes, most of them, perhaps, as with Bach's, have no organic relationship to the fugues, and appear to have come afterwards. Most players will prefer them to the fugues. Played separately, they are, indeed, quite complete in themselves. The work speaks for itself, even without the name of the composer!

JEANQUIRIT[7]

V

Frédéric Chopin:

Études, Opus 25

How could our museum fail to include Chopin, to whom we have so often pointed as to a rare star sighted late at night?

Who knows its course? Who knows where it leads, or how long or how brightly it will shine. Thus far its every appearance has displayed the same deep-dark glow, the same nuclear radiance, the same sharpness, all distinguishing it from other stars in such a way that any child would recognize it.

In discussing these études I have the great advantage of having heard them played by Chopin, himself—

'And very *à la Chopin* he played them too,' Florestan just whispered in my ear.

Imagine an aeolian harp, with all the scales, swept by the hand of an artist conjuring up all kinds of exotic ornaments, but in such a way that a deeper fundamental tone and a softly singing upper voice are ever discernible—imagine this, and you will have an approximate idea of his playing. No wonder that the études we love most are those we have heard him play, particularly the first one, in A flat—more a poem than an étude. It would be a mistake, however, to suppose that he played in such a way that you could hear every note. It was rather an undulation of the A flat chord, propelled aloft every now and again from the pedal. But through the harmonic veil one heard the wondrous melody full-voiced; only in the middle did there emerge from the chord a tenor voice, more distinctly, in conjunction with that main theme. Afterwards one felt as though he had just seen a beautiful image in a dream and was now, already half awake, trying to recall it. It is hard to talk about—and impossible to praise.

He went on to the Étude in F minor, the second of the set, and another that leaves the unforgettable impress of his individuality, so charming, dreamlike and soft, like the singing of a child in its sleep. Then came the Étude in F major, also beautiful, if less original in character than in figuration; the object here was the bravura display— the most amiable imaginable, and we praised him whole-heartedly. . . .

But of what use are descriptive words? The études are all symbols of his bold, inherent creative strength—true poetic images. Taken one by one they are not without some small blemishes, as a whole they are powerful and gripping.

Not to suppress my most candid opinion, the total substance of the earlier set strikes me as more important. There can be no suspicion, however, of a diminution of Chopin's artistic nature, or of retrogression, since most of the études of the new set originated about the same time. Only a few, notable for their greater mastery, are of recent date, among them the first, in A flat, and the final magnificent Étude in C minor.

That our friend is composing little at the moment, and nothing of larger dimensions, is, unfortunately, also true. The distractions of Paris may be partly to blame. But let us rather assume that, after so many storms, an artist's bosom requires some rest, and that later, newly strengthened, he will hurry off towards more distant suns. There are always new ones for genius to disclose.

EUSEBIUS

[1] Henselt, Adolf von (1814-1889), a pupil of Hummel at Weimar and Sechter in Vienna. He settled in St. Petersburg, where he was appointed Court Pianist and Teacher to the Imperial Children. Although in later years he seldom played in public, he was regarded by those who heard him as one of the greatest pianists of his time. The études have survived. Schumann dedicated to him his *Noveletten*.

[2] Sara, i.e. Sophie Kaskel, a correspondent in Dresden, who had contributed a piece about Henselt.

[3] Heller, Stephen (1814?-1888), Hungarian-born pianist and composer who, following initial successes as a virtuoso, settled for a time in Augsburg, whence he contributed correspondence to the *Neue Zeitschrift für Musik* over his Davidsbündler name of Jeanquirit (derived from the closing sentence of his first letter from Augsburg in April, 1836, in which he said of himself that he was no Jean Paul but rather 'a *Jean qui rit* or a *Paul qui pleure*'). From 1838 he lived in Paris, much admired as teacher, composer and critic. Berlioz said of him, 'At once a charming humorist and a learned musician, who has written so many admirable pianoforte works, and whose melancholy spirit and religious zeal for the true divinities of art have always had a powerful attraction for me.'

[4] Heller lived and studied in Vienna from 1824 to 1829.

[5] A pun on Heller's name which, in German, means 'brighter'.

[6] Reicha, Anton (1770-1836), now best remembered as having been the companion of Beethoven in both Bonn and Vienna. He later settled in Paris, succeeding Méhul as Professor of Composition at the Conservatoire and Boieldieu as member of the Académie. He was a prolific, if not notably successful, composer, and was the author of many theoretical treatises.

[7] Stephen Heller's Davidsbündler name, here used by Schumann for one of his own articles—and for obvious reasons.

THE EDITOR'S BALL

(A Report to Jeanquirit in Augsburg)[1]

(1837)

Believe it or not, dear friend, the editor of the *Neueste Musik-alische Zeitschrift* gives, at least once a year, a kind of art-historical ball. The invited assume that it is in their honour, but the sly old fox laughs behind their backs. What they do not know is that he simply escapes the drudgery of reading through a lot of dance music and at the same time is able to get an idea of how the various pieces go over with the public. In a word, what he is after is living criticism.

You should meet him. I had heard rumours about the hardly dance-able music that we were supposed to polish off with our feet. But can a young artist afford to decline such an invitation? Certainly not! On the contrary, we flocked solemnly on to the dance floor like lambs dolled up for the sacrifice. Besides, this editor has two daughters whose acquaintanceship might be useful—one of them uncommonly tall, who does a lot of notices for the periodical; the other and younger is a painter, and innocence itself. These young ladies, my friend, got me into no end of trouble!

You would have loved it! Composers wandering up and down, watchful, pretty mothers of dilettantes, the Ambassador of Something-or-Other with his sisters, music publishers in white tie and tails, a couple of rich Jewesses—and Davidsbündler lounging against pillars. In short, it was only with great effort that I was able to push my way through the crowd and carry off the giantess—Ambrosia is her name—for the first polonaise.—Here, by the way, is the programme:

Sequence of Dances

Grand Dramatic Polonaise, Opus 11	I. Nowakowski[2]
Waltz, Opus 18	F. Chopin
Four Mazurkas, Opus 8	I. Brzowski[3]
Six Four-Hand Waltzes	K. Zoellner[4]
Grand Polonaise, Opus 174	F. Ries
Bolero, Opus 19	F. Chopin
Three Four-Hand Polonaises, Opus 15	K. Kraegen[5]
Grand Bravura Waltz, Opus 6	F. Liszt

Four Mazurkas, Opus 5 . . . . .E. Wolff[6]
Two Polonaises, Opus 26 . . . . .F. Chopin

Ambrosia and I chatted while we danced, going on at a great rate
about what is the essential characteristic of the polonaise and how
typically German it is that even in dancing we follow the footsteps of
others and that in this respect Strauss is a true saviour ('And perhaps
only in this respect', said my partner) and how there is something sad
for me in the last measure of the polonaise, with the final cadence, and
so on.

'Since the conquest of Warsaw,' observed my companion, 'whenever I dance a polonaise I half expect a Cossack to come bursting in and
put an end to it—alas, the poor Poles! My sister never plays Chopin
without weeping!'[7]

'What noble sentiments,' I said, 'and how charmingly melodious is
the polonaise of this new Polish composer to which we are now dancing.'

'I find the trio most attractive,' she replied, 'but rather *à la Chopin*.'

It was the second time she had dragged the romantic school into the
conversation. She seemed to be feeling me out. Cleverly and gallantly
I endeavoured to make a good impression and gain as much credit as
possible for myself and future compositions. But it became more and
more of a burden as she gazed at me with those adoring eyes. At last,
thank God, the dance was over! Just as I was leaving the floor she
called me back and whispered:

'To be guided through the last Chopin polonaise by such a master
hand would——'

'Make me very happy,' I finished gallantly, and bowed deeply.

I had won a battle, but the evening was young. I sought out Beda,
the younger sister, for a Chopin waltz. It was the first time I had ever
seen this lovely creature, and I was the more surprised at her ready
acquiescence, since Eusebius, only a few moments before, and with
considerable embarrassment, had told me how she had indignantly
rebuffed him. Well, she danced with me! And if ever I danced on air
it was during those precious moments. I couldn't get much out of her,
to be sure, except an occasional 'yes', but this was always spoken so
soulfully and with so many fine shades of meaning that I just warbled
on like a nightingale. It seemed to me that she would rather say nothing
than make an issue of anything, and I was thus utterly at a loss to understand her rude treatment of Eusebius.

And now, as we were carried along body and soul by the dark flood of Chopin's wonderful waltz, and with Beda gazing ever more sadly into the crowd, I brought the conversation around to Chopin himself. Hardly had she heard the name when, for the first time, she turned her lovely great eyes straight at me—

'And you know him?'

I confessed that I did.

'And you have actually heard him? And have even heard him speak?'

And now I told her what an unforgettable sight it was to see him at the piano, like a dreaming soothsayer, and how, as he played, one became identified in one's own mind with his dream, and how he had an iniquitous habit, at the end of each piece, of running a finger from one end of the keyboard to the other in a disruptive glissando, as if to break the spell, and how he had to spare himself because of his delicate health, and so forth. She pressed herself ever more closely to me, seemingly prompted by a combination of anxiety and pleasure, and begged me to go on. O, Chopin, you charming heart-breaker! I have never envied you—but now? In fact, Jeanquirit, I was stupid, nothing but the brush that brought the sainted hero within kissing distance—yes, stupid!

'Would it be very childish of me,' she asked during the concluding stretto, 'if I were to confess that I have painted a picture of him, and without ever having seen him? I'll get it for you, and maybe you will tell me how close I have come—and not a word to anyone?

At these last words she pressed my hand. When the dance was finished I asked her for another. She had only the final Chopin polonaise free, and would gladly dance it with me. Dear friend, don't ask me to tell you how bored I was during all the intervening dances!

But I made an interesting discovery which will enable me to get back at that two-faced editor and host. I was pacing up and down in a half-lighted ante-room when my eye fell upon a tuning fork and a sheet of paper. There, to my astonishment, I read the following:

'Mazurka by Brzowski, odd, confused, often vulgar stuff, more nasal than chest tones, but not entirely uninteresting. Waltz by Zoellner, rather dull, and hardly danceable, but industrious and actually rather too good for dancing; might have been written by an organist for the weddings of fellow organists.' And so on.

I put the sheet back where I had found it, and wandered off. But curiosity got the better of me. Through a fold in a curtain I peered back into the little ante-room, and just in time to see the editor return, seat himself and resume his writing, from time to time banging the tuning fork on the table and holding it to his ear. As soon as a dance was ended he would jump to the ballroom door, open it slightly, assess the popular reaction, and then go back to his writing. My heart went out to the fellow. He was writing a notice!

Thus lost in looking and listening, I was suddenly surprised by someone coming up from behind me and clapping his hands over my eyes. I turned on the jokester and recognized a Flemish bassoon virtuoso, a certain Herr de Knapp—a creature with the face of a scandalmonger, not to mention a repulsively bald head and an obscenely turned nose. He is a miserable tootler who hates me because once in Brussels I said within his hearing that a bassoon virtuoso need not wear himself out on my account unless he could also play the fiddle like Paganini. In short, the very thought of him endows me with a Shakespearean vocabulary of invective.

'Excuse my little joke,' he said (he is a friend of the house, incidentally, and Ambrosia's suitor), 'but Fräulein Beda is beginning the *Bolero*.'

Reason enough to turn my back on the fellow! You know this tender, love-drenched composition, this image of Latin passion and shyness, of Latin abandon and reserve. And here, now, was Beda, pouring her heart out at the piano, the picture of her beloved pressed to her bosom. The very thought was too much for me, and I dashed off, dreaming only of the last polonaise. . . .

Events now began to pile up one on top of the other. Let me pass over a couple of polonaises (the composer himself was on hand, a gentle, agreeable person, rather like his polonaises). Ambrosia, in due course, tackled Liszt's *Bravura Waltz*—it was more threshed than mastered!—and worked up a bit of a sweat over it. Such a monster, I whispered in her ear, can only be mastered by rage. And I told her that she was quite right not to spare herself. She smiled back at me— adoringly!

There were still a few mazurkas to go before that dance with Beda which would decide the fate of the evening. The lovely tunes of these dances pursued me as I found myself once more before the curtain, behind which our editor was housed. But hardly had I sneaked a glance through the fold than I was seized again from behind, my eyes covered by a stranger's hands. It was de Knapp, of course, and I lost no time in telling him that it was bad enough to repeat a joke and worse to repeat one which had not been funny the first time. Since he doesn't understand much German, I repeated it in Flemish with my eyes.

'Excuse me, *mon cher*,' he stammered, 'but Fräulein Ambrosia is waiting for the polonaise.'

I suddenly became aware of my predicament! Was this not the dance that I had also promised to Beda? How could Ambrosia forgive me? Would not those cupid's arrows now be dipped in critical poison and shot in anger rather than in love? One look at Beda, however, and I reached for her hand, forsaking any less immediate laurels.

Dear friend, you know my capacity for both pain and champagne—but to abandon oneself to such music in such company, to soar with such a girl, sustained by shafts of light! I was dizzy with rapture, and carefully avoided reminding her of Chopin, lest I be tumbled from my lonely, blessed heights like a common criminal. And yet, when she asked me if she might show me the picture, I extended my hand automatically.

It was splendidly done, the head almost like Chopin's right down to the revolutionary curve of his mouth, the figure rather too big, but with the body bent backwards, the right eye covered by a hand, the other gazing boldly into the darkness. Lightning flashes in the background provided the illumination.

'Good,' I said, possibly a bit sharply, for she kept pressing me to tell her if the picture did not remind me of a troubled past. I could only answer:

'No, rather of a troubled future!'..

And I danced on, firmly, silently.

Ambrosia, who was sitting without a partner beside de Knapp, watched it all with trembling lips, and hastily withdrew. Shortly afterwards de Knapp whispered something in Beda's ear. She turned pale and begged to be excused, explaining that she could no longer dance with me. You can imagine my indignation! After the ball I overheard de Knapp saying something to a third person about 'outrageous behaviour towards the daughters of the house', and I challenged him forthwith. Pistols, of course. One look at his face restored my spirits!

But now hear what Eusebius told me, drawing me off secretively into a corner! I was responsible for his snub! It seems that Papa Editor had expressly forbidden Beda to dance with me (Florestan) as I was an arch-romantic, a Faust in three-quarter time, and to be shunned as one would shun a composition by Liszt. Because of our great resemblance to each other, Beda had confused us and had snubbed Eusebius instead. Hence her strange disappearance when de Knapp, at the behest of her father, had apprised her of the true state of affairs.

And this editor! This oaf, whose critical procedures with the tuning fork I shall duly expose to all the world! He stops me on the stairs and proposes that I write something for his *Neueste* about the dances we had just heard! He assures me, moreover, that he would like to attach me to his house (to Ambrosia, of course, who has no man, being one herself), and so forth. Jeanquirit, that I should mumble something stupid was to be expected; that, on the contrary, and all on account of Beda, I stood there like a lamb and said nothing—well, may heaven forgive me! And anyway, it was all Chopin's fault!

PS. Just as I thought—No. 37 of the *Neueste* carries a review of our *Carnaval*, describing it as 'another monstrous onion, so pitiful that one cannot even weep over it. Authors of such concoctions should at least get them out of range of sound and smell before they draw the bungs. Nor should they imagine that simply by adding a tail to a zero they automatically get a nine!' Etc.[9]

PPS. De Knapp got out of town last night!

---

[1] One of Schumann's most imaginative literary productions. It is a review of some two dozen piano pieces, all dances, worked into a short story. Of the cast of characters Ambrosia has not been identified. Beda is presumably Clara Wieck. De Knapp is a fractured anagram of the name of Karl Banck (1809–1889), a composer and critic who had been associated with Schumann on the *Neue Zeitschrift für Musik* and contributed to it under the Davidsbündler pseudonym of Serpentin. He and Schumann fell out at about this time, partly, it is believed, because Banck was Schumann's rival for Clara's affections.

[2] Nowakowski, Joseph (1800–1865), a celebrated Polish pianist.

[3] Brzowski, Joseph (1805–1888), Polish conductor and composer.

[4] Zoellner, Karl (1792–1836), a famous organ virtuoso.

[5] Kraegen, Karl (1797–1879), Court Pianist in Dresden.

[6] Wolff, Edouard (1816–1880), Polish pianist resident in Paris, where he was a contemporary and intimate friend of Chopin.

[7] Schumann refers to the ill-fated Polish uprising against the Russians of 1830–1831.

[8] I.e. B-E-D-A.

[9] This, too, is fictional. Schumann's *Carnaval* had not been published.

THE OLD CAPTAIN[1]

(1837)

YESTERDAY, WHEN THE storm was raging so furiously against my window, seeming to carry moaning bodies through the air, your image suddenly appeared to me, old poetic captain, and banished the storm from my mind!

As long ago as 183* a slender, dignified figure had entered into our circle—we hardly knew how. No one knew his name. No one asked him from where he came or where he went. He was called simply 'the old captain'. There were periods when we might not see him for weeks at a time; or he would come every day, particularly when there was music. Then he would sit quietly, in a corner, as if unseen, his head buried in his hands. Afterwards, he would make the most pertinent and acute comments.

'Eusebius,' I said one day, 'what we lack in our wild disordered life, is a harpist out of *Wilhelm Meister*.[2] How would it be if we were to accept the old captain as such and leave him his incognito?'

And for a long time so it was. But as little as he spoke of himself, carefully avoiding any discussion of his circumstances, we learned at least that he was a Herr von Breitenbach, a retired officer of the —— Army, with money enough to meet his needs and such a passion for artists that he could give his all for them, too. More important was that he had been to Rome and London, Paris and St. Petersburg, mostly on foot, and had seen and heard the most famous artists. He could also play Beethoven concertos charmingly, so it was said, and Spohr's concertos for the violin, which he carried with him on his travels, sealed under his jacket. Moreover, he painted portraits of all his friends, which he kept in an album, read Thucydides, worked out problems in mathematics, wrote marvellous letters, etc.

There was some truth in all of this, as we were able to determine on closer acquaintance. But as far as music was concerned, we were never able to hear him play—until one day when Florestan heard him by chance and came home to report in confidence:

'He plays horribly, and I owe him an apology for listening. It reminded me of a story of old Zelter. He was walking through the streets of Berlin one night with Chamisso.[3] They stopped before a house where a piano was being played. After they had listened for a while Zelter took Chamisso by the arm and said: "Come, his music is home-made!" '

And, indeed, it was perfectly natural that he should have had no technique. Just as his profoundly poetic eye could take in the heights and depths of Beethoven, so had he begun his musical studies, not with a teacher and scales, but with Spohr's *Gesangsszene* and Beethoven's last B flat sonata. We were assured that he had been working on these two pieces for a full ten years. He would often arrive in high spirits and report that it would soon go well, that the sonata was learning to obey him, and that we would soon hear it. At other times he would be despondent and confide that as often as he approached the summit just as often did he slip back. But he could not resist the temptation to try again.

If his ability as a performing musician could not, therefore, be rated very highly, it was the greater pleasure to see him listening to music. There was no one for whom I was happier to play. There was something inspiring about his mere listening. I dominated him, led him whither I wished, and yet I often had the feeling that it all originated with him. And then when he began to speak, his voice soft and clear, about the nobility of art, it was as if from some superior insight—so impersonal, poetic and true. The word 'criticize' was not in his vocabulary. If he was forced to hear something trivial, one could tell that for him it simply did not exist. As with a child who knows no sin, he was unaware of the commonplace.

Thus for years he came and went, always welcomed among us as a kind of unearthly benevolent spirit. Recently, he was absent for longer than usual. We assumed that he was off on one of his longer journeys on foot, which he undertook in all seasons. Then, one evening, while leafing through the newspapers, we ran across his obituary. Eusebius composed the following epitaph:

'Beneath these flowers I lie dreaming, a stringed-instrument, stilled. Myself no player, I become, under the hands of those who understand me, an eloquent friend. Try me, traveller, before continuing on your way. The more care you take with me, the more beautiful the tones that shall be your reward.'

---

[1] An obituary tribute to a Hauptmann von Breitenbach, a retired officer who

belonged to the select circle privileged to take part, as players or listeners, in
Schumann's so-called 'Quartet Mornings'.

[2] A character in Goethe's novel. Music-lovers have encountered him in
Ambroise Thomas' *Mignon*.

[3] Chamisso, Adelbert von (1781-1838), poet and naturalist, author of *Peter
Schlemihl's wundersame Geschichte*.

'THE HUGUENOTS'

(1837)

I FEEL TODAY like a doughty young warrior drawing his sword for the first time in a great cause!

It so happened that we have just experienced productions of the two most important works of the time, Meyerbeer's *The Huguenots* and Mendelssohn's *St. Paul*. It was in all probability the first time that they have been heard side by side, as if our little Leipzig, where weighty world issues have been settled in the past, were now being called upon to settle musical issues as well.[1]

Where to begin, where to end? The reader knows this journal's policies only too well, and will understand that when we speak of Mendelssohn there can be no talk of Meyerbeer, in such diametrically opposite directions do their respective paths lead. He will understand, too, that in order to assess them one need only attribute to the one what is lacking in the other—excepting only talent, which they have in common.

Meyerbeer's success in our musically healthy Germany is enough to make one question one's own sanity, particularly when honourable people, including musicians, even those who are delighted with Mendelssohn's less spectacular conquests, say that there is something to him. I heard *The Huguenots* for the first time while still under the spell of Schröder-Devrient's nobly projected Leonora.[2] Who does not look forward with pleasure and hope to something new? Had not Ries himself, and with his own hand, written that there was much in *The Huguenots* worthy of being ranked with Beethoven? What did others say? And myself?

I agree whole-heartedly with Florestan, who exclaimed, shaking his clenched fist at the score: 'I still reckoned Meyerbeer a musician when he wrote *Il Crociato*. With *Robert le Diable* I began to have my doubts. Now, with *The Huguenots*, I place him in Franconi's circus!'[3] I cannot describe or quell the loathing with which the whole thing filled us. Time and again we had to turn away in disgust. We were sheerly consumed with fury. After hearing it a few times I found better things in it, and much to condone. But the verdict remains the same. To those who dare compare it with *Fidelio* or similar works I can only

repeat that they know nothing about it! Nothing! Nothing! Not
that I shall attempt to convert them. It can't be done!

One astute critic has aptly characterized both the music and the
action by noting that it all takes place either in a brothel or in church. I
am no moralist, but it is too much for a good Protestant when he
hears his most hallowed song[4] bawled forth from the stage; too much
for him when the bloodiest drama in the history of his church is
reduced to a rustic farce simply to earn money and notoriety. The thing
is outrageous from beginning to end, from the overture with its
cheap and silly religiosity, to the end, when we are all supposed to be
burned alive.[5] What is left after *The Huguenots* but actually to execute
criminals on the stage and make a public exhibition of whores?

Just consider what happens, and where it all leads. In the first act we
have a company of males indulging in a drinking bout with—a nice
touch!—only one female, veiled, to be sure. In the second act we are
treated to a debauch of bathing women with—exhumed for the
Parisians—a lone man, blindfolded! In the third act we find licentious-
ness mixed with religion. In the fourth we have strangulation prepared,
and in the fifth we see it done—in a church! Debauchery, murder and
prayer—*The Huguenots* offers nothing else. One may search in vain for
a sustained pure thought, a truly Christian sentiment. Meyerbeer nails
heart to skin and says: 'That's it. You can reach out and touch it!' It
is all contrived, all make-believe and hypocrisy!

And the heroes and heroines—excepting Marcel and St. Bris, who
do not sink to quite such miserable depths! There is Nevers, the complete French profligate, who loves Valentine, gives her up, and then
marries her. And Valentine herself, who loves Raoul, marries Nevers,
swears to love him for ever and then, finally, gives herself to Raoul.
Ah, yes! Raoul, who loves Valentine, rejects her, and then returns to
her anyway. And finally the Queen,—Queen of all these puppets!
And one likes it because it charms the eye and comes from Paris. And
you straight-laced German maidens, do you not shut your eyes? The
shrewdest of all composers rubs his hands in glee.

To speak of the music itself volumes would not suffice. Every
measure is a work of calculation, every measure gives you something
to talk about. 'Astonish or titillate' is his slogan, and he can accomplish
it even with the mob. As for that interwoven chorale, which leaves the
French beside themselves, well, I confess that if any pupil were ever to
bring me such an example of counterpoint, I would, at best, suggest
that in the future he never do anything worse. How intentionally
shallow it all is, and how purposefully superficial—lest the yokelry miss

the point!—and how crude the patchwork when Marcel keeps intruding with *Ein' feste Burg*, etc.

Much is made of the consecration of the swords in the fourth act. I
grant that it is a dramatic touch, with some striking, imaginative turns:
the chorus, particularly, has great theatrical effect. Situation, setting
and instrumentation are all of a piece; and since the monstrous is
Meyerbeer's element, he has written it with fire and affection. But if
you examine the melody, what is it but a tricked-up *Marseillaise*?
And is it really such an achievement to get an effect from such resources
in such a spot? I have no objection to the marshalling of everything
available at the right moment, but one should not speak of magnificence when a dozen trombones, trumpets, ophicleides and the voices of
a hundred people singing in unison can be heard at some distance!

Here I must mention a Meyerbeer-esque refinement. He knows the
public too well not to realize that noise can grow tiresome. How
cleverly he avoids the pitfall! After such a racket he starts right off with
whole arias accompanied only by single instruments, as if to say:
'There, you Germans, see what I, too, can do with modest means!'
One cannot, unfortunately, deny him a certain *esprit*!

To go through it all in detail would take too long. And in any case
Meyerbeer's ultimate superficiality, want of originality and lack of
style are as familiar as his talent for fancy trimmings, the fabrication of
brilliant and dramatic episodes, his skill in instrumentation and the
great variety of his forms. With no trouble at all one can tick off
Rossini, Mozart, Hérold, Weber, Bellini and even Spohr as they pass
in review through his scores. In short, there is nothing in the literature
of music upon which he does not draw. What is his, and his alone, is
that celebrated, fatally throbbing, indecent rhythm that runs through
almost every theme in the opera.

As I have said, only hate could deny him much that is better, even
nobler and grander. Marcel's 'Battle Song' is effective, and the song
of the Page charming; the greater part of the third act, with its lively
folk scenes, holds one's interest. The first part of the duet between
Marcel and Valentine is well drawn, as is the Sextet; the comedy of the
'Mocking Chorus' is well handled; there is much originality in the
'Consecration of the Swords' in the fourth act, and the following duet
between Raoul and Valentine has workmanship and a nice flow of
musical ideas. But what does it all amount to against the vulgarity,
distortion, artificiality, immorality and non-musicality of the whole?
Thank God that we have, at least, reached the limit. There can be no
worse, unless the stage were to be transformed into a gallows. And the

anguished cry of a talent tortured by the times yields to the hope that things can only get better!

[1] I.e. the defeat of Napoleon at Leipzig in 1813.

[2] She also sang Valentine in *The Huguenots*.

[3] A famous Parisian circus director, about whom Börne had recently written.

[4] *Ein' feste Burg*.

[5] An allusion to the lines: 'Par le fer et l'incendie exterminons la race impie!' in the closing scene of the opera.

SCHUBERT'S GRAND DUO
AND THREE LAST SONATAS

(1838)

Time was when I spoke of Schubert reluctantly, and then only at night to the trees and the stars.

Who does not have his special enthusiasms? Delighted by this new spirit, whose wealth I thought to be without measure or bounds, and deaf to anything that might be counted against him, I could think of nothing else!

As one grows older and more demanding, the circle of one's favourites tends to contract. Who is the master about whom one's views remain unchanged throughout a lifetime? The proper appreciation of Bach, for instance, requires experience that youth cannot have, and the same is true even of Mozart. Mere musical studies do not suffice to achieve a full understanding of Beethoven; in certain years some one of his works will inspire us more than others. One thing is certain; ages are mutually attractive. Youthful enthusiasm is best understood by youth, the strength of the mature master by a mature man.

Schubert will always be the favourite of the former. He exemplifies what youth seeks—a brimming heart, bold ideas and impulsive action. He tells them about the things that most appeal to them—romantic stories, knights, maidens and adventures. He mixes wit and humour with it all, but not so much as to disturb the softer, fundamental mood. At the same time, he gives wings to the player's own fantasy as no other composer but Beethoven ever did. The easily imitable in many of his idioms may well invite imitation. One feels impelled to work out a thousand ideas which he merely implied. Thus it is, and thus it shall be for many years to come.

Ten years ago I would not have hesitated to number these most recently published works among the loveliest ever. And compared with contemporary achievements, I would do so today. But as examples of Schubert, I do not consider them to be in a class with his Quartet in D minor, his Trio in E flat, or many of his small songs and piano compositions. The Duo,[1] particularly, appears to me to have been done under Beethoven's influence. Indeed, I had always regarded it as the piano arrangement of a symphony, until a glance at the original

manuscript—in which it is described in his own handwriting as a
'four-hand sonata'—seemed to contradict me. I say 'seemed' advisedly,
for I still cannot entirely abandon the idea. One who wrote as much
as Schubert could not have been overly fussy about titles; and he may
hastily have written 'sonata' over something that was already complete
in his head as a symphony—not to mention the more prosaic possibility
that it was simply easier to find a publisher for a sonata than for a
symphony, particularly at a time when his name was only just beginning to be known.

Familiar as I am with his style and his way of treating the piano, and
comparing this work with his other sonatas, all of them so expressive
of the purest pianistic character, I cannot but regard it as an orchestral
work. One hears strings and winds, tutti, solos, the rumble of timpani,
the broad symphonic form. Even the Beethoven reminiscences—as in
the second movement, echoing the Andante of Beethoven's Symphony
No. 2, and as in the last, recalling the last movement of Beethoven's
Symphony No. 7, along with a few paler passages which appear to me
to have been casualties of transcription—seem similarly to support my
view.[2]

At the same time, I would wish to defend the Duo against the charge
that it is not well conceived as a composition for piano, or that it
makes demands of the instrument that the latter cannot satisfy. It is
simply that if one regards it as an arrangement of a symphony, one
sees it from a different point of view, in which case we are a symphony
the richer.

We have already mentioned the reminiscences of Beethoven. Well,
we all draw upon his treasure. But even without this illustrious pre-
decessor, Schubert would have been no other, although his individuality might have emerged more slowly. Thus, whoever has some
sensibility and schooling will recognize both Beethoven and Schubert
on the first page and distinguish between them. Compared with
Beethoven, Schubert is a feminine character, much more voluble,
softer and broader; or a guileless child romping among giants. Such is
the relationship of these symphonic movements to those of Beethoven.
Their intimacy is purely Schubertian. They have their robust moments,
to be sure, and marshal formidable forces. But Schubert conducts himself as wife to husband, the one giving orders, the other relying upon
pleas and persuasion.

All of this in relationship to Beethoven! Compared with others he is
man enough, the boldest and freest, indeed, of all the newer musicians.
It is in this spirit that one should take the Duo in hand. Its beauties are

not hard to find. They meet us more than halfway, and are the more appealing the more often we examine them. One has no choice but to love this poetic spirit. And as much as the Adagio may remind one of Beethoven, I know hardly another passage where Schubert has revealed more of himself. So true to life it is that at certain measures his name inadvertently escapes one's lips—and with that one has hit the mark.

We will agree, too, that the work sustains its high level from beginning to end, something which one should always demand, but which is rarely achieved nowadays. Modern musicians should all be familiar with such a piece, and if they find it difficult to understand many a contemporary work, or many another of the future, or have failed to comprehend the transitions, then it is nobody's fault but their own. The new, so-called romantic school did not emerge from the blue sky. There is a reason for everything.

The sonatas[3] are designated as Schubert's last works, and are remarkable enough in any case. A critic unaware of the date of their origin might judge them differently. I myself might have attributed them to an earlier period of the composer's development, continuing to regard the Trio in E flat as his last and most individual work. It would be superhuman, of course, were a composer such as Schubert, who composed so much and so continuously, to surpass himself with each new work, and these sonatas may, indeed, be his last works.

Whether they were written from his sickbed or not, I have been unable to determine. The music would suggest that they were.[4] And yet it is possible that one imagines things when the portentous designation, 'last works', crowds one's fantasy with thoughts of impending death. Be that as it may, these sonatas strike me as differing conspicuously from his others, particularly in a much greater simplicity of invention, in a voluntary renunciation of brilliant novelty—an area in which he otherwise made heavy demands upon himself—and in the spinning out of certain general musical ideas instead of adding new threads to them from phrase to phrase, as was otherwise his custom. It is as though there could be no ending, nor any embarrassment about what should come next. Even musically and melodically it ripples along from page to page, interrupted here and there by single more abrupt impulses—which quickly subside.

Whether my imagination, through its awareness of his final illness, has led me astray in arriving at this judgment I leave to soberer heads to decide. Such was the effect, however, that these sonatas had upon me. In any case, he closes cheerfully and easily and amiably, as if he could begin again the next day. It was not to be. But he could, at least, face the end with a serene countenance.

And if on his tombstone it is written that in him was lost 'a precious possession but even more precious hopes',[5] let us think gratefully only of the first. Nothing is to be gained from speculation about what might have been. He did enough. And all honour to such aspirations and such achievements!

[1] The Sonata (for four hands) in C, composed in 1825, published by Diabelli as Grand Duo, Opus 140, in 1838 and dedicated to Clara.

[2] Subsequent research has not sustained Schumann's opinion that it was planned as a symphony. Others, however, have reacted similarly, and it has been orchestrated three times, initially by Joachim. None of these orchestrations has survived.

[3] The Sonatas in C minor, A major and B flat, written in September, 1828. Schubert had intended to dedicate them to Hummel, but the publisher, Diabelli, dedicated them to Schumann.

[4] They weren't. Schubert's last days were devoted to correcting the proofs of the second part of *Die Winterreise*.

[5] By Grillparzer.

LUIGI CHERUBINI

String Quartet No. 1 in E flat

(1838)

Even among good musicians there is a considerable difference of opinion about Cherubini's quartets.

It is not, of course, a question of their being the work of a master. There can be no doubt about that. It is rather a question of style. Do they represent the true quartet style which we love and which we have come to regard as exemplary?

We are accustomed to the type of quartet developed by Haydn, Mozart and Beethoven. In recent years we have acknowledged Onslow and Mendelssohn as worthy successors following the same path. Now along comes Cherubini, a man aged in the aristocracy of the art and in his own artistic concepts, still the supreme harmonist of the time, an estimable, learned and always interesting Italian whose elegance of manners and strength of character have sometimes prompted me to compare him with Dante!

I confess that when I heard this quartet for the first time I felt uneasy about it, particularly after the first two movements. It was not what one expected. Parts of it seemed operatic and overloaded, other parts trivial, empty or capricious. It may have been the impatience of youth that made it difficult to grasp immediately the sense of an old man's often wayward speech; for at the same time my whole being reacted to the authority of a master. Then came the Scherzo, with its impulsive Spanish theme and extraordinary Trio, and, at last, the Finale, throwing off sparks in every direction like a diamond. There could be no doubt about its authorship, or that it was worthy of its author.

Many will react similarly. The special quality of his quartet style takes a bit of knowing. It is not, after all, our mother tongue. It is rather the language of a distinguished foreigner, for whom our regard increases as we learn to understand it.

PIANO CONCERTOS

(1839)

MUSIC FOR THE PIANO looms large in the recent history of the art. It usually gives us the first radiance of a new genius. Our most gifted contemporaries are pianists, an observation that has been applied to earlier epochs. Bach and Handel, Mozart and Beethoven, all grew up at the keyboard. Like sculptors, who first sketch their statues in miniature in softer substances, they, too, may often have sketched at the keyboard what they later worked out in grand dimensions in the tougher substance of the orchestra.

In the meantime the instrument itself has been brought near to perfection. With the advancing physical mechanics of piano playing and the bolder flight of piano composition, stemming from Beethoven, the instrument, too, has advanced in compass and significance. Should pedals be added, as on the organ (and I believe that this will come), the composer will have new prospects. Freeing himself more and more from dependence upon the supporting orchestra, he will be able to proceed with wealthier resources, a fuller voice and greater self-sufficiency. This separation of the piano from the orchestra is something we have seen coming for some time. Defying the symphony, contemporary piano playing seeks to dominate by its own means and on its own terms. This may well explain why the past few years have produced so few piano concertos; indeed, so few original compositions of any kind in which the piano plays an accompanying role.

This periodical has, from its beginning, reported on just about every new piano concerto that has come along. There can hardly have been more than sixteen or seventeen, a small number in comparison with former days. Thus do times change. What once was regarded as an enrichment of instrumental forms, as an important discovery, is now voluntarily abandoned. Surely it would have to be counted a loss if the piano concerto with orchestra were to pass from the scene. We cannot, on the other hand, contradict the pianists when they say: 'We do not need any help from other instruments, ours is most effective alone.' And so we must await the genius who will show us in a newer and more brilliant way, how orchestra and piano may be combined, how the soloist, dominant at the keyboard, may unfold the wealth of his instrument and his art, while the orchestra, no longer a mere spectator, may interweave its manifold facets into the scene.[1]

One thing, however, we could easily demand from the younger composers—namely, that as a substitute for the serious and worthy concerto form, they give us worthy solo pieces, that they desist from caprices and variations and give us beautifully, fully rounded and substantial allegro movements suitable for the opening of programmes. Until such a time we must continue to look to older compositions to find things designed to set a concert programme off in a properly artistic manner and to test properly an artist's superior qualities—to those splendid works of Mozart and Beethoven, or for more select audiences, to the works of that still insufficiently appreciated gentleman, Johann Sebastian Bach.

[1] Destined, of course, to be Schumann himself. The first movement of his Concerto in A minor was completed in 1841, the other two in 1845.

GOTTFRIED PREYER'S SYMPHONY

(1839)

WHEN THE GERMAN talks about symphonies, he speaks of Beethoven. For him the words 'symphony' and 'Beethoven' are synonymous and inseparable. They are his pride and his joy.

Just as Italy has its Naples, the Frenchman his revolution, the Englishman his sea voyage, etc., so the German has his Beethoven symphonies. He can forget that he can point to no great school of painting. With Beethoven he has recovered in spirit what he lost to Napoleon. He dares even to equate him with Shakespeare.

Beethoven's works having become a part of our innermost being—even certain of the symphonies have become popular—one would assume that they had left deep traces, and that these would be visible in the works of the succeeding generation, particularly in works of the same category. Such is not the case. We hear reminiscences, to be sure, although curiously enough, mostly of the earlier symphonies, as if each of them required a certain time to be understood and imitated. Reminiscences there are—too many and too strong. But mastery of the grand form, where ideas follow one another in rapid succession, bound together by an inner spiritual bond, is encountered—with certain exceptions—only rarely. The newer symphonies level out, for the greater part, into the overture style, particularly the first movements. The slow movements are there only because custom requires it. The scherzos are such in name only. The last movements no longer know what the earlier movements contained.

Berlioz was heralded as a phenomenon. In Germany we know next to nothing about him, and what we have learned by hearsay has appeared rather to frighten the Germans. It will be some time before we become thoroughly acquainted with him. Certainly he will not have laboured in vain. Such talents do not appear in isolation. The immediate future will tell. Schubert should also be mentioned, but even his achievements in the symphonic field have not become public.

A significant indication of the present level of talent was provided by the Vienna Prize Award. Say what one will, such contests can only be helpful; they can do no harm. And he knows little about creative impulses who imagines that they are not encouraged by inducements, even prosaic ones. Had someone offered a prize of precious diamonds

—such as are to be found in royal and imperial treasuries—while Mozart, Haydn and Beethoven were still alive, I bet that the masters would have done their best to get it. But then, of course, who would have judged?

Enough of that. The outcome of the Vienna contest is known, and although it is said that the winner was virtually sure of the prize before he even began his symphony (every contestant was secretly just as confident), still it must be acknowledged that as things now stand— that is, having heard a number of the other submissions—Lachner deserved the prize. The symphony here under discussion, also a competitor, would seem to offer further confirmation. It is by Gottfried Preyer.[1] That it has appeared in full score makes an immediately favourable impression. The composer, a Viennese, has made a name for himself through the popularity of some of his songs. In this respect Vienna is not unlike other big cities. A successful effort, even in such a small form, suffices to establish one as an important composer. What sells the most is the best. And so it happened that a publisher decided to print the score—a notable decision. Symphonies are an expensive and hazardous commodity, real drugs on the market, and publishers will not, as a rule, take them as a gift. In any case, the engraved score, clean and correct, lies open before us.

A few pages suffice to disclose a progressive young composer, initially somewhat ill at ease in the large, unfamiliar form, but gaining in security and courage as he gets under way. His aspirations must be doubly acknowledged in view of the fact that he lives in a city where little encouragement is vouchsafed the solid, serious or even profound average, where judgments for and against are largely determined by first impressions, and where the verdict is usually couched in terms of 'it appealed' or 'it did not appeal'. Thus it was after the première of *Christus am Ölberge* and *Fidelio*. They did not appeal, and that was the end of it.

This symphony, which has been played frequently in Vienna, 'appealed'. It even 'impressed', thanks to the veneer of scholarly working out which it often displays. The composer will understand us only if he is acquainted with our periodical through other issues than this, only if he knows its policies and the masters it rates most highly, knows what it expects of a symphony, particularly, and how it is chary of praise, being an organ of musicians for musicians.

Precisely this so-called 'work' betrays the first attempt—and the tendency of well-meaning beginners to give us rather too much of a good thing. As if it were essential to sweat out the whole art of counterpoint again, we are threatened from afar with fugal beginnings, mostly rattling around in the violins. We are exposed to three, four and even more themes, ranked one above the other, which we are supposed to follow individually. What we note is the composer's pleasure in finding his way back to the fundamental key without having disgraced himself. The writer knows all this from the best of experience—namely, his own. And what is the good of it all? Certainly Mozart 'worked', and Beethoven, too, but with what materials and at what places and for what reasons, and all as if it were mere child's play! Of course, they had to make their experiments, too; but they never wrote merely that the eye might see something on paper.

Sometimes I wish that a young composer might give us, just once, a light, merry symphony, in a major key, without trombones and doubled horns, but then of course, that is even more difficult. Only one who understands how to command large forces can play with them. Lest the above be held against us at some time in the future as evidence that we are against 'work', let it be said forthwith that we do favour 'work' and of the profoundest sort. But it should not be for its own sake, or of such a kind that we can pull it apart thread by thread. Gluck's saying that one should write nothing that is without effect, if taken in the right sense, is one of the most golden of rules, a true master's secret.

[1] Preyer, Gottfried (1807-1901), Viennese organist, composer, conductor and teacher.

FELIX MENDELSSOHN

Piano Concerto No. 2

(1839)

TRULY, HE REMAINS the same, striking out in his old happy stride!
No one has a lovelier smile on his lips than he!

This concerto,[1] to be sure, will offer virtuosos little in which to show
off their monstrous dexterity. Mendelssohn gives them almost nothing
to do that they have not already done a hundred times before. We
have often heard them complain about it. And not unjustly! A concerto
need not exclude opportunities to show off bravura in the novelty and
brilliance of its passages. But music comes first, and he who gives it to
us always and most richly shall earn our highest praise.

Music is the outflow of a benign spirit, regardless of whether it flows
in the presence of hundreds or in solitude. That is why Mendelssohn's
compositions are so irresistible when he plays them himself. The fingers
are only carriers, and could just as well be hidden from view. The ear
alone should receive, and the heart then decide. I often think that
Mozart must have played like that.

If it may be said in praise of Mendelssohn that he always gives us
such music, it cannot, at the same time, be denied that he does so in
some pieces more fleetingly, in others more emphatically. This concerto belongs among his more fleeting productions. Unless I am greatly
mistaken, he did it in a few days, perhaps even in a few hours. It is
like shaking a tree and having the ripe fruit fall at your feet without
further ado.

One will ask how it compares with his First Concerto. It's the same,
and yet not the same; the same because it comes from the same
practised master hand, different because it comes ten years later.
Sebastian Bach is discernible in the harmonization. The rest, melody,
form and instrumentation are all Mendelssohn.

Let us enjoy the fleeting, cheerful gift! It resembles one of those
works thrown off by the older masters while recuperating from one of
their greater exertions. Our younger master will certainly not forget
how the older ones would suddenly emerge with something magnificent—Mozart's Concerto in D minor, Beethoven's in G!

[1] In D minor, Opus 40.

FRIEDRICH KALKBRENNER

Études, Opus 145

(1839)

I SHALL BE hard put to find anything favourable to say about Kalkbrenner's[1] new études (*Études de Style et de Perfectionnement Composées pour servir de Complément à la Méthode*, etc.).

It may be that I am simply irritated by the legends that have reached us. We have heard, for instance, that Kalkbrenner always considers his latest compositions to be his best, and that he practises his own études, just like a student studying from himself—this last, in particular, aroused my curiosity! Be that as it may, I confess that these études depressed me. Imagination, where are you? Ideas? No answer! Almost nothing but dry formulas, beginnings, residue—the image of an ageing beauty.

Such is the fate of all who hang their art on an instrument. They charm as long as they are young, as long as they can offer something novel, something more scintillant. But then young talents come along. What was once astonishing brilliance has become child's play for all. But those who have grown accustomed to applause can no longer live without it, and they try to force it. Not one palm is touched to another; the audience merely smiles at what once left it gaping in astonishment.

As Kalkbrenner himself says, he has devoted a large part of his life to the mechanical development of his hands. This would throttle the composing of a Beethoven, not to speak of what it must do to an inferior talent. And then age exposes what the charms of youth could disguise: want of deeper, less one-sided knowledge, neglect of the study of great models. Could one imagine a Sebastian Bach or a Beethoven without imagination, they would still, even in old age, be able to produce something interesting, simply because they had studied and learned something. Those who have not learned may produce some agreeable things up to a certain age. But then they no longer have the strength to meet the requirements put upon them, and every attempt at camouflage merely renders the defects the more unsightly.

Of what use are these études? Certainly of none to the artist or to the composer, who has only to leaf through them to put them aside for ever! And of none even for virtuosos and students; the one will hardly find anything new, and the other will find nothing not better and more concisely presented in Kalkbrenner's earlier études. I can believe that in twenty-five pieces there are some nice things. But art is served only by the masterly. Whoever cannot supply this everywhere and at all times has no claim to be called a true artist. Among all these études not one is masterly, i.e. great in invention and execution. Better to pull out our honourable old Cramer, our finely cultivated Moscheles, our imaginative Chopin. We have no time to spend in the study of mediocre compositions!

[1] Kalkbrenner, Friedrich (1788-1849), one of the foremost pianists of the generation preceding Liszt and Chopin. He spent most of his life in Paris, where his father had settled as coach at the Opera. Chopin, when he arrived in Paris in 1831, was much taken with him. 'Just imagine,' he wrote to his friend Titus Woyciechowski in December, 1831, 'how curious I was to hear Herz, Liszt, Hiller and the rest—they are all nobodies compared with Kalkbrenner. I confess I have played as well as Herz, but I long to play like Kalkbrenner. If Paganini is perfection itself, Kalkbrenner is his equal in quite a different field. It is impossible to describe his calm, his enchanting touch, his incomparable evenness and the master which he reveals in every note. . . . He is a giant who tramples underfoot the Herzes and Czernys and, of course, me!' (From Hedley, *op. cit.*) Kalkbrenner made a proposition to Chopin that he become his pupil for three years, and Chopin seriously considered taking him up on it. In the end he decided against it, but apparently he attended some of Kalkbrenner's classes. Kalkbrenner himself was a great admirer of Chopin, assisting him in getting established in Paris, sending him pupils, assisting at his first concert, etc. Friedrich Wieck rather shared Chopin's high opinion of Kalkbrenner, describing him as 'the greatest—he comes nearest to my ideal'.

LISZT'S ÉTUDES

(1839)

Our subject is two sets of études by Liszt, and we may begin by letting the reader in on a discovery that can only heighten interest in them. We have, on the one hand, a set published by Hofmeister, designated as Opus 1 and described as *Travail de la Jeunesse*. On the other hand we have a set published by Haslinger under the heading, *Grandes Études*.[1] A more careful examination reveals that most of the pieces of the latter set are reworkings of the former, originally published some twenty years ago in Lyon and, because of the obscurity of the publisher, long since lost to sight and only recently reissued by Hofmeister.

While one cannot, therefore, properly describe the new set, expensively and handsomely prepared by Haslinger, as an original work, it will—and precisely on this account—be doubly interesting to the professional pianist, who thus may compare it with the two earlier versions. A comparison of them underscores the difference between piano playing as it was then and as it is now. The new version has gained in the wealth of resources, in brilliance and fullness, while, on the other hand, the elemental *naïveté* which animated the first youthful effusion is almost completely suppressed. Thus the new edition also provides a gauge of Liszt's present greatly matured manner of thought and feeling, and even a look into his more intimate spiritual life. The latter, admittedly, leaves us wondering whether we should not envy rather the boy than the man, who seems incapable of finding peace.

Opinions about Liszt's talent as a composer differ so greatly that it may not be inappropriate to go into its more important aspects right here where that talent is exposed from so many angles. Analysis is rendered difficult by the confusion surrounding the number and chronology of his compositions. Most of them bear no opus number at all, leaving the reviewer to guess at the date of their origin. Be that as it may, they all testify to an exceptional spirit, variously moved and variously moving. His own life is mirrored in his music. Removed from his fatherland at an early age, and deposited amidst the excitements of a big city, already much admired as child and boy, he often shows himself in his older compositions in a more melancholy mood, as if yearning for his German homeland, or, at the opposite extreme, more frivolous, as if frothed over by the light habits of the French.

He appears to have had no time for protracted study in composition; possibly, too, he has found no teacher worthy of him. He has studied, therefore, as a virtuoso, probably preferring the fluent tone to dry paper work, as lively musical natures often do. If he has raised himself as a player to astonishing heights, it follows that the composer in him has lagged behind, producing an imbalance that continues conspicuously to take its toll even in his latest works. Other phenomena have goaded him in other ways. First, he has been possessed of the idea of carrying over into music the romantic ideas of the French literary set, among whose leading lights he lived. Then the sudden apparition of Paganini spurred him on to improve himself as a pianist and to seek the ultimate in virtuosity.

Thus we see him (in his *Apparitions*,[2] for example) pondering the gloomiest fancies, but indifferent to the point of being *blasé* about it; while, on the other hand, letting himself go in the most wanton virtuosity, mocking, and reckless to the point of semi-madness. The example of Chopin, it would seem, first recalled him to his senses. Chopin, at least, has form; under the exotic images of his music there always runs the rosy thread of a melody. But by now it was too late for the extraordinary virtuoso to make up for what he had neglected as a composer. Possibly no longer content with himself as such, he sought refuge in others, in Beethoven and Schubert, whose works he could transcribe so brilliantly for piano. Or, in haste to do something of his own, he pulled out his earlier works, redecorating them with the pomp of his newly acquired virtuosity.

Accept the above as a view, as an attempt to explain Liszt's indistinct, often interrupted course as a composer as the consequence of the overriding demands of his virtuosity. I firmly believe that so eminently musical a nature as Liszt would have been a significant composer had he devoted as much time to composition and to himself as he, in fact, devoted to his instrument and to other masters. As to what may yet be expected of him, one can do no more than speculate. To gain the affections of his fatherland he would, of course, have to return to the brightness and simplicity that shine forth so benevolently from those older études. And in his compositions he would have to pursue a reverse course from the difficult to the easy. At the same time, we should not forget that what he is giving us here are *études*, and that the new complicated difficulties may be excused by the purpose of the exercise, which is, after all, the overcoming of the greatest difficulties.

¹ I.e. the *Études en forme de Douze Exercices pour Piano*, Opus 1, and the *Grandes Études*. Both sets were forerunners of the ultimate *Études d'Exécution Transcendante* of 1852. Schumann was wrong, of course, about the first set having been published 'twenty years ago'—in other words, in 1819 when Liszt was eight. They were published in 1827 not in Lyon, but in Marseille, when he was sixteen. The Haslinger edition was published in 1839.

² Three pieces dating from 1834.

FRANZ LISZT

Concerts in Dresden and Leipzig

(1840)

LISZT ARRIVED IN Dresden[1] last Saturday, rather the worse for wear, having just given six concerts in eight days in Prague. His visit can hardly have been anticipated anywhere with greater excitement than in this court city where piano music and piano playing are preferred to all other forms of music-making. The first recital was on Monday, before a distinguished audience that included several members of the royal family.

All eyes were focused upon the door where the artist would make his entrance. Pictures of him have enjoyed a wide circulation, and the painting by Kriehuber, which most strikingly captures his Jupiter-like profile, is excellent. But young Jupiter himself is interesting in a different way. It is fashionable now to speak of the prosaicness of our time, of jaded court and residence atmosphere, of railway mentality, etc. But let the right man appear, and his every move is noted with reverence. And so it was with Liszt, whose wondrous deeds were acclaimed twenty years ago, whose name we are accustomed to associate with those of the very greatest, and before whom, as with Paganini, all factions bow in unison, their differences for the moment apparently reconciled. There was a roar of acclaim as he entered. And then he began to play.

I had already heard him, but privately. It is one thing to hear an artist playing for a few friends, quite another to hear him before an audience. It is a different occasion—and a different artist. The beautiful, bright rooms, illuminated by candlelight, the bejewelled and decorated audience, all stimulate the giver as well as the given. The demon began to flex his muscles. He first played along with them, as if to feel them out, and then gave them a taste of something more substantial until, with his magic, he had ensnared each and every one and could move them this way or that as he chose.

It is unlikely that any other artist, excepting only Paganini, has the power to lift, carry and deposit an audience in such high degree. A Viennese writer has celebrated Liszt in a poem consisting of nothing but adjectives beginning with the individual letters of his name. It is a tasteless thing as poetry, but there is something to be said for it. Just as we are overwhelmed in leafing through a dictionary by an onslaught of letters and definitions, so in listening to Liszt are we overwhelmed by an onslaught of sounds and sensations. In a matter of seconds we have been exposed to tenderness, daring, fragrance and madness. The instrument glows and sparkles under the hands of its master. This has all been described a hundred times, and the Viennese, in particular, have tried to trap the eagle in every possible way—with winged pursuit, with snares, with pitchforks and with poems. It simply has to be heard—and seen. If Liszt were to play behind the scenes a considerable portion of poetry would be lost.

He played the whole programme alone, including the accompaniments for Mme. Schröder-Devrient,[2] probably the only artist who could survive in such company. They did the 'Erlkönig' and a few smaller songs of Schubert. Mendelssohn once had the notion of composing a whole concert programme, including an overture, vocal offerings and all the usual trappings. Liszt has something of the same idea. He gives his concerts pretty much alone.

I am ill-qualified to appraise the impression of this great artist in Dresden, having no experience with the local applause thermometer. The enthusiasm was described as extraordinary. The Viennese, among all Germans, is the least sparing of his hands, and treasures as a souvenir the slit glove with which he applauded Liszt. In northern Germany, as I have said, it is different.

Early Tuesday morning Liszt continues on to Leipzig. About his appearances there, more in our next.

II

I wish I could capture in words a picture of this extraordinary man, especially for those who cannot hope ever to see him in the flesh and who eagerly devour every word that is written about him. It is not easy! Least difficult is to speak of his outward appearance. It has been tried often enough. His head has been called Schiller-esque and Napoleonic, and such comparisons are in some way apt. All extraordinary men have one feature in common—namely, the suggestion of energy and will-power around the eye and mouth. Liszt bears a striking resemblance to Napoleon, pictured as a young general—pale, lean, striking in profile, the expressive centre of the countenance focused upward towards the hair-line. But to speak of his art is most difficult. It is no longer piano playing of this kind or that, but rather the utterance of a daring fellow, whose fate it is to conquer and rule, not with the dangerous tools of combat, but with the peaceful tools of art. Many and excellent artists have come our way in recent years, some of them our own, who can bear comparison with Liszt in this or that respect. In energy and daring none can touch him. Thalberg, particularly, was thought of as a competitor. But one had only to compare the two heads. I remember the observation of a well-known Viennese cartoonist who likened Thalberg's, not inaptly, to that of a beautiful countess with a man's nose. Of Liszt's head he said that any painter could use it as a model for a Greek god. Much the same could be said of their playing. Chopin comes closer, at least as a pianist. He is Liszt's equal in elfin tenderness and charm. Closest to him are Paganini and, among women, Malibran, from each of whom Liszt acknowledges having learned the most.

He began with the Scherzo and Finale of Beethoven's Pastoral Symphony. It was a wilful choice, and unfortunate on many grounds. In private, in a small room, this otherwise ultimately decent transcription may well let one forget the orchestra. In a large hall, and one, moreover, where we have heard the symphony played by the orchestra so often and so perfectly, the weakness of the instrument was painfully evident, especially where it was called upon to reproduce the big effects. A more modest arrangement, a mere suggestion, might have been more effective. One was aware, of course, that the instrument was presided over by a master. One was satisfied. We had at least seen him shake his mane. To abide by the metaphor, the lion soon showed a more imposing side. This was in a Fantasy on themes by Pacini,[3] which he played in an extraordinary manner. But I would gladly sacrifice all the reckless bravura for the tender utterance of the following étude. Excepting Chopin, I know of none who could approach him in this kind of playing. He concluded with the familiar *Grande Galope Chromatique* and added the *Grande Valse de Bravura* as an encore.

Exhaustion and indisposition prevented him from playing the concert promised for the following day.[4] Instead, there was a musical festival unlikely to be forgotten by Liszt or anyone else who was present. The host, none other than Mendelssohn, had chosen compositions unfamiliar to the guest of honour. There were the Schubert Symphony in C; the psalm, 'Wie der Hirsch schreit'; the overture, *Meeresstille und glückliche Fahrt*; three choruses from *St. Paul* and finally Bach's Concerto in D minor for Three Keyboard Instruments played by Liszt, Mendelssohn and Hiller. It was all as if totally improvised, done on the spur of the moment; three hours of the most beautiful music, the sort of thing one might not hear in years. The company parted in a high state of exhilaration, and the happiness reflected in every countenance expressed the gratitude of all to our host for this homage to the celebrated talent of another.

Liszt's most extraordinary accomplishment was yet to come: Weber's *Konzertstück*, with which he began his second recital. Both artist and audience appeared to be in a particularly lively mood, and the enthusiasm during the playing and at the close surpassed just about anything ever experienced here. And how Liszt went at the piece, with a strength and grandeur as if it concerned a battlefield manœuvre, increasing the tension from minute to minute until it seemed as though he were at the head of an orchestra and jubilantly directing it himself! At this moment he seemed, indeed, that field commander with whom, in outward appearance, at least, we have previously compared him, and the applause was mighty enough to have been a *'Vive l'Empereur!'* Afterwards he played a fantasy on themes from *The Huguenots*, Schubert's 'Ave Maria' and 'Serenade' and, as an encore, the 'Erlkönig'. The *Konzertstück*, however, remained his crowning achievement.

Whose idea it was to have a favourite singer present him with a bouquet of flowers at the close of the concert I do not know. Certainly it was not unearned. How mean and spiteful to carp at such attentions, as one of our local papers has seen fit to do! The pleasure that he gives is an artist's life-long goal. You listeners know little of all the pains his art costs him. He gives you the best that is in him, the full flower of his life, even perfection. Should we then begrudge him a simple floral wreath? Liszt was graciousness itself. Visibly pleased by the glowing reception accorded his second concert, he declared himself prepared to give a third for the benefit of any appropriate charity, leaving the choice to those acquainted with the local circumstances.

Thus it was that last Monday he played again, for the benefit of the Pension Fund for Aged and Ailing Musicians, having the previous day played a benefit concert in Dresden. The hall was jammed with listeners attracted by the cause, the choice of programme, the participation of our finest singers and, of course, by Liszt himself. Still tired from the journey, and from the concerts of the preceding days, he arrived from Dresden in the morning and went directly to the rehearsal, leaving himself little time for recuperation prior to the concert. This must be mentioned. No man is a god, and the visible strain under which Liszt played on this occasion was the natural consequence of all that he had been through. As a friendly gesture he had chosen compositions by three local composers—Mendelssohn, Hiller and myself.

Mendelssohn was represented by his newest piano concerto, Hiller by some études and I by selections from an older work called *Carnaval*. For the edification of many a bashful virtuoso let it be said that Liszt played them all virtually at sight. He was slightly familiar with the études and *Carnaval*;[5] Mendelssohn's concerto he had seen for the first time just a few days before the concert. With all the demands made upon him in the meantime he had no opportunity to prepare any of them. To certain doubts that I expressed as to whether such rhapsodic carnival life would make an impression upon so large an audience Liszt said only that he hoped so. I fear that he was too sanguine.

A few words here about this composition, which came about quite by accident. The name of a little town where a musical friend of mine lived contained all those letters of the scale which happen to correspond to letters of my own name.[6] This led to one of those little games that have been played every since Bach's time.[7] I finished the pieces one after another. This was during the carnival season in 1835, which found me in a serious frame of mind and in rather serious personal circumstances. Later on I gave the pieces new titles and called the whole thing *Carnaval*. There are things in them which may delight this person or that, but the musical moods change too quickly for a large audience to follow without being wakened every minute or two.

My amiable friend had not, as I have said, taken this into consideration. Sympathetically and wonderfully as he played, he may have reached a few individual listeners, but not the whole audience. It was different with the études, which are more familiarly cast; one in D flat and another in E minor, both tender and picturesque, were warmly received. The concerto was already familiar from performances by the composer himself. Liszt played it, as I have said, practically at sight. I know of no one who could easily do the same. He displayed the full brilliance of his virtuosity in his concluding piece, the *Hexameron*, a set of variations by Thalberg, Pixis, Herz and Liszt himself.[8] One can only wonder where he drew the strength to repeat half of it and then, to the delight of the audience, to add the *Grande Galope Chromatique*. I only wish that he might have offered something by Chopin, whose music he plays incomparably and with the utmost affection. In private he gladly plays anything requested of him. How often I have heard him on such occasions, and how I have admired him!

He left us Tuesday evening.

---

[1] In the autumn of 1839 it became known that the project of raising funds

for a Beethoven monument at Bonn had failed. Liszt, having just then reached the parting of the ways with Madame d'Agoult, decided to shoulder the project himself, and set off on an extended concert tour to raise the required funds. He began in Vienna, where he played six concerts, continuing on to Pressburg and Budapest, enjoying triumphs and honours beyond anything previously recorded in the history of music. He returned to Vienna, then moved on to Prague, Dresden and Leipzig. Schumann went to Dresden to hear him and make his acquaintance, and this article begins with his account of the first recital there on March 16, 1840.

[2] In other words, not quite alone. While Liszt may not have been the first artist to give a solo concert, it was he who established the solo recital as an institution.

[3] Pacini, Giovanni (1796–1867), composer of some ninety operas, one of which, *Niobe*, provided the themes for this Fantasy.

[4] There was more to it than that. High prices at the first concert and the failure of certain individuals to get the free tickets to which they felt themselves entitled aroused some hostility among the townspeople and some resentment on the part of Liszt. Mendelssohn reckoned, correctly, that an informal occasion of this character might help to break the ice.

[5] Liszt has been introduced to *Carnaval* by Clara in Vienna in 1838.

[6] I.e. Asch, on the border between Saxony and Bohemia, the home of Ernestine von Fricken, a piano pupil of Wieck, with whom Schumann had a tender relationship at that time and whom he seriously considered marrying. The letter H, it should be remembered, is B natural in German notation.

[7] I.e., variations on a theme derived from the note equivalents of the letters of a name, a favourite being B-A-C-H (with Bach himself setting the example). Schumann himself had played the game in his Opus 1, the so-called 'Abegg' Variations (1831) derived from the name of a young lady, Meta Abegg, whom he had met at a ball in Mannheim while still a student at Heidelberg. In his *Album für die Jugend*, Opus 68, he played it again, this time on the name of the composer, Niels Gade.

[8] Schumann omits Czerny and Chopin. The composition derived from a benefit concert given in Paris in 1837 under the auspices of Princess Belgiojoso in which all six participated, playing on six pianos. Each played a variation on a theme from Bellini's *I Puritani*. Liszt composed an introduction and a finale in addition to his own variation. Under the title of *Hexameron* the variations were subsequently published, and Liszt often played them in his recitals. He may have omitted the Czerny and Chopin variations on this occasion.

SCHUBERT'S SYMPHONY IN C

(1840)

A MUSICIAN VISITING Vienna for the first time may well rejoice in the festive street sounds and pause in admiration before St. Stephen's spire. But he will shortly be reminded how near to the city lies a churchyard dearer to him than any other of the city's sights, the place where almost side by side lie two of the greatest men his art has ever produced.[1]

Many young musicians will have wandered as I did[2] out to this churchyard in Währing to lay a wreath upon those graves, or even a mere wild rose such as the one I found planted on the spot where Beethoven finally found repose. Franz Schubert's grave was unadorned. So it was that one of my fondest wishes was fulfilled. I stayed for a long time contemplating the two hallowed graves, almost envying that Count O'Donel—if I have remembered the name correctly— who lies buried between them.[3]

To see a great man face to face for the first time, to grasp his hand, is one of life's most blessed experiences. It had not been my good fortune to encounter either of these artists, whom I admire most among the more recent composers, during his lifetime, and so I would have liked to have at my side during this pilgrimage some person who had been close to at least one of them, preferably one of their brothers. And then it occurred to me as I walked back to the city that Schubert's brother Ferdinand still lived, of whom Schubert thought so highly. I looked him up soon afterwards and found a strong resemblance, judging by the bust that rests by Schubert's grave. He was rather smaller, but sturdily built, his features expressing honesty and music alike. He knew me as an outspoken admirer of his brother, told me much and finally showed me some of his treasures—namely, those of Franz Schubert's compositions still in his hands. The assembled wealth set me to trembling with joy! Where to begin? Where to stop? He showed me, among other things, the scores of a number of symphonies, some still unheard, some examined and put away as too difficult and extravagant.

One must know Vienna, the problems of musical life there, the difficulty of assembling the resources required for the performance of large works, to understand how it could be possible that in the city where Schubert lived and worked little or nothing of his music is heard beyond his songs. Who knows how long the symphony now under discussion might have lain in darkness and dust had I not promptly arranged with Ferdinand to send it to Leipzig and to the management of the Gewandhaus concerts, or to Mendelssohn himself, whose keen eye rarely misses the most modestly budding beauty, much less the radiant full bloom? And so it was. The symphony arrived in Leipzig, was heard,[4] grasped, heard again and almost universally admired. The enterprising firm of Breitkopf & Härtel purchased the work and the rights, and thus we have it now complete with all the parts, with a full score, we hope, soon to follow for the use and enlightenment of the world.

Let me state at the outset: he who doesn't know this symphony knows little of Schubert. In view of what the world has already received from him this may seem hardly credible praise. It is so often said, and to the considerable annoyance of composers, that 'after Beethoven one should forgo symphonic ambitions', and it is true that most of those who have disregarded this advice have produced only lifeless mirrorings of Beethovenesque idioms, not to mention those sorry, dull symphonists who have managed a tolerable suggestion of the powdered wigs of Haydn and Mozart but not their heads. One may make an exception for single important orchestral works, but they have been more interesting for the light they have cast on the development of their composers than for any influence they have had on the public or on the evolution of the symphony. Berlioz belongs to France, and is only mentioned from time to time as an interesting foreigner and madman. I had suspected and hoped—and probably many others, too—that Schubert, who had shown such a sure sense of structure, such invention and such versatility in so many other forms, would also tackle the symphony from the flank and find the spot from which he could get at both it and the public. All this has now most wonderfully come to pass.

It was not his intention, to be sure, to continue Beethoven's Ninth Symphony. Industrious artist that he was, he produced symphony after symphony of his own. That the world is now suddenly confronted with his seventh without having known its predecessors or having been able to follow the progress that led to it is perhaps the only regrettable aspect of its publication and one which could contribute to its being misunderstood. Perhaps, on the other hand, it may lead to the release of the others. The smallest of them will have its Schubertian significance. Indeed, those Viennese who, a few years ago, offered a prize for a 'best' symphony need not have gone to such lengths or so far afield to find the laurels they coveted. Fine symphonies were lying piled up sevenfold in Ferdinand Schubert's little study in a Viennese suburb.[5] Here were laurels for the asking. So it goes. If one speaks to a Viennese of ——[6] he'll praise Vienna's Franz Schubert to the skies. But among themselves they have no very high opinion of either of them!

Be that as it may, we may refresh ourselves here in the fullness of the spirit that flows forth from this delightful work. Granted, this Vienna, with its St. Stephen's spire, its lovely women, girded by the Danube with countless ribbons, stretching out to the fertile plain and beyond to ever higher mountain ranges, with all its reminders of the greatest German masters—this Vienna cannot fail to provide rich nourishment for the musician's fantasy. I used to look down upon it from the hill-tops and think how Beethoven's restless eye must have strayed out to those distant alpine ranges, how Mozart must have dreamily followed the course of the Danube, everywhere losing itself in reed and wood, and how Papa Haydn must have looked up at St. Stephen's, shaking his head in disbelief at the spire's dizzy height. Put the Danube, St. Stephen's and the distant alps together and you have something of Vienna. Imagine the soft Catholic fragrance of incense, add the surrounding landscape, and you have something that vibrates strings within us that would never have sounded under any other circumstances. With this symphony of Schubert's, with its bright, blossoming, romantic life, the city stands before my eyes again, more distinctly than ever before, and I understand once more how, precisely in this surrounding, such works can be born.

I shall not attempt to give the symphony a programme. Persons of various ages choose too variously in their imagining of texts and pictures. The eighteen-year-old often hears something world-shaking in music which suggests to a grown man no more than a local incident. The composer himself may have had nothing else in mind than to get down the best music that was in him. But one likes to believe that the outside world, bright today, dark tomorrow, often penetrates to the spiritual recesses of the poet and musician, and to hear such a symphony as this is to concede that it carries hidden away within it more than mere lovely song, more than mere joy and sorrow expressed in conventional musical terms. It is to concede that it guides us to a new realm. Here, beside sheer musical mastery of the technique of composition is life in every fibre, colour in the finest shadings, meaning everywhere, the acutest etching of detail, and all flooded with a romanticism which we have encountered elsewhere in Franz Schubert. And this heavenly length, like a fat novel in four volumes by Jean Paul—never-ending, and if only that the reader may go on creating in the same vein afterwards.[7] How refreshing is their sense of inexhaustible wealth where with others one always fears the ending, troubled by a presentiment of ultimate disappointment.

One would be at a loss to explain how Schubert suddenly came by this sovereign command of the orchestra were it not known that this symphony was preceded by six[8] others and that it was written in his prime. It is still evidence of an extraordinary talent that he who heard so little of his own instrumental work during his lifetime could achieve such an idiomatic treatment both of individual instruments and of the whole orchestra, securing an effect as of human voices and chorus in discourse. This resemblance to the human voice I have never encountered so deceptively and so strikingly except in much of Beethoven. It is the reverse of Meyerbeer's treatment of the singing voice. The symphony's utter independence of Beethoven's symphonies is another indication of its masculine origin. One sees here how rightly and wisely Schubert's genius manifests itself. Aware of his more modest resources, he avoids the grotesque forms and bold proportions of Beethoven's later works. He gives us something charmingly and yet still very originally formed, never departing too far from the central idea and always returning to it. So it must appear, at least, to one who has heard it and studied it often. The brilliance and novelty of the instrumentation, the breadth and expanse of the form, the striking changes of mood, the whole new world into which we are transported—all this may be confusing to the listener, like any initial view of the unfamiliar. But there remains a lovely aftertaste, like that which we experience at the conclusion of a play about fairies or magic. There is always the feeling that the composer knew exactly what he wanted to say and how to say it, and the assurance that the gist will become clearer with time.

This sense of security is established right at the beginning in the splendid, romantic introduction, although everything is still veiled in secrecy. Brilliantly novel, too, is the transition to the Allegro; we are aware of no change of tempo, but suddenly without knowing how, we have arrived. To break down the individual movements into their constituent parts would amuse neither ourselves nor the reader. One would have to write out the whole symphony to get an idea of its novel character. Only the second movement, speaking to us in such touching tones, I cannot pass over in silence, especially that passage where a horn is heard as from a distance. It seems to come from another sphere. Here everything listens, as if a heavenly spirit were wandering through the orchestra.

The symphony made an effect here like that of none other since Beethoven's. Artists and art-lovers were united in its praise. From the master who had so carefully prepared it I heard words which I should have liked to pass on to Schubert as the ultimate in joyous tidings. It may be years before the symphony establishes itself in Germany. That it will be forgotten or overlooked one need not fear. It bears within it the seed of eternal youth.

Thus my visit to the grave, which, in turn, led me to a relative of the deceased, brought me a second reward. The first I harvested on the day of the visit when I found on Beethoven's grave a steel pen which I have treasured ever since and which I use on special occasions—such as this![9]

[1] I.e. the Ortsfriedhof, or District Cemetery of Währing.

[2] Schumann had moved to Vienna in the autumn of 1838, hoping to arrange for the transfer of the *Neue Zeitschrift für Musik* to that city in the course of 1839. He felt that this was necessary to establish himself as a man of substance in the eyes of Wieck, who was opposing his marriage to Clara because of what he described as Schumann's insufficient means. The venture ran into many official and bureaucratic obstacles and had to be abandoned, Schumann returning to Leipzig in the spring of 1839.

[3] Schubert, on his deathbed, had expressed the wish to be buried next to Beethoven. The nearest available lot, however, was four graves away. Between them were the remains of Barons von Wssehrd and von Hardtmuth and those of Count Odonel and Countess O'Donnell (not O'Donnel, as Schumann spells it). The bodies of Beethoven and Schubert were exhumed for scientific measurements in 1863 and reinterred. They were removed to the Zentralfriedhof, or Central Cemetery, in 1888, where they now lie, side by side. The District Cemetery in Währing no longer exists. It was the site of what is now appropriately named Schubert Park.

[4] On March 21, 1839, and repeated in December, 1839, and in March and April, 1840, Mendelssohn, of course, conducting.

[5] I.e. Wieden, now No. 6 Kettenbrüchengasse. Curiously, Schumann fails to note that it is also the house where Schubert died.

[6] I.e. Mendelssohn.

[7] Schumann conceived his own *Papillons* as a continuation of Jean Paul's *Flegeljahre*.

[8] Actually by seven. Schumann could not, of course, have known of the Eighth, or Unfinished Symphony, which was still in the possession of Schubert's

friend Anselm Hüttenbrenner in Graz. It was first introduced to the public by Johann Herbeck with the Vienna Philharmonic in 1865. The number can be augmented by including the *Gastein* Symphony, attributed to 1822, of which no trace has ever been found, and the incomplete Symphony in E of 1822.

[9] And for the autograph copy of his own Symphony in B flat.

THE MUNICIPAL AND COMMUNAL MUSICAL
SOCIETY OF THE CITY OF KYRITZ

(1840)

THE CITY OF Kyritz[1] has long been distinguished by its love of music. Just as there are some localities where everyone plays chess, and others that have their own theatres, so Kyritz resembled one big musical conservatory, with the sounds of a variety of instruments descending— or rising—from every window at every hour of the day or night.

From Cantor to Nightwatchman everyone was musical. It would be a mistake, however, to assume from this that Kyritz was a haven of harmony. Rather, it had long harboured contending—and contentious —forces. Indeed, it was here, one Walpurgis night, that a party of blaring and fiddling partisans assembled before the door of Regimental Drum-Major Fresser (an avowed romanticist) and proceeded, with their chief at their head, to the home of Chief Organ-Blower Kniff[2] (leader of the opposition), there to serenade him with the Overture to Berlioz' *Les Francs Juges*,[3] among other merry ditties. Kniff and his followers countered with the Overture to Boieldieu's[4] *Le Calife de Bagdad*. An awful racket it was, a battle between the old and the new. All Kyritz was in ferment.

But more important events were yet to come, and things grew ever more complicated. Who in Kyritz did not know Lippe, the friseur? He was likely to be seen at any hour of the day in one or another of the little streets of the town, a Janissary Jack-of-all-Instruments and master of none. He had trimmed the hair of Lafont[5] and hundreds of others in Paris, and was back now where he had come from—not without some official encouragement from the French authorities. A conniving windbag he was, right now courting Fresser's daughter, while assuring Kniff that he had no fonder desire than to see Fresser and all his romanticists fried alive. Deep down in his heart he cursed them all and hoped, by playing one off against the other, to emerge himself as Kyritz's musical dictator and make off with Fresser's pretty Sabina.

Ah, Kyritz! How blind you were when you gave credence to an article in the Kyritz Weekly Intelligencer signed, 'G.S.' and reading more or less as follows:

'Music, which should bless us with the harmony of the ever beautiful and seal the bond between God and mankind, has recently been the cause of some unfortunate occurrences in this worthy community. Would it not be possible to put an end to such contentions through a union of all local celebrities? Might this not best and most easily be achieved by a formal establishment of a Kyritz Municipal and Communal Musical Society, such as exists in most other cities of this country, with corresponding and also honorary memberships? And might not our estimable Mayor Kaulfuss be disposed to be its official sponsor?'

This is how things stood with Lippe—namely, bad! His debts were numerous and his clients few. He played the way he barbered, i.e. superficially, although it should be added that in the former he displayed the more industry, in the latter the more talent. All his life he had wavered between the tonal and the tonsorial arts. More recently he had been devoting all his energy to music, since every Kyritzer with either his own hair or a wig on his head was a fugitive from his tonsorial ministrations.

Never had anyone seen him expend such energy as on the day after this notice appeared. Dashing through the streets, scattering flocks of geese, ducks and chickens in his wake, he flew from house to house, threatening all and sundry with honorary membership. Even you, most worthy Kaulfuss, wavered for a moment—and then capitulated, even giving Lippe your wig to be trimmed. Other wigs followed. Lippe was beside himself with joy, urging on the Fressers and the Kniffs in turn in order to make the most of the thing for himself.

Storm clouds hung heavy over Kyritz. Everyone was puffing and blowing and fiddling like mad. Then in the middle of it all somebody suddenly cried out: 'Where's Lippe, that miserable scoundrel and windbag?' They found him under a street lamp—and here we shall let a merciful curtain descend upon the scene. Seldom can a human being have been gone over with such—unison! Every instrument was played at him. The horn players blew in his ear, violinists fiddled into his teeth, two little kettledrums were hung from his feet, etc., until Fresser, satisfied with his victory, blew the retreat.

In the midst of the tumult a couple of Davidsbündler wandered to the gate which separated the contending parties. Lippe was dragged back to the suburb where he lived, more dead than alive, while the Davidsbündler, still laughing, noted down what you, dear reader, have just read!

FLORESTAN

¹ Although Kyritz is presumably Leipzig, this little essay was, in fact, a satire directed at Gustav Schilling (1803-1881), founder of a 'Deutscher National-verein für Musik und ihre Wissenschaften' (German National Union for Music and Its Sciences) and publisher, from 1839 to 1842, of the *Jahrbücher des deutschen Nationalverein für Musik und ihre Wissenschaften* (Yearbooks of the German National Union for Music and its Sciences). Schilling had settled in Stuttgart in 1830 as Director of the Stöpel School of Music and had acquired, in addition to an apparently legitimately earned doctorate from the University of Halle, the high-sounding title of Councillor to the Princely Court of Hohenzollern-Hechingen. Among his many publications were *Polyphonomos oder die Kunst zur Erwerbung einer vollständigen Kenntniss der Harmonie in 36 Stunden* (Polypho-nomos, or the Art of Achieving a Complete Knowledge of Harmony in 36 Hours); an *Enzyklopaedie der gesammten musikalischen Wissenschaften oder Universal-Lexikon der Tonkunst* (Encyclopedia of all the Musical Sciences, or Universal Lexicon of the Art of Music); an *Allgemeine Generalbass Lehre* (General Instruction in Thoroughbass), and a *Musikalisches Handwörterbuch nebst einigen vorangeschickten allgemein philosophisch-historischen Bemerkungen über die Tonkunst, insbesondere für Klavierspieler bearbeitet* (Musical Pocket Dictionary with some Introductory General Philosophical and Historical Observations about the Art of Music, Especially Arranged for Piano Players), all of which prompted Schumann, in his letters of the period, to describe Schilling as the 'Stuttgarter Universaldoktor' and as 'having a way with words and titles'. Schumann was annoyed at being accused, in the *Universal-Lexikon*, of 'pre-mature striving for the extraordinary', and by being listed, without his know-ledge or consent, as a corresponding member of the *Nationalverein*. In a letter to Clara, dated February 2, 1840, he promises to 'take my (ironic) knife to Schil-ling, too'. He had previously written to Heinrich Dorn (April 14, 1839): 'What do you make of this Stuttgarter Universaldoktor, whose ambitions are growing ever more presumptuous? With his hand lifted limply in self-defence he reminds me of an angry apprentice who has just had his ears boxed—but he is a thorough rascal.' In a letter to Zuccalmaglio (April 27, 1839) he calls Schilling an 'arch windbag who, in my opinion, hasn't an inkling of what music is all about'. Schilling is, of course, the Lippe of Schumann's feuilleton, and just to make sure that his readers got the point, he even has Lippe sign his proclamation with the initials G. S. Schumann's description of Lippe as having returned from Paris 'not without encouragement from the French authorities' was oddly prophetic—unless Schilling had already had troubles with the law missing from the historical record. In any case, he was compelled, because of criminal charges, to emigrate to New York in 1857, and further difficulties with the Law prompted him to move on to Montreal, where he lived in obscurity for many years. He died in Nebraska. Berlioz met Schilling in Stuttgart in 1842 and found him quite different from what Schilling's title of 'Dr.' had led him to expect. 'He is not old,' he wrote at the time, 'does not wear spectacles, has fine black hair of his own, is full of animation, speaks loudly and rapidly, almost like pistol shots, and is a smoker, not a snuff-taker. He received me very kindly,

at once gave me all the necessary information about my concert, never said a word about fugues or canons, showed no contempt either for *The Huguenots* or *William Tell*, and expressed no aversion to my music before hearing it.'

[2] I.e. Fink, editor of the *Allgemeine Musikalische Zeitung*, who had, as Schumann doubtless knew, collaborated with Schilling in his *Universal-Lexikon*.

[3] Berlioz' first major instrumental work. He was so set up by a compliment on it from a member of the orchestra that he walked home as in a dream, not looking where he was going, and sprained his ankle. 'I get a pain in my foot now when I hear that piece', he wrote in his *Memoirs*. 'Perhaps it gives others a pain in their heads.'

[4] Boieldieu, François Adrien (1775-1834), a famous French opera composer of the older school. His most famous work was *La Dame Blanche*.

[5] Lafont, Charles Philippe (1781-1839), one of the foremost French violinists of his generation.

CHOPIN'S SONATA

(1841)

To examine the first phrases of this sonata and still be in any doubt about its authorship would hardly bespeak the discerning eye of the connoisseur.

Only Chopin begins in this fashion—and in this fashion only Chopin ends; with dissonance through dissonance to dissonance. And yet how much beauty there is in this work!

That he should have called it a 'sonata' suggests a joke, if not sheer bravado. He seems to have taken four of his most unruly children and put them together, possibly thinking to smuggle them, as a sonata, into company where they might not be considered individually presentable.[1]

Assume, for example, that some provincial cantor came to a metropolitan music centre to buy music. He is shown the newest things, but will have none of them. Finally, some bright fellow shows him a 'sonata'. 'Aha,' he exclaims, 'that is something for me, an echo of the good old days!' He buys it and tries it out at home. I should be gravely mistaken if, after laboriously negotiating the first page, he were not to swear by all the musical saints that this was no proper sonata and probably godless at that. But Chopin will have achieved his objective. He will have got into the cantor's house. Who can tell whether, under the same roof, and years later, a romantically inclined grandson may not come upon it, dust it off, play it through and think to himself: 'The fellow wasn't so wrong after all!'

With the foregoing we have already delivered half a verdict. Chopin no longer writes what could as easily be had from anyone else. He is true to himself, and he has his good reasons.

It is too bad that most pianists, including even cultivated ones, cannot see or judge beyond what they can master with their own fingers. Instead of first scanning such difficult pieces they pick them out and struggle through them bar by bar. They have hardly discerned the crudest structural relationships when they lay them aside as 'queer' and 'confused'. Chopin, particularly, rather like Jean Paul, has his crotchety passages and parentheses where it is inadvisable to tarry too long lest the trail be lost.

In this sonata one encounters such obstacles on almost every page, and Chopin's frequently wilful and disordered progressions make them even more difficult to decipher. He does not like to enharmonize, if I may use such a term, and the result is showers of sharps and flats of a density normally welcome only in the most significant cases. Sometimes he is right. But often enough he only confuses, estranging, as we have said, a good portion of the lay public, which prefers not to be for ever mystified and harried. This sonata, characteristically, has a signature of five flats, or B flat minor, a tonality not notable for its great popularity. And the first three bars give us E natural and A natural and C sharp and G sharp!

Following this eminently Chopinesque beginning comes one of those stormy, passionate movements abundantly familiar to us from Chopin's earlier work. This must be heard often, and be well played. But there is beautiful song in this first movement, too. Indeed, it would seem as if the Polish national aftertaste which clung to most of his earlier music were vanishing, as if he were inclining, via Germany, towards Italy. It is known that Chopin and Bellini were friends, that they knew one another's works, and that this was not without artistic influence on them both. But it is really no more than a modest nod. As soon as the song is sung the Pole flashes forth again in all his bold originality. Certainly Bellini never would nor could have dared the interwoven chords encountered after the close of the first episode of the second part. Thus, the ending of the whole movement is anything but Italian—which reminds me of Liszt and his remark that Rossini and his confrères always closed with 'Your most humble servant!' Chopin's cadences express a different sentiment!

The second movement is merely a continuation of this mood—bold, intelligent and imaginative. The Trio is tender and dream-like, thoroughly Chopinesque. A Scherzo it is in name only, like many of Beethoven's. What follows is still more sombre, a funeral march with something even repulsive about it. An adagio, in D flat, say, would have had an immeasureably more beautiful effect. For what we then get in the last movement under the heading of 'Finale' is more mockery than music. And yet one must confess that from this songless and cheerless movement there breathes a special and dreadful spirit, suppressing with resolute fist every inclination to resist. We hear it through, spellbound and without complaint—but without praise, too, for music it is not. Thus the sonata ends as it began, enigmatically, a sphinx, smiling, mocking——

---

[1] There is no historical evidence to support this assumption.

SIGISMOND THALBERG

(*A Charity Recital for the Musicians' Pension Fund*)

(1841)

I N T H E C O U R S E O F his flight through Germany, Thalberg flapped his wings over Leipzig, depositing rubies and other precious stones, like the wings of that angel in one of Rückert's poems. They fell into the hands of the needy, too, as the master wished it.

It is difficult to say something new about one who has been so showered with praise. But there is one thing that every ambitious virtuoso is glad to hear—namely, that he has made progress since his last visit. And of Thalberg we can truthfully say that he has advanced astonishingly in the two years since we last heard him. His playing is, if possible, even freer, more charming and more adventurous. Thus he seemed to be equally well received by all sections of the audience. That feeling of well-being, which he himself may well have enjoyed, was communicated to all.

True virtuosity, to be sure, offers more than mere dexterity and stunts; it, too, can reflect the player, in this case one of those chosen and favoured by fortune, basking in wealth and brilliance. Thus he began his career, thus he has pursued it, and thus he will end it, attended by happiness—and dispensing it. Of this the entire concert, every number that he played, was proof. It never seemed that the audience was there to judge; it was there to enjoy. And one was as secure in his pleasure as the master in his playing.

The compositions were all new. There was a Serenade and Minuet from *Don Giovanni*, a Fantasy on Italian Themes, a big Étude, and a Capriccio on Themes from *La Sonnambula*—all of them ultimately effective transcriptions of original melodies peering out amiably from their shelter of scales and arpeggios. The *Don Giovanni* arrangement in particular was ingeniously made, and its performance surprisingly beautiful. Purely as a composition, the Étude struck me as the most valuable. It is based on a charming theme of Italian folksong character, and the final variation, with its thrilling triplets and Thalberg's inimitable playing, will hardly be forgotten by those who heard it.

Once more, all honour to him for the concert, the memory of which remains as a souvenir of Thalberg as artist and man, and may he soon be reunited once again with his admirers!

[1] Thalberg, Sigismond (or Sigismund), (1812-1871), after Liszt the most spectacular piano virtuoso of a generation rich in spectacular pianists. He was the illegitimate son of Prince Moritz Dietrichstein and the Baroness von Wetzlar. His name, invented by his mother, represented a combination of the German words 'Thal' (valley) and 'Berg' (mountain). He was famous for the elegance both of his person and of his playing. For a description of Thalberg as instructive as it is charming see Arthur Loesser's *Men, Women and Pianos* (Simon & Schuster, New York, 1954. Victor Gollancz Ltd, London, 1955).

ALEXANDER DREYSCHOCK

Grand Fantasy

(1841)

THE FIRST MAJOR WORK by this young keyboard hero about whom we have been reading so much in the newspapers!

And we must confess, more in sorrow than in anger, that nothing so tasteless has come our way for a long time. What poverty of invention! What expense of effort to disguise lack of talent! What prettifying of the most trivial commonplaces!

Has the young virtuoso no friend to tell him the truth, no one who can disregard his clever fingers and point out to him how vapid, how utterly negligible it all is?

There is a rumour afoot that he is a sworn enemy of Beethoven and can see nothing in him. We don't know; but his composition gives us no reason to doubt it. If he would just learn from Beethoven! Or not even that! He can learn something from third- and fourth-rate masters, from Strauss and Lanner!

Unfortunately, we doubt that our good advice will be understood; for this Fantasy betrays, not so much the beginner, as an inherent creative sterility. Even this might be tolerable. But when impotence is so pretentiously heralded it is impossible to contemplate the spectacle with equanimity. What Dreyschock[1] accomplishes a a virtuoso is one thing; his leaps, his tricks, the bravura with which he plays everything, may delight the listener—for a while. But the time comes when these blandishments pale—and what does this type of virtuoso have then?

[1] Dreyschock, Alexander (1818-1869), whose debut in Paris in 1843 prompted one reviewer to speak of a 'trinity' with Liszt as the father, Thalberg as the son and Dreyschock as the holy ghost. He had a powerful left hand, and liked to show it off in his own Fantasy on God Save the King for left hand alone.

CHOPIN

Two Nocturnes, Opus 37; Ballade, Opus 38; Waltz, Opus 42[1]

(1841)

CHOPIN COULD PUBLISH everything anonymously. One would recognize him immediately. This implies praise and censure at once—the one for his talent, the other for his aspirations. Inherent in everything he does is that significant originality which, once displayed, leaves no doubt as to the master's identity. He produces, moreover, an abundance of new forms which, in their tenderness and daring alike, deserve admiration. Always novel and inventive in externals, he remains the same in the construction of his compositions and in special instrumental effects, so that one fears that he may not surpass what he has already achieved. The latter, to be sure, is enough to enter his name ineradicably in the history of modern art, although his influence is restricted to music for the piano. With his gifts he could have achieved more, and have extended his influence upon the further growth of our art in general.

Let us be thankful for what we have. What he has accomplished has been so fine, and he still gives us so much! Certainly we would congratulate any other artist who had accomplished half as much. To earn the name of poet one need not produce thick volumes. One may earn the title with one or two poems, and Chopin has written such, among them the nocturnes noted above. They are distinguished from his earlier ones essentially by simpler ornamentation, by a quieter charm. We know how it used to be with Chopin—all tinsel, gold leaf and pearls. He is different now, and older. He still loves his finery, but it is of the more thoughtful sort, from behind which the nobility of poetry shines through the more amiably. One cannot deny him the most exquisite taste. It means nothing to theorists, of course. They just look for fifths, and take umbrage at every offender. They could learn a lot from Chopin, particularly about fifths!

We have yet to note the Ballade as a remarkable piece. Chopin has already written one under that title, one of his most daring and characteristic compositions. The new one is quite different, inferior to the first as a work of art, but hardly less fanciful and imaginative. The passionate intermediate episodes appear to be afterthoughts. I remember very well when Chopin played it here and closed in F major; now he closes in A minor. He told us then how he was prompted to his ballades by poems of Mickiewicz. Conversely, a poet might easily be inspired to set words to his music. It evokes the most intimate thoughts.

The waltz, finally, is, like the earlier ones, a salon piece of the noblest sort. Florestan says that if he were to play it for dancing, at least half the females would have to be countesses. He is right, of course. It is an aristocrat through and through.

[1] I.e. the Nocturnes in G major and G minor; the Ballade in F and the Waltz in A flat.

MENDELSSOHN'S 'SCOTTISH' SYMPHONY

(1842)

ALL OF US who have rejoiced in Mendelssohn's brilliant career thus far, looked forward to the new symphony with the utmost interest.[1] It was properly regarded as virtually his first venture into the symphonic field.[2] His true first symphony, in C minor, belongs to his tenderest youth. His second, written for the London Philharmonic Society, has not been published. The *Hymn of Praise* is a symphonic cantata, and cannot be regarded as a purely instrumental work. Thus only the symphony—opera excepted—is missing from the opulent wreath of his creations. In all other categories he has already demonstrated his fruitfulness.

We know from others that the new symphony was begun many years ago, during his sojourn in Rome,[3] but only recently completed. This is pertinent to an evaluation of its special character. It is as if one had suddenly found a faded leaf in a book laid aside and long forgotten. Memories similarly faded are suddenly revived, and so compellingly that now the present fades. Something of the kind must have transpired in Mendelssohn's imagination when he found among his papers those old tunes of lovely Italy. Consciously or unconsciously a tender tone-painting emerged, which, rather like the description of a journey through Italy in Jean Paul's *Titan*, might make one forget, for a while, one's misfortune in never having seen this blessed land.

It has often been said that the whole symphony is animated by a characteristic folk spirit. Only someone totally wanting in imagination could fail to note it. And it is this uniquely charming flavour—as with Franz Schubert's symphony—that assures it a special place in the symphonic literature. It has nothing of the traditional symphonic afflatus, nothing of the customary large-scaled breadth, nothing that might suggest a composer set on outdoing Beethoven. It is closer, particularly in character, to Schubert's symphony, with the distinction that where Schubert's evokes the image of a wild, gypsy-like existence, Mendelssohn's transplants us in soil exposed to the Italian sky. Which is to say that the new symphony's charm is of more conventional cast and speaks in less exotic inflections—but not to deny that Schubert's boasts certain other virtues, notably greater powers of invention.

In its basic outlines Mendelssohn's symphony is further distinguished by the inner homogeneity of all four movements. Even the melodic treatment of the principal theme of each of the four movements is consistent. This is evident in a first, fleeting comparison. Thus it emerges, more than any other symphony, as a tightly integrated whole. In none of the various movements is there any considerable deviation in character, tonality or rhythm. The composer himself, as he has stated in a preface, wishes the work to be played without long pauses between the movements.

As for the purely musical aspects of the composition, there is no doubting the master's hand. In beauty and delicacy of its structure overall, as well as in structural detail, it ranks with his overtures; nor is it less rich in charming instrumental effects. Every page of the score offers evidence anew of Mendelssohn's skill in recalling older ideas, in ornamenting a reprise in such a way that the original appears in a new light. And how rich and interesting are the details, free of all excesses and of bourgeois pedantry!

The effect of the symphony upon the public will always depend in part upon the greater or lesser virtuosity of the orchestra. This is true of all music, of course, but in this case doubly so, where the power of the full orchestra matters less than the cultivated delicacy of the individual instruments. Important above all are fine winds. Most irresistible is the Scherzo. Nothing more imaginative has been written in recent years. The instruments literally seem to speak.

The end of the whole symphony will excite controversy. Many will expect it to appear in the guise of the fast movement. In fact, it recalls the first, circumferentially rounding off the whole. We find it sheerly poetic, the proper evening for a lovely morning.[4]

---

[1] It was first performed under the composer's direction at a Gewandhaus Concert in Leipzig on March 3, 1842.

[2] Not quite so properly. His first symphony, in C minor, belonged, as Schumann observes, to Mendelssohn's earliest youth. It was introduced at a Philharmonic Concert in the Argyll Rooms on May 25, 1829, and was dedicated to the Philharmonic Society. The second, in D major, was written, not for the London Philharmonic Society, but for the tercentenary of the Augsburg Confessional in 1830, hence its more familiar designation as the 'Reformation' Symphony. The third was the 'Italian' Symphony, first performed by the London Philharmonic on May 13, 1833.

[3] Actually it was begun in 1829 and not in Italy, but in Edinburgh, hence the designation 'Scottish'. It was at Holyrood Palace, Mendelssohn wrote, 'that I

found the beginning of my "Scottish" Symphony'. All that he wrote down at that time, however, was the first sixteen bars of the Introduction. During his sojourn in Italy in 1830-1831 he worked on both the 'Italian' and the 'Scottish' Symphonies.

⁴ The reference is to an extra movement in the form of a coda, considered a striking novelty at the time.

LOUIS SPOHR

Sixth and Seventh Symphonies[1]

(1843)

We have before us two new symphonies by Spohr, both published within a span of three years. The first of them (the sixth of
seven[2]) was discussed at some length in these pages following its first
performance in Leipzig. At that time we said:

'It remains an oddity, certainly, that in our time so many attempts
have been made to conjure up for us the good old days. There is
nothing to be said against it. These attempts have a certain validity as
studies. Besides, our generation has recently shown a taste for rococo.
But Spohr of all people, Spohr, the finished, fully-rounded master,
who has never said a thing that did not spring from his innermost heart
and whose work can be recognized in the first measure—this, indeed,
is interesting! The result is about what one might have expected. He
has addressed himself to the external problem of adjusting himself to
a variety of styles. For the rest he is the same master whom we have
so long known and loved. Indeed, the unusual milieu brings his
individuality even more strikingly to the fore, just as any really distinguished person never so easily betrays his identity as when masked.
Napoleon had hardly arrived at a *bal masqué* before he folded his
arms. Like wildfire the word ran through the room: "The Emperor!"
Similarly with this symphony, one could hear in every corner of the
hall: "Spohr!" '[3]

Now that we have the published score before us we find ourselves
with little to add. Individual lovely touches are to be found in everything of Spohr, the more easily the better one knows him. We would
wish only to modify certain ironically intended observations about the
last movement in that earlier review. Its mirror image of modern times
strikes us less glaringly now. Haven't many things changed in the
intervening three years? Yes. And we hope that this estimable master's
declining years may be brightened by the first rays of a better epoch
than is reflected in the final movement of his symphony.

The best contradiction is Spohr's own in the shape of his newest
symphony. It is remarkable in many ways. In individuality of conception, in form and in its mode of expression it is comparable, among

Spohr's other works, only with the earlier symphony, *Weihe der Töne*. Again he has chosen a central theme, to which, this time, he gives the not very explicit heading, 'Worldly and Godly in Human Life'. He develops it through three movements, each with its own sub-motto. Thus, the first movement describes the world of the child, the second the perils of manhood and the last the triumph of good over evil.[4]

We confess to a bias against this sort of creation and share it, perhaps, with hundreds of learned men, many of whom have singular ideas about the process of composition and never fail to cite Mozart as an example of one who composed without thinking of anything in particular. If a composer shows me his composition along with such a programme I say: 'First show me that you can make beautiful music; after that I may well like your programme.'

There is, after all, a difference, whether it is Goethe or some other poet who chooses to abandon terminal rhymes. Similarly, no one will argue away the beauties of Spohr's symphony, if only because it is one thing if a Spohr sets himself an exceptional task and quite another if a beginner tries it. We have been all through this with the *Weihe der Töne*. Now the dispute is flaring up anew. Should composers be thinking of anything while composing or not? The philosophers make it out to be worse than it is. They err in supposing that a composer who works from an idea sits down like a preacher on a Saturday afternoon, sketches out his sermon in the usual three parts and then develops it accordingly. With a musician the creative process is utterly different. If he is working from an idea or an image he can feel at ease in his work only if the image or idea comes to him in the form of beautiful melodies born by those same unseen hands that carried Goethe's 'golden pails'. So, hold on to your prejudices, but take care not to count a student's daubs against the work of masters.

To put it briefly then, this newest symphony of Spohr is flooded with enchantment as is hardly any other. We cannot say that we encounter any particularly great or new thoughts, or even any that we have not encountered previously in Spohr. But this purity, this transfiguration of sound, will hardly be found elsewhere. The intensified charm of the coloration is attributable in good measure to the use of a double orchestra. This is another of those ideas that do not occur to everyone, or that everyone could manage if they did. For if it takes a master to score for the orchestra it takes an even greater master to score for two. The undertaking is unlikely to find many imitators, nor would emulation necessarily be desirable. It would be interesting to know what Beethoven would have made of such a thing. Something colossal, probably. But we doubt that it would have appealed to him. It is more appropriate to the character of a master in refinement and tenderness like Spohr than to the lusty Beethoven. It was Spohr, after all, who wrote the first double quartet.

So let us follow him—in art, in life and in his aspirations! The industry evident in every line of the score is absolutely touching. Let us welcome him among the great German masters as a shining example to us all!

---

[1] I.e. No. 6 in G major, or 'Historical' Symphony, so called because of its survey of a variety of period styles, and No. 7 in C major for Two Orchestras.

[2] There were to be two more, No. 8, in G minor, and No. 9, better known as 'The Four Seasons'.

[3] Referring to Spohr's experiments with 'programme' music, and after noting that Spohr was a contemporary of Beethoven and senior to Schubert, Sir Hubert Parry, in his thoughtful essay on 'Symphony' in *Grove's Dictionary*, says: 'Two of these are such curiosities as to deserve description. The sixth, Opus 116, in G major, is called "Historische Symphonie", and the four movements are supposed to be illustrations of four distinct musical periods. The first is called the Period of Handel and Bach, and dated 1720; the second, the Period of Haydn and Mozart, and dated 1780 (i.e. before any of the greatest instrumental works of either Haydn or Mozart were produced); the third is the Period of Beethoven, and dated 1810; and the fourth, "Allerneueste Periode", and dated 1840. This last title seems to imply that Spohr regarded himself as belonging to a different generation from Beethoven. . . . The last movement, representing the then "latest period", has, of course, no names appended. Spohr probably did not intend to imitate anyone, but was satisfied to write in his own manner, of which the movement is not a highly satisfactory example. It is perhaps rather to the composer's credit that his own characteristics should peep out at all corners in all the movements, but the result can hardly be called an artistic success. However, the experiment deserves to be recorded and described as unique among works by composers of such standing and ability as Spohr; and the more so as it is not likely to be often heard in the future.'

[4] To continue with Sir Hubert: 'His next symphony (No. 7 in C major, Opus 121) is in many respects as great a curiosity of a totally different description. It is called "Irdisches und Göttliches im Menschenleben", and is a double symphony in three movements for two orchestras. The first movement is called "Kinderwelt", the second "Zeit der Leidenschaften", and the last (Presto) "Endlicher Sieg des Göttlichen". In the first two, the second orchestra, which is the fuller of the two, is little more than an accompaniment to the first. In the last it has a good deal of work to do, uttering chiefly vehement and bustling passages in contrast with quiet and sober passages by the first orchestra.

The idea seems to be to depict the divine and the worldly qualities more or less by the two orchestras: the divine being given to the smaller orchestra of solo instruments, and the worldly to the fuller orchestra. The treatment of the instrumental forces is on the whole very simple; and no very extraordinary effects seem to be aimed at.'

RUDOLPH WILLMERS

(1843)

WILLMERS[1] HAS ALREADY made a name for himself as a brilliant pianist and gifted composer, and this periodical has previously had occasion to express its interest in his accomplishments.[2] Thus we regret it doubly to see him now proceeding along a path that we have designated time and again as wholly reprehensible and on which he cannot possibly escape the fate that time ordains for all that is vain, fashionable and superficial.

From him of all people, who has been well schooled, who can distinguish between Beethoven and Bellini, we expected better things. Indeed, in his newer pieces even mere virtuosity is not displayed at its best. No one can deny Liszt, for example, his genius in the assembling of mechanical difficulties, in the invention of truly novel instrumental effects, etc. Nor can Thalberg be denied a certain elegant charm and a shrewd recognition of effects. Hence his attractiveness and the enthusiasm that he invariably arouses. Willmers' compositions, on the other hand, are characterized by a singular aridity and pedantry, as if he were not himself quite at ease with his fine manners, as if he heard from afar the admonishing thunder of his old teacher in Dessau,[3] who would hardly rejoice in such aspirations. It is this aridity—the Liszt-Thalberg style and the same difficulties, but without their charm—that prompts us to believe that his compositions will hardly find, even in those circles at which they are aimed, the favour which Liszt and Thalberg have enjoyed and—from the standpoint of virtuosity—earned.

There are, in our opinion, only two routes of escape open to Willmers. Either he can turn away from the path of insipidity upon which he is now embarked, or he can surrender himself to the Devil altogether. In the latter case he must outdo his predecessors in vulgarity. He must write twenty-part chords, be unembarrassed by fifths and octaves, and find a form designed to make Liszt's most tortured excursions seem like the gurgle of an innocent babe. In a word, he must forget that there are, in art, such things as nobility, beauty and eternity.

He will not want for laurels and publishers. We have only one fear: that it will not last long. The public itself pulls apart the wreaths it has plaited in order to plait them anew and in a different shape for someone who knows how to be more amusing. He should ponder all this, and change his ways while there is still time. It is possible to fritter away even the goodwill of one's colleagues, and then it is twice as hard to clamber back, to regain respectability. He should think it over. . . .

[1] Willmers, Heinrich Rudolph (1821-1878), a pupil of Hummel in Weimar and of Friedrich Schneider in Dessau.

[2] Including a charming testimonial in 1835, which read as follows:

'How gladly I accommodate the desire of Herr Willmers, of Copenhagen, to copy from the Archives of the Davidsbündler some reference to his fourteen-year-old son Rudolph:

' "Far more astonishing than his playing of compositions studied with Hummel was the musical talent reflected in his improvising. Eusebius gave him the horn theme from the first movement of the Symphony in C minor. The boy was hesitant and uncertain at first, not knowing whether it belonged to B flat or E flat, and felt his way through the harmonies with such charming embarrassment that it was a joy to behold. Little by little he began to perceive the significance of the four notes and a stream of flowers, lightning flashes and pearls poured from his fingers. Take note of him, said Master Raro when he had finished. He will have something to tell you one of these days."

'Thus it stands in the Twentieth Book of the Davidsbündler.

FLORESTAN.'

Schumann reviewed favourably a set of études, Opus 1, published in 1839. From then on it is obvious that he felt himself betrayed, hence the bitter tone of the review translated here, covering a variety of tone paintings, fantasies, variations, etc. Indeed, Schumann was so angry that when he was editing his writings for the Collected Works ten years later he deleted from the testimonial quoted above a valedictory: 'With special pleasure and with bright hopes for his future we introduce him today for the first time as a composer in this periodical.'

[3] I.e. Friedrich Schneider.

ROBERT FRANZ

(1843)

ABOUT ROBERT FRANZ'S[1] Lieder there is quite a lot to be said. They are, for one thing, by no means an isolated phenomenon. Indeed, they are intimately related to the whole development of our art in the past ten years.

We all know that between 1830 and 1835 a reaction set in against the prevailing taste. It was not really a very severe battle. The enemy was the fad of superficial virtuosity manifest in every category of music, but especially in piano playing, granting such exceptions as Weber and Loewe. And it was in the field of piano playing that the first attacks were launched. Pieces featuring scintillant passages were replaced by more thoughtful conceptions influenced by the examples of Bach and Beethoven. The number of their disciples grew, and the impulse spread to other fields. In that of the Lied spadework had already been done by Franz Schubert, although rather in the manner of Beethoven; the achievements of the north Germans betrayed rather the influence of Bach. An encouraging factor was the emergence of a new school of German poetry. Rückert[2] and Eichendorff,[3] although they had bloomed somewhat earlier, were taken up by musicians; most favoured, however, were Uhland[4] and Heine.[5] Thus emerged a more artistic and more thoughtful type of song, something of which earlier composers, of course, could have had no inkling, since it was essentially the musical reflection of a new poetic spirit.

The Lieder of Robert Franz belong to this nobler new category. The kind of wholesale song fabrication that rejoices equally in a clumsy jingle and a poem by Rückert is beginning to be recognized for what it is. If the general public is still blind to the progress already made, the more enlightened have been aware of it for some time. In fact, the Lied may well be the only form in which important progress has been made since Beethoven. Compare, for instance, the industry that has gone into encompassing the content of a poem right down to the individual word in these songs of Franz with the indolence of the older procedure where the poem was, at best, of secondary concern. Or compare the whole harmonic projection of the one with the tottering accompaniment formulas of the other. Only the narrow-minded can fail to note the contrast.

The foregoing just about describes the essential characteristics of Robert Franz's Lieder. He aims for something more than merely agreeable sounding music. He seeks to recreate the poem in all its vital depth. These are distinctive Lieder, quite different from any others. But one who has begun so well should not be surprised if the future should levy higher requirements. Success in small forms often leads to one-sidedness, to mannerisms. May the young artist shield himself against such tendencies by trying his hand at new forms. He should seek another outlet for his rich imagination than the solo voice. We shall follow his career with sympathetic interest.

[1] Franz, Robert (1815-1892). Like Willmers, he was a pupil of Friedrich Schneider; like Schumann he had to overcome stubborn parental resistance to his becoming a professional musician, and like both Schumann and Willmers his later years were beset by mental and nervous disorders. He wrote almost nothing but songs, but of these he wrote some 350, all of them limited in scope, style and expression by his aversion to any kind of emotional extravagance. Like Schumann, he laid much stress upon the piano accompaniment. The songs here reviewed comprised his first published work. Schumann's notice did much to call attention to him and gain him the sponsorship of Mendelssohn and Liszt. It also furthered his appointment as organist at the Ulrichskirche in Halle, where he was born and where he died.

[2] Rückert, Friedrich (1788-1866), poet and orientalist, famous for his translations or adaptations of Chinese and other oriental lyrics.

[3] Eichendorff, Joseph Freiherr von (1788-1857), poet and novelist. *Aus dem Leben eines Taugenichts* was his most famous work. Many of his lyrics were set by Schubert and Schumann.

[4] Uhland, Johann Ludwig (1781-1862), one of the earliest of the great German romantic poets.

[5] Heine, Heinrich (1797-1856), the most outstanding of the German romanticists, critics, satirists and even (in his correspondence from Paris) journalists.

NIELS GADE

(1843)

A FRENCH NEWSPAPER reported recently: 'A young Danish composer is making something of a sensation in Germany; his name is Gade.[1] He travels frequently from Copenhagen to Leipzig on foot, his violin strapped to his back. He is said to be the living image of Mozart.'

The first and the last sentences are correct. Some fiction has crept into the middle. The young Dane did, indeed, arrive in Leipzig a few months ago (although not on foot), and his Mozart-like head, with its shock of hair, looking as if it had been carved from granite, blended well with the sympathy previously aroused in local music circles by his 'Ossian' overture and his First Symphony.

Of the factual circumstances of his life there is little to report. Born in Copenhagen in 1817, the son of a native instrument-maker, he may well have dreamt away his early years more among instruments than among people. He received his first musical instruction from one of those not uncommon teachers who lay more stress upon mechanical industry than upon talent; nor does this teacher appear to have been particularly satisfied with his progress. He learned guitar, violin and piano, a bit of each, without notably distinguishing himself. Only later did he find better-grounded teachers in Wexschall[2] and Berggreen.[3] He occasionally enjoyed the counsel of the excellent Weyse.[4]

He composed a variety of works, of which he now has a rather low opinion. Some of them were presumably the outbursts of a fevered imagination. Later he was engaged as violinist in the Royal Orchestra in Copenhagen, and here he had the opportunity of learning those secrets of the instruments which he sometimes passes on to us in his instrumental compositions. This practical schooling, denied to many and not always properly understood by others, was the principal factor in his achievement of that mastery of instrumentation which is indisputably his.

With his overture, *Nachklänge aus Ossian*, awarded the prize of the Copenhagen Musical Society, with Spohr and Franz Schneider as the judges, he came to the attention of his art-loving king.[5] Like many another of his talented countrymen, he received a truly regal grant for travel abroad, and headed straight for Leipzig, where he was then first introduced to the larger musical world. He is still here, but will be leaving shortly for Paris, to continue on from there to Italy. Thus we now seize the opportunity, while his image is fresh in our consciousness, of presenting certain features of this excellent young man's artistic physiognomy. Nothing quite like him has come our way among the younger composers for a long time.

It would be a great mistake to assume from his physical resemblance to Mozart a corresponding musical affinity, as truly striking as the former may be. We have to do here with an entirely new musical personality. In fact, it would seem that the nations bordering on Germany were seeking emancipation from German dominion. This may annoy the German chauvinists, but to those of deeper insight and greater understanding of human nature it seems both natural and welcome. Thus Chopin represents Poland and Bennett represents England, while in Holland Verhulst[6] gives promise of providing his country with a worthy voice. There are similar national stirrings in Hungary. While they all look to the German nation as the first and most beloved music teacher, no one should be surprised if they seek a characteristic musical language for their own countries, and without any disloyalty to the maxims of their teacher. For no country in the world has masters comparable to the greatest of ours, nor would anyone wish to deny it.

In the north, too, we have already noted the emergence of national tendencies. Linblad,[7] in Stockholm, has transcribed his old folksongs, and Ole Bull, while not a creative talent of the first class, attempted to export echoes of his mother country. And then the newly emerging and important Scandinavian poets cannot have failed to provide a powerful stimulus to young musicians, assuming that the latter had not already been reminded by their mountains and lakes, their runes and northern lights, that the north is entitled to a language of its own.

Gade, too, has been educated by the poets of his fatherland. He knows them all and loves them. The old tales and sagas accompanied him upon his childhood outings, and Ossian's mighty harp rang clear from England's shores. Thus we hear in his music, and first in this very 'Ossian' overture, an unmistakably Nordic character. But at the same time Gade himself would certainly be the last to deny his debt to the German masters. The great industry which he has devoted to their works (he knows them pretty much through and through) has been rewarded with the gift that they bestow on all who demonstrate their loyalty—with the blessing of mastery.

Among more recent composers he has been influenced particularly by Mendelssohn, as is evident in certain of his instrumental combinations, especially in the *Nachklänge aus Ossian*. The symphony contains reminiscences of Schubert. But an utterly original melodic idiom asserts itself throughout, with national characteristics never before encountered in the higher categories of instrumental music. The symphony is in every way superior to the overture, in natural resources as well as in technical mastery.

One hopes that the composer does not succumb to his own nationalism, that his 'aurora-borealic' fantasy, as someone has described it, will prove itself rich and many-sided, that he will focus his attention on other areas of nature and life. Indeed, one is tempted to say to all artists: achieve originality and then cast it off as a snake casts off its old skin when it begins to grow too tight.

But the future is obscure. Things usually happen contrary to our expectations. But at least we can give voice to our hopes, and state that from this distinguished talent we expect the ripest beauty. And as if the accident of a name had predestined him for music, as with Bach, it should be noted that the four letters of his name are those of the open strings of the violin. Let no one dismiss this modest symbol of providential favour, nor the other—namely, that with the employment of four clefs,[8] all the letters of his name can be expressed by a single note. Cabalists will have no difficulty working it out.

[1] Gade, Niels Vilhelm (1817-1890), Danish composer, a protégé of Mendelssohn and, from 1844 until Mendelssohn's death in 1847, his deputy as conductor of the Gewandhaus concerts in Leipzig. He actually succeeded Mendelssohn, but returned to his native Copenhagen in 1848, to remain there for the rest of his life. He was conductor of the Musikverein and, in 1861, became Director of Music to the Court.

[2] Wexschall, Frederik Thorkildson (1798-1845), distinguished Danish violinist. He was a pupil of Spohr and teacher of Gade and Ole Bull.

[3] Berggreen, Andreas Peter (1801-1880), organist at the Church of the Holy Trinity, Copenhagen.

[4] Weyse, Christoph Ernst Friedrich (1774-1842), a German from Hamburg-Altona, who settled in Copenhagen, devoting himself primarily to sacred music, but finding time also for operas, symphonies and chamber music. He was Gade's instructor in composition. Berggreen wrote his biography.

[5] In 1841.

[6] Verhulst, Jean (1816-1891), like Gade a protégé of Mendelssohn and, it should be added in both cases, of Schumann, with whom he kept up a lively

correspondence and whose concert tour with Clara through Holland in 1853 he sponsored. He was in Leipzig from 1838 until 1842, where Mendelssohn had secured him a position as conductor of the Euterpe Concerts. Upon his return to Holland he was appointed Musical Director to the Court, and was for many years the leading figure of Dutch musical life, as conductor, composer and teacher, in The Hague, Rotterdam and Amsterdam.

[7] Linblad, Adolf Frederik (1801-1878), a pupil of Zelter in Berlin. He was a prolific composer, his best works being his songs, which were so beloved that he became known as the 'Swedish Schubert'. He was also the first teacher of Jenny Lind, 'the Swedish Nightingale'.

[8] I.e. with two staves crossing each other at right angles and with a clef designation at each terminal, providing a G in the tenor clef, an A in the treble clef, a D in the alto clef (reading upside down from left to right) and an E in the bass clef.

You, MY FRIEND, will be the first, of course, to hear from me about *A Midsummer Night's Dream*. We saw it yesterday for the first time in almost 300 years.[1] That the theatre director chose a winter evening for it spoke for his good judgment. In a true summer evening one would prefer *The Winter's Tale*, for obvious reasons.

There were many, I can assure you, who came to Shakespeare simply to hear Mendelssohn. For me it was rather the other way round. I know perfectly well that Mendelssohn is not to be compared with those inferior actors who put on airs whenever chance lands them in the company of the great. His music—the overture excepted—is intended merely as an accompaniment, an interlocutor and, at the same time, a bridge between Bottom and Oberon, without which a passage into the realm of the fairies would hardly be possible. Music must have performed a similar function in Shakespeare's time. Whoever expected more of it will have been disappointed. This music is even more reticent than that to *Antigone*,[2] where the choruses compelled the composer to greater opulence. With the progress of the plot proper, i.e. with the fortunes of the four young lovers, it is otherwise unconcerned. At one point it depicts in pleading inflexions Hermia's search for her beloved. This is a splendid piece. For the rest the music accompanies the fairies. Here Mendelssohn is in his element, and incomparable, as I hardly need to tell you.

About the Overture, the world has long been of one mind.[3] It is decked in the blossoms of youth as hardly any other work of this composer—the finished master daring his first high flight at just the right moment. I was touched by the way in which bits of the overture recur in the other pieces, composed so much more recently. Only the Finale, repeating the close of the Overture almost note for note, found me dissenting. The composer's intention to round it all off is obvious. But I found it too contrived. This scene, above all, should have been adorned with his freshest inspiration. Here, where music could have achieved its greatest effect, I had expected something original and freshly composed. Just picture the scene: elves crawling into the house through every gap and fissure to dance their rounds, Puck at their head, declaiming, 'I am sent with broom before, to sweep the dust behind the door', and Oberon, 'With this field-dew consecrate', etc.! It is impossible to conceive of anything better suited to music. If Mendelssohn had only written something new for it!

Thus, it seemed to me that the conclusion fell short of the ultimate effect. One remembered, of course, the many charming pieces that had gone before. There are probably still those who find Bottom's ass's head amusing and the enchantment of the green forest at night and the confusion therein unforgettable; the play as a whole seemed more a curiosity. For the rest, you may be sure, the music is fine and fanciful enough, right from the first entrance of Puck and the fairies. The instruments tease and joke as if the fairies themselves were playing them. One hears brand new sounds. Ultimately lovely, too, is the following song of the elves, with the concluding words, 'So, good night, with lullaby', as is, indeed, everything that has to do with the fairies. There is even a march in it (the first, I believe, that Mendelssohn has written).[4] It comes before the end of the last act, and reminds one somewhat of the march in Spohr's *Weihe der Töne*. It could have been more original, but it has an utterly charming trio. . . .

[1] In Potsdam, October 18, 1843, in the Tieck translation.

[2] Opus 55, composed at the request of Friedrich Wilhelm IV of Prussia, and first performed in Berlin under the composer's direction in 1841.

[3] It had been composed and first performed in 1826.

[4] The now famous 'Wedding March'.

ROBERT SCHUMANN

Concerto without Orchestra

(1843)

Wʜɪʟᴇ ᴏɴ ᴛʜᴇ subject of the latest concertos, it would seem appropriate to report on a so-called Concerto without Orchestra, just published by Haslinger, which those rascals Florestan and Eusebius have attributed to the undersigned. I shall punish them for this unauthorized use of my name by saying not a word about their Opus 14.[1] At the same time, certain passages from the letter of a beloved master (to whom, by the way, the work is dedicated)[2] strike me as being too important to permit of their being entirely suppressed. He says, among other things:

'One wonders what may have prompted the title. It presents rather the characteristics of a big sonata than the requirements of a concerto, a big sonata of the kind we associate with Beethoven and Weber. In concertos, unfortunately, we are accustomed to expect some concessions to brilliant virtuosity or flirtatious elegance of execution. No such concessions could have been made in this work without compromising your conceptual intention. The predominant earnestness and passion are incompatible with the expectations of a contemporary concert audience, which does not want to be deeply moved and has neither the capacity nor the sense of consecration required to grasp and comprehend such harmonies and ingenious obscurities. A proper appreciation of such things is restricted to ears and temperaments attuned to the loftier inflexions of artistic heroes.

'Much of the harmonization employs dissonances whose subsequent resolution brings balm only to an experienced ear. Anticipations and suspensions, whose development often becomes clear only after the second or third bar, are frequently harsh, although justified. In order not to be disturbed or abused by them, one must be an experienced musician who senses in advance and anticipates how every contradiction resolves itself. I think of a statesman who, amidst the tumultuous revelry of a court ball, seems to be focusing his eyes and ears on everything and yet actually concentrates on those few in whom he has a diplomatic interest.'

There it is. Now, Florestan and Eusebius, make yourselves worthy of such benevolent judgment and from now on see to it that you are as strict with yourselves as you so often are with others.

ROBERT SCHUMANN

[1] Originally conceived and now known as the Sonata in F minor.

[2] I.e. Moscheles. Schumann had similarly called upon Moscheles for a review of his Sonata in F sharp minor.

NEW PATHS

(1853)

MANY YEARS HAVE passed since I have been heard from in the *Neue Zeitschrift für Musik*, an arena so rich in memories for me—indeed, almost as many years as I once devoted to editing it—namely, ten. I have often been tempted to speak out, despite strenuous creative activity. A number of important new talents have come along in the meantime, a musical era has appeared to be in the offing, heralded by many rising young artists, even though the latter may be known to a rather small circle. Following their progress with the utmost interest, I felt certain that from such developments would suddenly emerge an individual fated to give expression to the times in the highest and most ideal manner, who would achieve mastery, not step by step, but at once, springing like Minerva fully armed from the head of Jove. And now here he is, a young fellow at whose cradle graces and heroes stood watch. His name is Johannes Brahms.

He comes from Hamburg, where he had been working in quiet obscurity, initiated by an excellent and inspired teacher into the most difficult canons of the art.[1] He was recommended to me by an eminent and famous master.[2] Even in his external appearance he displays those characteristics which proclaim: here is a man of destiny! Seated at the piano, he began to disclose most wondrous regions. It was also most wondrous playing, which made of the piano an orchestra of mourning or jubilant voices. There were sonatas, more like disguised symphonies; songs, whose poetry would be intelligible even to one who didn't know the words, although a profound vocal line flows through them all; a few piano pieces, partly of a demoniac character, charmingly formed; then sonatas for violin and piano, string quartets, etc.—all so different one from another that each seemed to flow from a separate source.[3] And finally it seemed as though he himself, a surging stream incarnate, swept them all together into a single waterfall, sending aloft a peaceful rainbow above the turbulent waves, flanked on the shores by playful butterflies and the voices of nightingales.[4]

When once he lowers his magic wand over the massed resources of chorus and orchestra, we shall have in store for us wonderful insights into the secret of the spiritual world. May the highest genius lend him strength; and well it may, for in him resides a second genius—namely, that of modesty. His contemporaries greet him as he sets off into a world which may bring him pain, but which will surely bring him laurels and palms as well. We welcome him as a staunch combatant.

Every age has a secret society of congenial spirits. Draw the circle tighter, you who belong to one another, that the truth of art may shine ever more clearly, spreading joy and blessings everywhere!

R. S.

[1] Eduard Marxsen, of Altona (1806-1887).

[2] Joseph Joachim.

[3] It is impossible from this description to determine precisely what Brahms actually played. In a letter to *Breitkopf & Härtel* of November 3, 1853, Schumann lists the following as pieces that Brahms wishes to have published: a String Quartet, Opus 1; a volume of six songs, Opus 2; a large Scherzo for Pianoforte, Opus 3; a volume of six songs, Opus 4 and a grand Sonata for Pianoforte in C major, Opus 5. The opus numbers, of course, no longer apply. One recognizes, however, at least the Sonata in C major, Opus 1, a volume of six songs, Opus 3, and the Scherzo for Pianoforte, Opus 4.

[4] Schumann seems to have been fond and proud of this rather high-flown metaphor. In a letter to Joachim, undated, but certainly written in very early October, 1853, he says of Brahms: 'Or one could compare him with a mighty river which, like Niagara, displays itself at its most beautiful when tumbling from the heights in a waterfall, sending up a rainbow from the waves, surrounded by butterflies at play and accompanied by the voices of nightingales.' Subsequent letters to Joachim show him to have been at work on the article on October 13 and to have finished it the next day.

INDEX

INDEX

A CATALOG OF SELECTED
DOVER BOOKS
IN ALL FIELDS OF INTEREST

A CATALOG OF SELECTED DOVER
BOOKS IN ALL FIELDS OF INTEREST

DRAWINGS OF REMBRANDT, edited by Seymour Slive. Updated Lippmann, Hofstede de Groot edition, with definitive scholarly apparatus. All portraits, biblical sketches, landscapes, nudes. Oriental figures, classical studies, together with selection of work by followers. 550 illustrations. Total of 630pp. 9⅛ × 12¼.
21485-0, 21486-9 Pa., Two-vol. set $25.00

GHOST AND HORROR STORIES OF AMBROSE BIERCE, Ambrose Bierce. 24 tales vividly imagined, strangely prophetic, and decades ahead of their time in technical skill: "The Damned Thing," "An Inhabitant of Carcosa," "The Eyes of the Panther," "Moxon's Master," and 20 more. 199pp. 5⅜ × 8½. 20767-6 Pa. $3.95

ETHICAL WRITINGS OF MAIMONIDES, Maimonides. Most significant ethical works of great medieval sage, newly translated for utmost precision, readability. Laws Concerning Character Traits, Eight Chapters, more. 192pp. 5⅜ × 8½.
24522-5 Pa. $4.50

THE EXPLORATION OF THE COLORADO RIVER AND ITS CANYONS, J. W. Powell. Full text of Powell's 1,000-mile expedition down the fabled Colorado in 1869. Superb account of terrain, geology, vegetation, Indians, famine, mutiny, treacherous rapids, mighty canyons, during exploration of last unknown part of continental U.S. 400pp. 5⅜ × 8½. 20094-9 Pa. $6.95

HISTORY OF PHILOSOPHY, Julián Marías. Clearest one-volume history on the market. Every major philosopher and dozens of others, to Existentialism and later. 505pp. 5⅜ × 8½. 21739-6 Pa. $8.50

ALL ABOUT LIGHTNING, Martin A. Uman. Highly readable non-technical survey of nature and causes of lightning, thunderstorms, ball lightning, St. Elmo's Fire, much more. Illustrated. 192pp. 5⅜ × 8½. 25237-X Pa. $5.95

SAILING ALONE AROUND THE WORLD, Captain Joshua Slocum. First man to sail around the world, alone, in small boat. One of great feats of seamanship told in delightful manner. 67 illustrations. 294pp. 5⅜ × 8½. 20326-3 Pa. $4.50

LETTERS AND NOTES ON THE MANNERS, CUSTOMS AND CONDITIONS OF THE NORTH AMERICAN INDIANS, George Catlin. Classic account of life among Plains Indians: ceremonies, hunt, warfare, etc. 312 plates. 572pp. of text. 6⅛ × 9¼. 22118-0, 22119-9 Pa. Two-vol. set $15.90

ALASKA: The Harriman Expedition, 1899, John Burroughs, John Muir, et al. Informative, engrossing accounts of two-month, 9,000-mile expedition. Native peoples, wildlife, forests, geography, salmon industry, glaciers, more. Profusely illustrated. 240 black-and-white line drawings. 124 black-and-white photographs. 3 maps. Index. 576pp. 5⅜ × 8½. 25109-8 Pa. $11.95

THE BOOK OF BEASTS: Being a Translation from a Latin Bestiary of the Twelfth Century, T. H. White. Wonderful catalog real and fanciful beasts: manticore, griffin, phoenix, amphivius, jaculus, many more. White's witty erudite commentary on scientific, historical aspects. Fascinating glimpse of medieval mind. Illustrated. 296pp. 5⅜ × 8¼. (Available in U.S. only)   24609-4 Pa. $5.95

FRANK LLOYD WRIGHT: ARCHITECTURE AND NATURE With 160 Illustrations, Donald Hoffmann. Profusely illustrated study of influence of nature—especially prairie—on Wright's designs for Fallingwater, Robie House, Guggenheim Museum, other masterpieces. 96pp. 9¼ × 10¾.   25098-9 Pa. $7.95

FRANK LLOYD WRIGHT'S FALLINGWATER, Donald Hoffmann. Wright's famous waterfall house: planning and construction of organic idea. History of site, owners, Wright's personal involvement. Photographs of various stages of building. Preface by Edgar Kaufmann, Jr. 100 illustrations. 112pp. 9¼ × 10.
        23671-4 Pa. $7.95

YEARS WITH FRANK LLOYD WRIGHT: Apprentice to Genius, Edgar Tafel. Insightful memoir by a former apprentice presents a revealing portrait of Wright the man, the inspired teacher, the greatest American architect. 372 black-and-white illustrations. Preface. Index. vi + 228pp. 8¼ × 11.   24801-1 Pa. $9.95

THE STORY OF KING ARTHUR AND HIS KNIGHTS, Howard Pyle. Enchanting version of King Arthur fable has delighted generations with imaginative narratives of exciting adventures and unforgettable illustrations by the author. 41 illustrations. xviii + 313pp. 6⅛ × 9¼.   21445-1 Pa. $5.95

THE GODS OF THE EGYPTIANS, E. A. Wallis Budge. Thorough coverage of numerous gods of ancient Egypt by foremost Egyptologist. Information on evolution of cults, rites and gods; the cult of Osiris; the Book of the Dead and its rites; the sacred animals and birds; Heaven and Hell; and more. 956pp. 6⅛ × 9¼.
        22055-9, 22056-7 Pa., Two-vol. set $21.90

A THEOLOGICO-POLITICAL TREATISE, Benedict Spinoza. Also contains unfinished *Political Treatise.* Great classic on religious liberty, theory of government on common consent. R. Elwes translation. Total of 421pp. 5⅜ × 8½.
        20249-6 Pa. $6.95

INCIDENTS OF TRAVEL IN CENTRAL AMERICA, CHIAPAS, AND YUCATAN, John L. Stephens. Almost single-handed discovery of Maya culture; exploration of ruined cities, monuments, temples; customs of Indians. 115 drawings. 892pp. 5⅜ × 8½.   22404-X, 22405-8 Pa., Two-vol. set $15.90

LOS CAPRICHOS, Francisco Goya. 80 plates of wild, grotesque monsters and caricatures. Prado manuscript included. 183pp. 6⅜ × 9⅜.   22384-1 Pa. $4.95

AUTOBIOGRAPHY: The Story of My Experiments with Truth, Mohandas K. Gandhi. Not hagiography, but Gandhi in his own words. Boyhood, legal studies, purification, the growth of the Satyagraha (nonviolent protest) movement. Critical, inspiring work of the man who freed India. 480pp. 5⅜ × 8½. (Available in U.S. only)
        24593-4 Pa. $6.95

ILLUSTRATED DICTIONARY OF HISTORIC ARCHITECTURE, edited by Cyril M. Harris. Extraordinary compendium of clear, concise definitions for over 5,000 important architectural terms complemented by over 2,000 line drawings. Covers full spectrum of architecture from ancient ruins to 20th-century Modernism. Preface. 592pp. 7½ × 9⅝. 24444-X Pa. $14.95

THE NIGHT BEFORE CHRISTMAS, Clement Moore. Full text, and woodcuts from original 1848 book. Also critical, historical material. 19 illustrations. 40pp. 4⅝ × 6. 22797-9 Pa. $2.50

THE LESSON OF JAPANESE ARCHITECTURE: 165 Photographs, Jiro Harada. Memorable gallery of 165 photographs taken in the 1930's of exquisite Japanese homes of the well-to-do and historic buildings. 13 line diagrams. 192pp. 8⅜ × 11¼. 24778-3 Pa. $8.95

THE AUTOBIOGRAPHY OF CHARLES DARWIN AND SELECTED LETTERS, edited by Francis Darwin. The fascinating life of eccentric genius composed of an intimate memoir by Darwin (intended for his children); commentary by his son, Francis; hundreds of fragments from notebooks, journals, papers; and letters to and from Lyell, Hooker, Huxley, Wallace and Henslow. xi + 365pp. 5⅜ × 8. 20479-0 Pa. $5.95

WONDERS OF THE SKY: Observing Rainbows, Comets, Eclipses, the Stars and Other Phenomena, Fred Schaaf. Charming, easy-to-read poetic guide to all manner of celestial events visible to the naked eye. Mock suns, glories, Belt of Venus, more. Illustrated. 299pp. 5¼ × 8¼. 24402-4 Pa. $7.95

BURNHAM'S CELESTIAL HANDBOOK, Robert Burnham, Jr. Thorough guide to the stars beyond our solar system. Exhaustive treatment. Alphabetical by constellation: Andromeda to Cetus in Vol. 1; Chamaeleon to Orion in Vol. 2; and Pavo to Vulpecula in Vol. 3. Hundreds of illustrations. Index in Vol. 3. 2,000pp. 6⅛ × 9¼. 23567-X, 23568-8, 23673-0 Pa., Three-vol. set $37.85

STAR NAMES: Their Lore and Meaning, Richard Hinckley Allen. Fascinating history of names various cultures have given to constellations and literary and folkloristic uses that have been made of stars. Indexes to subjects. Arabic and Greek names. Biblical references. Bibliography. 563pp. 5⅜ × 8½. 21079-0 Pa. $7.95

THIRTY YEARS THAT SHOOK PHYSICS: The Story of Quantum Theory, George Gamow. Lucid, accessible introduction to influential theory of energy and matter. Careful explanations of Dirac's anti-particles, Bohr's model of the atom, much more. 12 plates. Numerous drawings. 240pp. 5⅜ × 8½. 24895-X Pa. $4.95

CHINESE DOMESTIC FURNITURE IN PHOTOGRAPHS AND MEASURED DRAWINGS, Gustav Ecke. A rare volume, now affordably priced for antique collectors, furniture buffs and art historians. Detailed review of styles ranging from early Shang to late Ming. Unabridged republication. 161 black-and-white drawings, photos. Total of 224pp. 8⅜ × 11¼. (Available in U.S. only) 25171-3 Pa. $12.95

VINCENT VAN GOGH: A Biography, Julius Meier-Graefe. Dynamic, penetrating study of artist's life, relationship with brother, Theo, painting techniques, travels, more. Readable, engrossing. 160pp. 5⅜ × 8½. (Available in U.S. only) 25253-1 Pa. $3.95

HOW TO WRITE, Gertrude Stein. Gertrude Stein claimed anyone could understand her unconventional writing—here are clues to help. Fascinating improvisations, language experiments, explanations illuminate Stein's craft and the art of writing. Total of 414pp. 4⅝ × 6⅜. 23144-5 Pa. $5.95

ADVENTURES AT SEA IN THE GREAT AGE OF SAIL: Five Firsthand Narratives, edited by Elliot Snow. Rare true accounts of exploration, whaling, shipwreck, fierce natives, trade, shipboard life, more. 33 illustrations. Introduction. 353pp. 5⅜ × 8½. 25177-2 Pa. $7.95

THE HERBAL OR GENERAL HISTORY OF PLANTS, John Gerard. Classic descriptions of about 2,850 plants—with over 2,700 illustrations—includes Latin and English names, physical descriptions, varieties, time and place of growth, more. 2,706 illustrations. xlv + 1,678pp. 8½ × 12¼. 23147-X Cloth. $75.00

DOROTHY AND THE WIZARD IN OZ, L. Frank Baum. Dorothy and the Wizard visit the center of the Earth, where people are vegetables, glass houses grow and Oz characters reappear. Classic sequel to Wizard of Oz. 256pp. 5⅜ × 8. 24714-7 Pa. $4.95

SONGS OF EXPERIENCE: Facsimile Reproduction with 26 Plates in Full Color, William Blake. This facsimile of Blake's original "Illuminated Book" reproduces 26 full-color plates from a rare 1826 edition. Includes "The Tyger," "London," "Holy Thursday," and other immortal poems. 26 color plates. Printed text of poems. 48pp. 5¼ × 7. 24636-1 Pa. $3.50

SONGS OF INNOCENCE, William Blake. The first and most popular of Blake's famous "Illuminated Books," in a facsimile edition reproducing all 31 brightly colored plates. Additional printed text of each poem. 64pp. 5¼ × 7. 22764-2 Pa. $3.50

PRECIOUS STONES, Max Bauer. Classic, thorough study of diamonds, rubies, emeralds, garnets, etc.: physical character, occurrence, properties, use, similar topics. 20 plates, 8 in color. 94 figures. 659pp. 6⅛ × 9¼. 21910-0, 21911-9 Pa., Two-vol. set $14.90

ENCYCLOPEDIA OF VICTORIAN NEEDLEWORK, S. F. A. Caulfeild and Blanche Saward. Full, precise descriptions of stitches, techniques for dozens of needlecrafts—most exhaustive reference of its kind. Over 800 figures. Total of 679pp. 8⅛ × 11. Two volumes. Vol. 1 22800-2 Pa. $10.95 Vol. 2 22801-0 Pa. $10.95

THE MARVELOUS LAND OF OZ, L. Frank Baum. Second Oz book, the Scarecrow and Tin Woodman are back with hero named Tip, Oz magic. 136 illustrations. 287pp. 5⅜ × 8½. 20692-0 Pa. $5.95

WILD FOWL DECOYS, Joel Barber. Basic book on the subject, by foremost authority and collector. Reveals history of decoy making and rigging, place in American culture, different kinds of decoys, how to make them, and how to use them. 140 plates. 156pp. 7⅞ × 10¾. 20011-6 Pa. $7.95

HISTORY OF LACE, Mrs. Bury Palliser. Definitive, profusely illustrated chronicle of lace from earliest times to late 19th century. Laces of Italy, Greece, England, France, Belgium, etc. Landmark of needlework scholarship. 266 illustrations. 672pp. 6⅛ × 9¼. 24742-2 Pa. $14.95

ILLUSTRATED GUIDE TO SHAKER FURNITURE, Robert Meader. All furniture and appurtenances, with much on unknown local styles. 235 photos. 146pp. 9 × 12.
22819-3 Pa. $7.95

WHALE SHIPS AND WHALING: A Pictorial Survey, George Francis Dow. Over 200 vintage engravings, drawings, photographs of barks, brigs, cutters, other vessels. Also harpoons, lances, whaling guns, many other artifacts. Comprehensive text by foremost authority. 207 black-and-white illustrations. 288pp. 6 × 9.
24808-9 Pa. $8.95

THE BERTRAMS, Anthony Trollope. Powerful portrayal of blind self-will and thwarted ambition includes one of Trollope's most heartrending love stories. 497pp. 5⅜ × 8½.
25119-5 Pa. $8.95

ADVENTURES WITH A HAND LENS, Richard Headstrom. Clearly written guide to observing and studying flowers and grasses, fish scales, moth and insect wings, egg cases, buds, feathers, seeds, leaf scars, moss, molds, ferns, common crystals, etc.—all with an ordinary, inexpensive magnifying glass. 209 exact line drawings aid in your discoveries. 220pp. 5⅜ × 8½.
23330-8 Pa. $3.95

RODIN ON ART AND ARTISTS, Auguste Rodin. Great sculptor's candid, wide-ranging comments on meaning of art; great artists; relation of sculpture to poetry, painting, music; philosophy of life, more. 76 superb black-and-white illustrations of Rodin's sculpture, drawings and prints. 119pp. 8⅜ × 11¼.
24487-3 Pa. $6.95

FIFTY CLASSIC FRENCH FILMS, 1912–1982: A Pictorial Record, Anthony Slide. Memorable stills from Grand Illusion, Beauty and the Beast, Hiroshima, Mon Amour, many more. Credits, plot synopses, reviews, etc. 160pp. 8¼ × 11.
25256-6 Pa. $11.95

THE PRINCIPLES OF PSYCHOLOGY, William James. Famous long course complete, unabridged. Stream of thought, time perception, memory, experimental methods; great work decades ahead of its time. 94 figures. 1,391pp. 5⅜ × 8½.
20381-6, 20382-4 Pa., Two-vol. set $19.90

BODIES IN A BOOKSHOP, R. T. Campbell. Challenging mystery of blackmail and murder with ingenious plot and superbly drawn characters. In the best tradition of British suspense fiction. 192pp. 5⅜ × 8½.
24720-1 Pa. $3.95

CALLAS: PORTRAIT OF A PRIMA DONNA, George Jellinek. Renowned commentator on the musical scene chronicles incredible career and life of the most controversial, fascinating, influential operatic personality of our time. 64 black-and-white photographs. 416pp. 5⅜ × 8¼.
25047-4 Pa. $7.95

GEOMETRY, RELATIVITY AND THE FOURTH DIMENSION, Rudolph Rucker. Exposition of fourth dimension, concepts of relativity as Flatland characters continue adventures. Popular, easily followed yet accurate, profound. 141 illustrations. 133pp. 5⅜ × 8½.
23400-2 Pa. $3.50

HOUSEHOLD STORIES BY THE BROTHERS GRIMM, with pictures by Walter Crane. 53 classic stories—Rumpelstiltskin, Rapunzel, Hansel and Gretel, the Fisherman and his Wife, Snow White, Tom Thumb, Sleeping Beauty, Cinderella, and so much more—lavishly illustrated with original 19th century drawings. 114 illustrations. x + 269pp. 5⅜ × 8½.
21080-4 Pa. $4.50

SUNDIALS, Albert Waugh. Far and away the best, most thorough coverage of ideas, mathematics concerned, types, construction, adjusting anywhere. Over 100 illustrations. 230pp. 5⅜ × 8½.   22947-5 Pa. $4.00

PICTURE HISTORY OF THE NORMANDIE: With 190 Illustrations, Frank O. Braynard. Full story of legendary French ocean liner: Art Deco interiors, design innovations, furnishings, celebrities, maiden voyage, tragic fire, much more. Extensive text. 144pp. 8⅜ × 11¾.   25257-4 Pa. $9.95

THE FIRST AMERICAN COOKBOOK: A Facsimile of "American Cookery," 1796, Amelia Simmons. Facsimile of the first American-written cookbook published in the United States contains authentic recipes for colonial favorites—pumpkin pudding, winter squash pudding, spruce beer, Indian slapjacks, and more. Introductory Essay and Glossary of colonial cooking terms. 80pp. 5⅜ × 8½.
24710-4 Pa. $3.50

101 PUZZLES IN THOUGHT AND LOGIC, C. R. Wylie, Jr. Solve murders and robberies, find out which fishermen are liars, how a blind man could possibly identify a color—purely by your own reasoning! 107pp. 5⅜ × 8½. 20367-0 Pa. $2.00

THE BOOK OF WORLD-FAMOUS MUSIC—CLASSICAL, POPULAR AND FOLK, James J. Fuld. Revised and enlarged republication of landmark work in musico-bibliography. Full information about nearly 1,000 songs and compositions including first lines of music and lyrics. New supplement. Index. 800pp. 5⅜ × 8¼.
24857-7 Pa. $14.95

ANTHROPOLOGY AND MODERN LIFE, Franz Boas. Great anthropologist's classic treatise on race and culture. Introduction by Ruth Bunzel. Only inexpensive paperback edition. 255pp. 5⅜ × 8½.   25245-0 Pa. $5.95

THE TALE OF PETER RABBIT, Beatrix Potter. The inimitable Peter's terrifying adventure in Mr. McGregor's garden, with all 27 wonderful, full-color Potter illustrations. 55pp. 4¼ × 5½. (Available in U.S. only)   22827-4 Pa. $1.75

THREE PROPHETIC SCIENCE FICTION NOVELS, H. G. Wells. *When the Sleeper Wakes, A Story of the Days to Come* and *The Time Machine* (full version). 335pp. 5⅜ × 8½. (Available in U.S. only)   20605-X Pa. $5.95

APICIUS COOKERY AND DINING IN IMPERIAL ROME, edited and translated by Joseph Dommers Vehling. Oldest known cookbook in existence offers readers a clear picture of what foods Romans ate, how they prepared them, etc. 49 illustrations. 301pp. 6⅛ × 9¼.   23563-7 Pa. $6.00

SHAKESPEARE LEXICON AND QUOTATION DICTIONARY, Alexander Schmidt. Full definitions, locations, shades of meaning of every word in plays and poems. More than 50,000 exact quotations. 1,485pp. 6½ × 9¼.
22726-X, 22727-8 Pa., Two-vol. set $27.90

THE WORLD'S GREAT SPEECHES, edited by Lewis Copeland and Lawrence W. Lamm. Vast collection of 278 speeches from Greeks to 1970. Powerful and effective models; unique look at history. 842pp. 5⅜ × 8½.   20468-5 Pa. $10.95

THE BLUE FAIRY BOOK, Andrew Lang. The first, most famous collection, with many familiar tales: Little Red Riding Hood, Aladdin and the Wonderful Lamp, Puss in Boots, Sleeping Beauty, Hansel and Gretel, Rumpelstiltskin; 37 in all. 138 illustrations. 390pp. 5⅜ × 8½.
21437-0 Pa. $5.95

THE STORY OF THE CHAMPIONS OF THE ROUND TABLE, Howard Pyle. Sir Launcelot, Sir Tristram and Sir Percival in spirited adventures of love and triumph retold in Pyle's inimitable style. 50 drawings, 31 full-page. xviii + 329pp. 6½ × 9¼.
21883-X Pa. $6.95

AUDUBON AND HIS JOURNALS, Maria Audubon. Unmatched two-volume portrait of the great artist, naturalist and author contains his journals, an excellent biography by his granddaughter, expert annotations by the noted ornithologist, Dr. Elliott Coues, and 37 superb illustrations. Total of 1,200pp. 5⅜ × 8.
Vol. I 25143-8 Pa. $8.95
Vol. II 25144-6 Pa. $8.95

GREAT DINOSAUR HUNTERS AND THEIR DISCOVERIES, Edwin H. Colbert. Fascinating, lavishly illustrated chronicle of dinosaur research, 1820's to 1960. Achievements of Cope, Marsh, Brown, Buckland, Mantell, Huxley, many others. 384pp. 5¼ × 8¼.
24701-5 Pa. $6.95

THE TASTEMAKERS, Russell Lynes. Informal, illustrated social history of American taste 1850's–1950's. First popularized categories Highbrow, Lowbrow, Middlebrow. 129 illustrations. New (1979) afterword. 384pp. 6 × 9.
23993-4 Pa. $6.95

DOUBLE CROSS PURPOSES, Ronald A. Knox. A treasure hunt in the Scottish Highlands, an old map, unidentified corpse, surprise discoveries keep reader guessing in this cleverly intricate tale of financial skullduggery. 2 black-and-white maps. 320pp. 5⅜ × 8½. (Available in U.S. only)
25032-6 Pa. $5.95

AUTHENTIC VICTORIAN DECORATION AND ORNAMENTATION IN FULL COLOR: 46 Plates from "Studies in Design," Christopher Dresser. Superb full-color lithographs reproduced from rare original portfolio of a major Victorian designer. 48pp. 9¼ × 12¼.
25083-0 Pa. $7.95

PRIMITIVE ART, Franz Boas. Remains the best text ever prepared on subject, thoroughly discussing Indian, African, Asian, Australian, and, especially, Northern American primitive art. Over 950 illustrations show ceramics, masks, totem poles, weapons, textiles, paintings, much more. 376pp. 5⅜ × 8. 20025-6 Pa. $6.95

SIDELIGHTS ON RELATIVITY, Albert Einstein. Unabridged republication of two lectures delivered by the great physicist in 1920–21. Ether and Relativity and Geometry and Experience. Elegant ideas in non-mathematical form, accessible to intelligent layman. vi + 56pp. 5⅜ × 8½.
24511-X Pa. $2.95

THE WIT AND HUMOR OF OSCAR WILDE, edited by Alvin Redman. More than 1,000 ripostes, paradoxes, wisecracks: Work is the curse of the drinking classes, I can resist everything except temptation, etc. 258pp. 5⅜ × 8½. 20602-5 Pa. $3.95

ADVENTURES WITH A MICROSCOPE, Richard Headstrom. 59 adventures with clothing fibers, protozoa, ferns and lichens, roots and leaves, much more. 142 illustrations. 232pp. 5⅜ × 8½.
23471-1 Pa. $3.95

PLANTS OF THE BIBLE, Harold N. Moldenke and Alma L. Moldenke. Standard reference to all 230 plants mentioned in Scriptures. Latin name, biblical reference, uses, modern identity, much more. Unsurpassed encyclopedic resource for scholars, botanists, nature lovers, students of Bible. Bibliography. Indexes. 123 black-and-white illustrations. 384pp. 6 × 9. 25069-5 Pa. $8.95

FAMOUS AMERICAN WOMEN: A Biographical Dictionary from Colonial Times to the Present, Robert McHenry, ed. From Pocahontas to Rosa Parks, 1,035 distinguished American women documented in separate biographical entries. Accurate, up-to-date data, numerous categories, spans 400 years. Indices. 493pp. 6½ × 9¼. 24523-3 Pa. $9.95

THE FABULOUS INTERIORS OF THE GREAT OCEAN LINERS IN HISTORIC PHOTOGRAPHS, William H. Miller, Jr. Some 200 superb photographs capture exquisite interiors of world's great "floating palaces"—1890's to 1980's: *Titanic, Ile de France, Queen Elizabeth, United States, Europa,* more. Approx. 200 black-and-white photographs. Captions. Text. Introduction. 160pp. 8⅜ × 11¾. 24756-2 Pa. $9.95

THE GREAT LUXURY LINERS, 1927–1954: A Photographic Record, William H. Miller, Jr. Nostalgic tribute to heyday of ocean liners. 186 photos of Ile de France, Normandie, Leviathan, Queen Elizabeth, United States, many others. Interior and exterior views. Introduction. Captions. 160pp. 9 × 12. 24056-8 Pa. $9.95

A NATURAL HISTORY OF THE DUCKS, John Charles Phillips. Great landmark of ornithology offers complete detailed coverage of nearly 200 species and subspecies of ducks: gadwall, sheldrake, merganser, pintail, many more. 74 full-color plates, 102 black-and-white. Bibliography. Total of 1,920pp. 8⅜ × 11¼. 25141-1, 25142-X Cloth. Two-vol. set $100.00

THE SEAWEED HANDBOOK: An Illustrated Guide to Seaweeds from North Carolina to Canada, Thomas F. Lee. Concise reference covers 78 species. Scientific and common names, habitat, distribution, more. Finding keys for easy identification. 224pp. 5⅜ × 8½. 25215-9 Pa. $5.95

THE TEN BOOKS OF ARCHITECTURE: The 1755 Leoni Edition, Leon Battista Alberti. Rare classic helped introduce the glories of ancient architecture to the Renaissance. 68 black-and-white plates. 336pp. 8⅜ × 11¼. 25239-6 Pa. $14.95

MISS MACKENZIE, Anthony Trollope. Minor masterpieces by Victorian master unmasks many truths about life in 19th-century England. First inexpensive edition in years. 392pp. 5⅜ × 8½. 25201-9 Pa. $7.95

THE RIME OF THE ANCIENT MARINER, Gustave Doré, Samuel Taylor Coleridge. Dramatic engravings considered by many to be his greatest work. The terrifying space of the open sea, the storms and whirlpools of an unknown ocean, the ice of Antarctica, more—all rendered in a powerful, chilling manner. Full text. 38 plates. 77pp. 9¼ × 12. 22305-1 Pa. $4.95

THE EXPEDITIONS OF ZEBULON MONTGOMERY PIKE, Zebulon Montgomery Pike. Fascinating first-hand accounts (1805–6) of exploration of Mississippi River, Indian wars, capture by Spanish dragoons, much more. 1,088pp. 5⅜ × 8½. 25254-X, 25255-8 Pa. Two-vol. set $23.90

A CONCISE HISTORY OF PHOTOGRAPHY: Third Revised Edition, Helmut Gernsheim. Best one-volume history—camera obscura, photochemistry, daguerreotypes, evolution of cameras, film, more. Also artistic aspects—landscape, portraits, fine art, etc. 281 black-and-white photographs. 26 in color. 176pp. 8⅜ × 11¼.
25128-4 Pa. $12.95

THE DORÉ BIBLE ILLUSTRATIONS, Gustave Doré. 241 detailed plates from the Bible: the Creation scenes, Adam and Eve, Flood, Babylon, battle sequences, life of Jesus, etc. Each plate is accompanied by the verses from the King James version of the Bible. 241pp. 9 × 12.
23004-X Pa. $8.95

HUGGER-MUGGER IN THE LOUVRE, Elliot Paul. Second Homer Evans mystery-comedy. Theft at the Louvre involves sleuth in hilarious, madcap caper. "A knockout."—Books. 336pp. 5⅜ × 8½.
25185-3 Pa. $5.95

FLATLAND, E. A. Abbott. Intriguing and enormously popular science-fiction classic explores the complexities of trying to survive as a two-dimensional being in a three-dimensional world. Amusingly illustrated by the author. 16 illustrations. 103pp. 5⅜ × 8½.
20001-9 Pa. $2.00

THE HISTORY OF THE LEWIS AND CLARK EXPEDITION, Meriwether Lewis and William Clark, edited by Elliott Coues. Classic edition of Lewis and Clark's day-by-day journals that later became the basis for U.S. claims to Oregon and the West. Accurate and invaluable geographical, botanical, biological, meteorological and anthropological material. Total of 1,508pp. 5⅜ × 8½.
21268-8, 21269-6, 21270-X Pa. Three-vol. set $25.50

LANGUAGE, TRUTH AND LOGIC, Alfred J. Ayer. Famous, clear introduction to Vienna, Cambridge schools of Logical Positivism. Role of philosophy, elimination of metaphysics, nature of analysis, etc. 160pp. 5⅜ × 8½. (Available in U.S. and Canada only)
20010-8 Pa. $2.95

MATHEMATICS FOR THE NONMATHEMATICIAN, Morris Kline. Detailed, college-level treatment of mathematics in cultural and historical context, with numerous exercises. For liberal arts students. Preface. Recommended Reading Lists. Tables. Index. Numerous black-and-white figures. xvi + 641pp. 5⅜ × 8½.
24823-2 Pa. $11.95

28 SCIENCE FICTION STORIES, H. G. Wells. Novels, *Star Begotten* and *Men Like Gods*, plus 26 short stories: "Empire of the Ants," "A Story of the Stone Age," "The Stolen Bacillus," "In the Abyss," etc. 915pp. 5⅜ × 8½. (Available in U.S. only)
20265-8 Cloth. $10.95

HANDBOOK OF PICTORIAL SYMBOLS, Rudolph Modley. 3,250 signs and symbols, many systems in full; official or heavy commercial use. Arranged by subject. Most in Pictorial Archive series. 143pp. 8⅜ × 11.   23357-X Pa. $5.95

INCIDENTS OF TRAVEL IN YUCATAN, John L. Stephens. Classic (1843) exploration of jungles of Yucatan, looking for evidences of Maya civilization. Travel adventures, Mexican and Indian culture, etc. Total of 669pp. 5⅜ × 8½.
20926-1, 20927-X Pa., Two-vol. set $9.90

DEGAS: An Intimate Portrait, Ambroise Vollard. Charming, anecdotal memoir by famous art dealer of one of the greatest 19th-century French painters. 14 black-and-white illustrations. Introduction by Harold L. Van Doren. 96pp. 5⅜ × 8½.
25131-4 Pa. $3.95

PERSONAL NARRATIVE OF A PILGRIMAGE TO ALMANDINAH AND MECCAH, Richard Burton. Great travel classic by remarkably colorful personality. Burton, disguised as a Moroccan, visited sacred shrines of Islam, narrowly escaping death. 47 illustrations. 959pp. 5⅜ × 8½.   21217-3, 21218-1 Pa., Two-vol. set $17.90

PHRASE AND WORD ORIGINS, A. H. Holt. Entertaining, reliable, modern study of more than 1,200 colorful words, phrases, origins and histories. Much unexpected information. 254pp. 5⅜ × 8½.   20758-7 Pa. $4.95

THE RED THUMB MARK, R. Austin Freeman. In this first Dr. Thorndyke case, the great scientific detective draws fascinating conclusions from the nature of a single fingerprint. Exciting story, authentic science. 320pp. 5⅜ × 8½. (Available in U.S. only)   25210-8 Pa. $5.95

AN EGYPTIAN HIEROGLYPHIC DICTIONARY, E. A. Wallis Budge. Monumental work containing about 25,000 words or terms that occur in texts ranging from 3000 B.C. to 600 A.D. Each entry consists of a transliteration of the word, the word in hieroglyphs, and the meaning in English. 1,314pp. 6⅞ × 10.
23615-3, 23616-1 Pa., Two-vol. set $27.90

THE COMPLEAT STRATEGYST: Being a Primer on the Theory of Games of Strategy, J. D. Williams. Highly entertaining classic describes, with many illustrated examples, how to select best strategies in conflict situations. Prefaces. Appendices. xvi + 268pp. 5⅜ × 8½.   25101-2 Pa. $5.95

THE ROAD TO OZ, L. Frank Baum. Dorothy meets the Shaggy Man, little Button-Bright and the Rainbow's beautiful daughter in this delightful trip to the magical Land of Oz. 272pp. 5⅜ × 8.   25208-6 Pa. $4.95

POINT AND LINE TO PLANE, Wassily Kandinsky. Seminal exposition of role of point, line, other elements in non-objective painting. Essential to understanding 20th-century art. 127 illustrations. 192pp. 6½ × 9¼.   23808-3 Pa. $4.50

LADY ANNA, Anthony Trollope. Moving chronicle of Countess Lovel's bitter struggle to win for herself and daughter Anna their rightful rank and fortune—perhaps at cost of sanity itself. 384pp. 5⅜ × 8½.   24669-8 Pa. $6.95

EGYPTIAN MAGIC, E. A. Wallis Budge. Sums up all that is known about magic in Ancient Egypt: the role of magic in controlling the gods, powerful amulets that warded off evil spirits, scarabs of immortality, use of wax images, formulas and spells, the secret name, much more. 253pp. 5⅜ × 8½.   22681-6 Pa. $4.00

THE DANCE OF SIVA, Ananda Coomaraswamy. Preeminent authority unfolds the vast metaphysic of India: the revelation of her art, conception of the universe, social organization, etc. 27 reproductions of art masterpieces. 192pp. 5⅜ × 8½.
24817-8 Pa. $5.95

CHRISTMAS CUSTOMS AND TRADITIONS, Clement A. Miles. Origin, evolution, significance of religious, secular practices. Caroling, gifts, yule logs, much more. Full, scholarly yet fascinating; non-sectarian. 400pp. 5⅜ × 8½.
23354-5 Pa. $6.50

THE HUMAN FIGURE IN MOTION, Eadweard Muybridge. More than 4,500 stopped-action photos, in action series, showing undraped men, women, children jumping, lying down, throwing, sitting, wrestling, carrying, etc. 390pp. 7⅞ × 10⅝.
20204-6 Cloth. $19.95

THE MAN WHO WAS THURSDAY, Gilbert Keith Chesterton. Witty, fast-paced novel about a club of anarchists in turn-of-the-century London. Brilliant social, religious, philosophical speculations. 128pp. 5⅜ × 8½.
25121-7 Pa. $3.95

A CEZANNE SKETCHBOOK: Figures, Portraits, Landscapes and Still Lifes, Paul Cezanne. Great artist experiments with tonal effects, light, mass, other qualities in over 100 drawings. A revealing view of developing master painter, precursor of Cubism. 102 black-and-white illustrations. 144pp. 8¾ × 6⅝.
24790-2 Pa. $5.95

AN ENCYCLOPEDIA OF BATTLES: Accounts of Over 1,560 Battles from 1479 B.C. to the Present, David Eggenberger. Presents essential details of every major battle in recorded history, from the first battle of Megiddo in 1479 B.C. to Grenada in 1984. List of Battle Maps. New Appendix covering the years 1967–1984. Index. 99 illustrations. 544pp. 6½ × 9¼.
24913-1 Pa. $14.95

AN ETYMOLOGICAL DICTIONARY OF MODERN ENGLISH, Ernest Weekley. Richest, fullest work, by foremost British lexicographer. Detailed word histories. Inexhaustible. Total of 856pp. 6½ × 9¼.
21873-2, 21874-0 Pa., Two-vol. set $17.00

WEBSTER'S AMERICAN MILITARY BIOGRAPHIES, edited by Robert McHenry. Over 1,000 figures who shaped 3 centuries of American military history. Detailed biographies of Nathan Hale, Douglas MacArthur, Mary Hallaren, others. Chronologies of engagements, more. Introduction. Addenda. 1,033 entries in alphabetical order. xi + 548pp. 6½ × 9¼. (Available in U.S. only)
24758-9 Pa. $11.95

LIFE IN ANCIENT EGYPT, Adolf Erman. Detailed older account, with much not in more recent books: domestic life, religion, magic, medicine, commerce, and whatever else needed for complete picture. Many illustrations. 597pp. 5⅜ × 8½.
22632-8 Pa. $8.50

HISTORIC COSTUME IN PICTURES, Braun & Schneider. Over 1,450 costumed figures shown, covering a wide variety of peoples: kings, emperors, nobles, priests, servants, soldiers, scholars, townsfolk, peasants, merchants, courtiers, cavaliers, and more. 256pp. 8⅜ × 11¼.
23150-X Pa. $7.95

THE NOTEBOOKS OF LEONARDO DA VINCI, edited by J. P. Richter. Extracts from manuscripts reveal great genius; on painting, sculpture, anatomy, sciences, geography, etc. Both Italian and English. 186 ms. pages reproduced, plus 500 additional drawings, including studies for *Last Supper, Sforza* monument, etc. 860pp. 7⅞ × 10¾. (Available in U.S. only) 22572-0, 22573-9 Pa., Two-vol. set $25.90

THE ART NOUVEAU STYLE BOOK OF ALPHONSE MUCHA: All 72 Plates from "Documents Decoratifs" in Original Color, Alphonse Mucha. Rare copyright-free design portfolio by high priest of Art Nouveau. Jewelry, wallpaper, stained glass, furniture, figure studies, plant and animal motifs, etc. Only complete one-volume edition. 80pp. 9⅜ × 12¼. 24044-4 Pa. $8.95

ANIMALS: 1,419 COPYRIGHT-FREE ILLUSTRATIONS OF MAMMALS, BIRDS, FISH, INSECTS, ETC., edited by Jim Harter. Clear wood engravings present, in extremely lifelike poses, over 1,000 species of animals. One of the most extensive pictorial sourcebooks of its kind. Captions. Index. 284pp. 9 × 12. 23766-4 Pa. $9.95

OBELISTS FLY HIGH, C. Daly King. Masterpiece of American detective fiction, long out of print, involves murder on a 1935 transcontinental flight—"a very thrilling story"—NY Times. Unabridged and unaltered republication of the edition published by William Collins Sons & Co. Ltd., London, 1935. 288pp. 5⅜ × 8½. (Available in U.S. only) 25036-9 Pa. $4.95

VICTORIAN AND EDWARDIAN FASHION: A Photographic Survey, Alison Gernsheim. First fashion history completely illustrated by contemporary photographs. Full text plus 235 photos, 1840–1914, in which many celebrities appear. 240pp. 6½ × 9¼. 24205-6 Pa. $6.00

THE ART OF THE FRENCH ILLUSTRATED BOOK, 1700–1914, Gordon N. Ray. Over 630 superb book illustrations by Fragonard, Delacroix, Daumier, Doré, Grandville, Manet, Mucha, Steinlen, Toulouse-Lautrec and many others. Preface. Introduction. 633 halftones. Indices of artists, authors & titles, binders and provenances. Appendices. Bibliography. 608pp. 8⅜ × 11¼. 25086-5 Pa. $24.95

THE WONDERFUL WIZARD OF OZ, L. Frank Baum. Facsimile in full color of America's finest children's classic. 143 illustrations by W. W. Denslow. 267pp. 5⅜ × 8½. 20691-2 Pa. $5.95

FRONTIERS OF MODERN PHYSICS: New Perspectives on Cosmology, Relativity, Black Holes and Extraterrestrial Intelligence, Tony Rothman, et al. For the intelligent layman. Subjects include: cosmological models of the universe; black holes; the neutrino; the search for extraterrestrial intelligence. Introduction. 46 black-and-white illustrations. 192pp. 5⅜ × 8½. 24587-X Pa. $6.95

THE FRIENDLY STARS, Martha Evans Martin & Donald Howard Menzel. Classic text marshalls the stars together in an engaging, non-technical survey, presenting them as sources of beauty in night sky. 23 illustrations. Foreword. 2 star charts. Index. 147pp. 5⅜ × 8½. 21099-5 Pa. $3.50

FADS AND FALLACIES IN THE NAME OF SCIENCE, Martin Gardner. Fair, witty appraisal of cranks, quacks, and quackeries of science and pseudoscience: hollow earth, Velikovsky, orgone energy, Dianetics, flying saucers, Bridey Murphy, food and medical fads, etc. Revised, expanded In the Name of Science. "A very able and even-tempered presentation."—The New Yorker. 363pp. 5⅜ × 8. 20394-8 Pa. $6.50

ANCIENT EGYPT: ITS CULTURE AND HISTORY, J. E Manchip White. From pre-dynastics through Ptolemies: society, history, political structure, religion, daily life, literature, cultural heritage. 48 plates. 217pp. 5⅜ × 8½. 22548-8 Pa. $4.95

SIR HARRY HOTSPUR OF HUMBLETHWAITE, Anthony Trollope. Incisive, unconventional psychological study of a conflict between a wealthy baronet, his idealistic daughter, and their scapegrace cousin. The 1870 novel in its first inexpensive edition in years. 250pp. 5⅜ × 8½.   24953-0 Pa. $4.95

LASERS AND HOLOGRAPHY, Winston E. Kock. Sound introduction to burgeoning field, expanded (1981) for second edition. Wave patterns, coherence, lasers, diffraction, zone plates, properties of holograms, recent advances. 84 illustrations. 160pp. 5⅜ × 8¼. (Except in United Kingdom)   24041-X Pa. $3.50

INTRODUCTION TO ARTIFICIAL INTELLIGENCE: SECOND, EN-LARGED EDITION, Philip C. Jackson, Jr. Comprehensive survey of artificial intelligence—the study of how machines (computers) can be made to act intelligently. Includes introductory and advanced material. Extensive notes updating the main text. 132 black-and-white illustrations. 512pp. 5⅜ × 8½.   24864-X Pa. $8.95

HISTORY OF INDIAN AND INDONESIAN ART, Ananda K. Coomaraswamy. Over 400 illustrations illuminate classic study of Indian art from earliest Harappa finds to early 20th century. Provides philosophical, religious and social insights. 304pp. 6⅜ × 9⅜.   25005-9 Pa. $8.95

THE GOLEM, Gustav Meyrink. Most famous supernatural novel in modern European literature, set in Ghetto of Old Prague around 1890. Compelling story of mystical experiences, strange transformations, profound terror. 13 black-and-white illustrations. 224pp. 5⅜ × 8½. (Available in U.S. only)   25025-3 Pa. $5.95

ARMADALE, Wilkie Collins. Third great mystery novel by the author of *The Woman in White* and *The Moonstone*. Original magazine version with 40 illustrations. 597pp. 5⅜ × 8½.   23429-0 Pa. $7.95

PICTORIAL ENCYCLOPEDIA OF HISTORIC ARCHITECTURAL PLANS, DETAILS AND ELEMENTS: With 1,880 Line Drawings of Arches, Domes, Doorways, Facades, Gables, Windows, etc., John Theodore Haneman. Sourcebook of inspiration for architects, designers, others. Bibliography. Captions. 141pp. 9 × 12.   24605-1 Pa. $6.95

BENCHLEY LOST AND FOUND, Robert Benchley. Finest humor from early 30's, about pet peeves, child psychologists, post office and others. Mostly unavailable elsewhere. 73 illustrations by Peter Arno and others. 183pp. 5⅜ × 8½.
22410-4 Pa. $3.95

ERTÉ GRAPHICS, Erté. Collection of striking color graphics: *Seasons, Alphabet, Numerals, Aces* and *Precious Stones*. 50 plates, including 4 on covers. 48pp. 9⅜ × 12¼.   23580-7 Pa. $6.95

THE JOURNAL OF HENRY D. THOREAU, edited by Bradford Torrey, F. H. Allen. Complete reprinting of 14 volumes, 1837–61, over two million words; the sourcebooks for *Walden*, etc. Definitive. All original sketches, plus 75 photographs. 1,804pp. 8½ × 12¼.   20312-3, 20313-1 Cloth., Two-vol. set $80.00

CASTLES: THEIR CONSTRUCTION AND HISTORY, Sidney Toy. Traces castle development from ancient roots. Nearly 200 photographs and drawings illustrate moats, keeps, baileys, many other features. Caernarvon, Dover Castles, Hadrian's Wall, Tower of London, dozens more. 256pp. 5⅜ × 8¼.
24898-4 Pa. $5.95

AMERICAN CLIPPER SHIPS: 1833–1858, Octavius T. Howe & Frederick C. Matthews. Fully-illustrated, encyclopedic review of 352 clipper ships from the period of America's greatest maritime supremacy. Introduction. 109 halftones. 5 black-and-white line illustrations. Index. Total of 928pp. 5⅜ × 8½.
25115-2, 25116-0 Pa., Two-vol. set $17.90

TOWARDS A NEW ARCHITECTURE, Le Corbusier. Pioneering manifesto by great architect, near legendary founder of "International School." Technical and aesthetic theories, views on industry, economics, relation of form to function, "mass-production spirit," much more. Profusely illustrated. Unabridged translation of 13th French edition. Introduction by Frederick Etchells. 320pp. 6⅛ × 9¼. (Available in U.S. only)
25023-7 Pa. $8.95

THE BOOK OF KELLS, edited by Blanche Cirker. Inexpensive collection of 32 full-color, full-page plates from the greatest illuminated manuscript of the Middle Ages, painstakingly reproduced from rare facsimile edition. Publisher's Note. Captions. 32pp. 9⅜ × 12¼.
24345-1 Pa. $4.95

BEST SCIENCE FICTION STORIES OF H. G. WELLS, H. G. Wells. Full novel The Invisible Man, plus 17 short stories: "The Crystal Egg," "Aepyornis Island," "The Strange Orchid," etc. 303pp. 5⅜ × 8½. (Available in U.S. only)
21531-8 Pa. $4.95

AMERICAN SAILING SHIPS: Their Plans and History, Charles G. Davis. Photos, construction details of schooners, frigates, clippers, other sailcraft of 18th to early 20th centuries—plus entertaining discourse on design, rigging, nautical lore, much more. 137 black-and-white illustrations. 240pp. 6⅛ × 9¼.
24658-2 Pa. $5.95

ENTERTAINING MATHEMATICAL PUZZLES, Martin Gardner. Selection of author's favorite conundrums involving arithmetic, money, speed, etc., with lively commentary. Complete solutions. 112pp. 5⅜ × 8½.   25211-6 Pa. $2.95

THE WILL TO BELIEVE, HUMAN IMMORTALITY, William James. Two books bound together. Effect of irrational on logical, and arguments for human immortality. 402pp. 5⅜ × 8½.   20291-7 Pa. $7.50

THE HAUNTED MONASTERY and THE CHINESE MAZE MURDERS, Robert Van Gulik. 2 full novels by Van Gulik continue adventures of Judge Dee and his companions. An evil Taoist monastery, seemingly supernatural events; overgrown topiary maze that hides strange crimes. Set in 7th-century China. 27 illustrations. 328pp. 5⅜ × 8½.   23502-5 Pa. $5.95

CELEBRATED CASES OF JUDGE DEE (DEE GOONG AN), translated by Robert Van Gulik. Authentic 18th-century Chinese detective novel; Dee and associates solve three interlocked cases. Led to Van Gulik's own stories with same characters. Extensive introduction. 9 illustrations. 237pp. 5⅜ × 8½.
23337-5 Pa. $4.95

Prices subject to change without notice.

Available at your book dealer or write for free catalog to Dept. GI, Dover Publications, Inc., 31 East 2nd St., Mineola, N.Y. 11501. Dover publishes more than 175 books each year on science, elementary and advanced mathematics, biology, music, art, literary history, social sciences and other areas.